ROUTLEDGE LIBRARY EDITIONS: CHRISTIANITY

Volume 2

BRIDGE TO ISLAM

BRIDGE TO ISLAM
A Study of the Religious Forces of Islam and Christianity in the Near East

ERICH W. BETHMANN

LONDON AND NEW YORK

This edition first published in 2021
by Routledge
2 Park Square, Milton Park, Abingdon, Oxon OX14 4RN

and by Routledge
52 Vanderbilt Avenue, New York, NY 10017

Routledge is an imprint of the Taylor & Francis Group, an informa business

First published 1953 Allen & Unwin. Copyright 1953 Erich W. Bethmann

All rights reserved. No part of this book may be reprinted or reproduced or utilised in any form or by any electronic, mechanical, or other means, now known or hereafter invented, including photocopying and recording, or in any information storage or retrieval system, without permission in writing from the publishers.

Trademark notice: Product or corporate names may be trademarks or registered trademarks, and are used only for identification and explanation without intent to infringe.

British Library Cataloguing in Publication Data
A catalogue record for this book is available from the British Library

ISBN: 978-0-367-62307-4 (Set)
ISBN: 978-1-003-10879-5 (Set) (ebk)
ISBN: 978-0-367-62372-2 (Volume 2) (hbk)
ISBN: 978-0-367-63150-5 (Volume 2) (pbk)
ISBN: 978-1-003-10913-6 (Volume 2) (ebk)

Publisher's Note
The publisher has gone to great lengths to ensure the quality of this reprint but points out that some imperfections in the original copies may be apparent.

Disclaimer
The publisher has made every effort to trace copyright holders and would welcome correspondence from those they have been unable to trace.

BRIDGE TO ISLĀM

A STUDY OF THE RELIGIOUS FORCES
OF ISLĀM AND CHRISTIANITY
IN THE NEAR EAST

BY

ERICH W. BETHMANN

LONDON
GEORGE ALLEN & UNWIN LTD
RUSKIN HOUSE · MUSEUM STREET

FIRST PUBLISHED IN GREAT BRITAIN
IN 1953
Copyright in the U.S.A.

This book is copyright under the Berne Convention. Apart from any fair dealing for the purposes of private study, research, criticism or review, as permitted under the Copyright Act 1911, no portion may be reproduced by any process without written permission. Enquiry should be made to the publisher.

*Printed in Great Britain
in 11 point Baskerville type
by C. Tinling & Co., Ltd.,
Liverpool, London and Prescot*

PREFACE

After having spent twenty years in mission service in the Middle East, on my return to the West I was asked innumerable questions about Islām and Christianity and the relationship between these two great forces. Many of these questions revealed that the average Westerner has only a scant knowledge of the situation in the Middle East.

This volume will be an answer to some of these questions. It is hoped that it will be a contribution in its own small way to a better understanding and a more correct evaluation of our fellow men in the Near East. Its aim is to throw some light upon the spiritual background of the people in those lands and to draw attention to the multiple influences which have been at work and which have contributed to create the delicate relationships between Islām and Christianity.

The author is fully aware that in order to treat such a subject adequately a volume three to five times this size would be required. But such a work would be too cumbersome for the general reader, and its appeal would be limited to the specialist. This little volume, however, is not written for the specialist in the field of Islāmic studies, but for the general reader, and in a special sense for all those who look forward to a life of usefulness in the lands of Islām.

Although extensive research has been undertaken, and all facts stated are based on authorities, many topics are for obvious reasons only touched upon and not exhaustively treated. Short monographs such as these on the different countries of the Near East are but pencil sketches and are not intended to give the minute details of the paintings of an old master. Here, too, we should mention that the spiritual aspects and influences are stressed and not the material achievements.

To sum it up, this little work is not written to give ready answers to all the manifold problems of these lands, but rather to arouse an interest, stimulate thinking, and, if possible, to kindle the desire for further investigation and awaken the urge to make a contribution to a solution.

In order to facilitate further study a list of books besides the bibliography has been added. This may prove a help for the inquirer.

In the transliteration of Arabic names, the system of the Library of Congress, Washington, D.C., has been followed.

I would like to extend a special note of gratitude to all who have helped me in the preparation of this little volume. First of all, thanks are due to Miss O. Lattof, librarian of the Near East Section of the Library of Congress, to Miss Thelma Wellman, who had to struggle through the hand-written copy, and to Mrs. E. Howard and Miss J. Neuffer who spent many an extra hour in addition to their strenuous work to give it the finishing touch. Last but not least, my gratitude is due to Professor M. E. Kern, who made it possible for me to complete this project by allowing me sufficient free time to finish it.

THE AUTHOR

ACKNOWLEDGMENTS

Acknowledgment is hereby made to the following publishers for kind permission to quote from the books as listed. The publisher, author, and title of each book is given in full.

Clarendon Press: Sir Thomas and Guillaume Arnold, THE LEGACY OF ISLAM (1931) (Through Oxford University Press).

Columbia University Press: James Thayer Addison, THE CHRISTIAN APPROACH TO THE MOSLEM (1942).

Thomas Y. Crowell Company: Paul W. Harrison, THE ARAB AT HOME (1924).

Encyclopædia Britannica: Pope Urban II, THE HISTORIANS' HISTORY OF THE WORLD.

Funk & Wagnalls Company: S. M. Zwemer, D.D., RAYMOND LULL (1902).

Harper & Brothers: W. Wilson Cash, CHRISTENDOM AND ISLAM (1937).

Longman's, Green & Company, Inc.: J. J. Considine, ACROSS A WORLD (1942).

The Odyssey Press, Inc.: Nevill Barbour, PALESTINE, STAR OR CRESCENT? (1947).

Oxford University Press: A. H. Hourani, MINORITIES IN THE ARAB WORLD (1947). Dante Alighieri, THE DIVINE COMEDY OF DANTE ALIGHIERI (1933).

Charles Scribner's Sons: Tor Andræ, MOHAMMED, THE MAN AND HIS FAITH.

State Department, Washington, D.C.: Report, RECENT EDUCATIONAL ADVANCES IN EGYPT, April 18, 1946, Dr. Ruth C. Sloan.

University of Chicago Press: Wilbur W. White, THE PROCESS OF CHANGE IN THE OTTOMAN EMPIRE (1937).

World Dominion Press: William Harold Storm, WHITHER ARABIA (1938).

KEY TO TRANSLATION OF ARABIC LETTERS

ā for Arabic aliph ا pronounced like a in calm
ī "   "   ye ى   "   " ee " deed
ū "   "   wau و   "   " oo " root
ay " "   aliph-ye combination   " y " by
' "   "   hamza indicates syncopated break between syllables
' "   "   'ayn ع no equivalent in English
dh " "   dhal ذ pronounced like th in that
th " "   tha ث   "   " th in thief
gh " "   ghayn غ   "   " guttural r
kh " "   kha خ   "   " a Dutch guttural h
ḥ "   "   ḥa ح   "   " guttural h
ḍ "   "   ḍad ض no equivalent
ṭ "   "   ṭa ط   "   "
ṣ "   "   ṣad ص   "   "
ẓ "   "   ẓa ظ   "   "

All other letters are pronounced as their equivalents in English.

CONTENTS

Preface	page	5
1. *A First Glimpse*		11
2. *Islām, Its Founder and His Message*		15
3. *How Muslims Picture Muḥammad Today*		37
4. *Fundamentals of Islām*		44
5. *Jesus in Islām*		55
6. *Ideas Regarding Predestination and Sin*		65
7. *Religious Liberty in Islām*		71
8. *Interrelationship Between Islām and Christianity*		80
9. *Arabia*		102
10. *Al Yaman, Aden, and Ḥaḍramaut*		109
11. *'Omān and the Persian Gulf States*		118
12. *'Irāq*		124
13. *Syria and Lebanon*		136
14. *Palestine and Transjordan*		157
15. *Egypt*		166
16. *Turkey*		181
17. *Irān*		187
18. *The Bridge and Its Builders*		200
Appendix		215
Bibliography		219
Index		230

CHAPTER ONE

A FIRST GLIMPSE

THE road descends sharply from the eastern gate of the city into a narrow valley, crosses a small brook, and leads into a garden—a garden with age-old olive trees, gnarled and weather-beaten, which, spreading their bent and moss-grown branches widely, create a mild and subdued light amidst the glare of an ever-present, blazing sun. A hushed stillness seems to rest in the shade of these old trees. It is neither the stillness of the forest, nor the silence of death, but the quietness and serenity of a place where a soul fought its deepest struggle and won its greatest victory. The garden's name is Gethsemane. The path leads out of the garden again, winding upward between thorny hedges of prickly pears to the flat top of a mountain. We turn around, and before us lies Jerusalem, with its maze of streets and alleys, its turreted walls and bastions. In the foreground spreads a large open area on which the temple once stood. Today the rock of Moriah is crowned by the beautiful Mosque of 'Umar, and a little farther to the south the minarets of the likewise famous Al Aqsa mosque point toward heaven. Here and there church spires rise above the medley of flat and slanting roofs, and far to the west and north-west stretches the rugged, restless sky line of the modern city.

While we are still looking at the town with all its life and activity, a haze seems to swallow it, and out of the mist pictures pass before our eyes: A small fortress appears, which for centuries has withstood the onrush of the nomads from the eastern shore of the Jordan. Now it is beleaguered by a determined foe, who has made up his mind to force its gates by might or by ruse. Soon David becomes master of the stronghold of the Jebusites, and begins to build Zion in its place. Under the dynasty of David, Jerusalem becomes a mighty city. Prophets, priests, and kings ride through its gates. Suddenly there appears before us a gaunt figure, standing on the hilltop, thundering against this city, against its carelessness, and its gaiety, preaching doom and destruction, preaching the wrath of Jehovah. Not long afterward the armies of Nebuchadnezzar enter the mighty city, blinding its king, taking captive its nobles, and razing its powerful walls.

The haze thickens again, blotting out the vision. Suddenly we hear the sound of marching columns: Roman legions tramp over the old cobblestones, and plant the Roman eagle in this sacred place. Then we see before the palace of Pilate, the foreigner, a nation condemning its greatest Son to an ignominious death, screaming in wild frenzy that His blood be upon them and their children.

Again the city is totally destroyed, but out of its ruin rises a new community, a community of those who follow this Nazarene cross-bearer. They build their churches and venerate the place where His bruised body was laid. Jerusalem now has become the holy city for the Christians.

Centuries pass, and out of the sandy regions of the East another storm sweeps over these ancient hills and dales. Jerusalem cannot long withstand its vehemence and opens her gates. The victorious Arabs ride in to take possession of the sacred ground from which Muhammad, on the celestial horse Burāq, started on his journey through the heavenly spaces. Again Jerusalem becomes a holy city—the holy city of Islām. The crescent is planted beside the cross.

Bitter tales of persecution reach the far-distant lands of the West. One day the iron men of France, of Germany, and of England stand before the ancient walls to recapture the city for Jesus their Lord, and to stand guard over the empty sepulchre, the symbol of a triumphant Christendom. Yet their sojourn is not for long. The knights have to give way against overwhelming odds; the crescent again rules unchallenged.

The successive pictures of our reverie vanish, and before us lies Jerusalem, the modern city, the three-times holy city, wedded to its past. Though full of unrest, bloodshed, and strife, it is still the city of God. It has raised, and still raises, the highest aspirations in millions of hearts. For its possession more men

A FIRST GLIMPSE

have been willing to die than for the possession of any other place. This is just one little glimpse of the many-coloured spectrum of the Near East.

We could take our vantage point at many another place, and a similar multicoloured picture would pass before our eyes. We could stand on the Birs Nimrud near the ruins of the so-called Tower of Babel, and out of the flat plains, simmering in the midday sun, there would rise like mirages the Sumerians, with their ancient culture; Hammurabi, the wise law-giver and ruler; Babylon, the mighty city of Nebuchadnezzar, with Daniel its one time prime minister. Alexander the Great, with his youthful Macedonian horsemen, would encamp on those far-stretching plains. The Sassanids of Persia, with their pomp and splendour, would build a wonderful city on the banks of the mighty Tigris, to be overrun, ruined, and wrecked by the fierce horsemen of the desert. But the very sons and grandsons of those horsemen would build, a little farther upstream, another dream city Baghdad—gorgeous, beautiful, luxurious, the marvel city of its day. Yet, vanity of vanities, the day came when the Mongols stormed over these same plains, sacked the city, and built pyramids of the skulls of the slain victims. In this materialistic day, this country is again of interest to all the world, because under it is a vast lake of oil.

That is another of the manifold pictures of the Near East. Therefore if you should ever set your foot on these lands, step carefully. You will be standing on soil drenched with the blood of many generations and saturated with the wisdom of many sages. Remember, whatsoever was revealed to men about God has been revealed in these regions. Whatsoever man thought about God and about life was thought here first, be it polytheism or monotheism, formalism or mysticism, righteousness by works or righteousness by faith. Therefore step carefully in these lands, lest you make yourself a laughing-stock—tolerated but despised.

* * * * * *

The moment we set our feet on land in any of the countries, from Morocco in the west to Afghanistan in the east, a multitude of new and strange pictures will crowd into our view, and leave their imprint on our minds. But soon, like a dominant colour in a spectrum, one feature will hold the attention, because its influence seems to permeate all aspects of life, intangible but nevertheless distinctly perceptible.

Here are black-robed, veiled figures silently walking in one of the narrow streets; there, in the courtyard, men in long rows are making strange genuflections at exactly defined intervals. Then, again, amidst the din and noise of the market, a melodious voice cries certain sentences from the top of a tower into the four directions of the wind. We try to become familiar with all these strange and foreign sounds and sights.

We try to come closer to the people, because, after all, the people are the chief object of our interest. Yet the harder we try, the more evasive they seem to become. One day, walking through a street, we notice eyes staring at us, and in their depth glows fanatical, hardly concealed hatred. We have learned some of the language, and we hear horrible curses. At first we do not mind, until we suddenly discover that these curses are aimed at us. We are surprised, perhaps startled, because we have done nothing to offend. We have never spoken a word to them. They are strangers to us. Why this unmotivated hate? Why this enmity?

In the course of time, we have made some acquaintances, and have even won some friends. They are very polite and friendly. They invite us to their houses; and we invite them to ours. However, in spite of all their friendliness and their winning smiles, there is somewhere an unseen but keenly felt barrier which seems to be ever present. There seems to be no possibility of overcoming it or of removing it. This strange influence meets us wherever we turn; it seems to surround and encompass us until it haunts us. It permeates the whole atmosphere. We feel the utter foreignness of these people, the impossibility of becoming one with them. The fear wells up that we shall ever remain an unassimilated element in their midst.

What is the reason for this strange phenomenon? There is only one answer to it. We have entered into a foreign world—foreign not only in its language, but also in its thinking and feeling, in its whole outlook. We have entered the dominion of 'Dār al-Islām.' It is Islām which surrounds us at every step and every turn.

CHAPTER TWO

ISLĀM, ITS FOUNDER AND HIS MESSAGE

WHAT is Islām? This is a simple enough question to ask, but there is no equally simple answer. First there are some important facts to consider:

Islām is the latest of all great world religions. It appeared on the scene later than Judaism, Buddhism, or Christianity. It sprang up in the full light of history. It spread more rapidly than any of the other great religions. In one hundred years it had carved out an empire reaching from Spain and North Africa to India.

It is the only religion which clashed with Christianity and conquered a large part of the latter's former territory. It never receded from a country in which it had taken root, except from Spain. It still commands, and holds, the loyalty of over 300,000,000 adherents today. It is still progressing. It is a special mode of life. It is one of the great religio-political world forces to be reckoned with. It is the one great unsolved mission problem of the present-day Christian church.

The foregoing represents quite an array of facts—hard facts which cannot be ignored, and which must always be taken into consideration. Every one who takes an interest in these Middle Eastern countries, for one reason or another, and who wants to acquire more than a superficial knowledge of the people therein, has to keep these facts in mind. There are a multitude of other problems which can hardly be correctly understood and evaluated if these basic facts are not given due consideration.

Many questions will rise immediately in our minds. For instance, what caused the rise of Islām? How could Islām gain such a following? What circumstances made it possible?

Islām sprang up in one of the remote corners of the earth, in one of the neglected countries which lie far away from the main course of traffic and the general stream of civilization. It sprang up in Arabia, a country of deserts, of wide-open spaces and a few oases—a country of wandering tribes, the Beduins, and a few trade centres, the population of which lived on the business of caravans.

THE INFLUENCE OF THE DESERT

Islām, coming from Arabia, is therefore primarily the religion of the desert, and, although it has undergone many changes in the course of the centuries, it still carries with it the flavour of the glorious deserts of that land. If one would comprehend two of the basic thoughts in Islām, he has to take into account the tremendous impact of the desert upon man in forming and moulding his whole psychological structure. And I venture to say that long before Muhammad, the founder of Islām, gave expression to these ideas in masterly fashion, they lay dormant in the heart of every son of the desert. It needed only the spark of ingenuity to kindle them to an ever-blazing fire.

There is practically no scenery on earth which impresses the soul more overwhelmingly with the omnipotence of God than the desert. Here nature in its bareness and nakedness shows its primeval grandeur. There is no living creature—no tree, no bush, to arrest the eye. Nothing is here to which the soul can cling for refuge—nothing except a lifeless sea of sand, and dunes, and ranges of eroding rock. Here, in this vastness of space, in this extreme solitude, life's most cherished dreams and ambitions suddenly appear trivial and meaningless, and from the depths of the being comes the cry: 'God! God—Almighty omnipotent God! In Thee alone is life, and Thou alone knowest its meaning.'

Yet another thought is brought home with inescapable force, and fills the heart with awe—the utter inadequacy of human cleverness and efficiency. One feels the absurdity of self-reliance and self-assurance in surroundings such as these. None of the lofty attributes man likes to flatter himself that he possesses would help him in the desert. For instance, if the water gave out in his waterskin, or if he should lose his path in the shifting sands of the desert and pass the life-giving well, only a benevolent providence, which might turn at any moment into a cruel fate, could lead him across a lonely track. And only God could bring to pass his meeting, at the decisive moment, with a fellow traveller in a country where for weeks he might not encounter a human soul. It is willed by Allah whether he lives or dies. The powerlessness of man and the importance of Kismet, or Fate, are the two basic thoughts deeply embedded in Islām, whose messenger was Muhammad, the son of the desert, the orphan boy of Makka [Mecca].

MUHAMMAD IN THE EYES OF HIS CRITICS

Who was Muhammad? What was he like—the founder of Islām? Any person who has influenced history deeply will be alternately praised or blamed, depending altogether upon the point of view of the reviewer, the temper of his time, and the school of thought to which he belongs. But seldom indeed has a person drawn upon himself such contradictory evaluation as has Muhammad.

Most of the older church fathers considered him a heretic, as, for example, John of Damascus in *De Hæresibus* writes:

'From that time until now a false prophet arose for them, surnamed Mamed, who, having happened upon the Old and New Testament, in all likelihood through association with an Arian monk, organized his own sect.'[1]

Dante placed him in the ninth gulf of hell, and describes his horrible predicament in most vivid language:

> 'No cask that middle board or stave forewent
> Was cleft so wide as one I saw,
> Ripped from the chin clean down to fundament.
> . . . .
> While I am gazing at him full of wonder,
> He eyes me, and both hands in breast he plants,
> Saying: "Look how I tear myself asunder.
> How mangled is Muhammad! In advance of me
> With weeping goes along Alee,
> Cleft chin to forelock in the countenance.
> And all the others whom thou here dost see
> Were sowers of scandal and schismatic feud
> While living, and hence are cleft so cruelly." '[2]

A sower of scandal and schism—that is the verdict of Dante on Muhammad.

Savonarola denounces him as absolutely unreasonable, a criminal, an adulterer and robber of the people.[3] Luther was very much interested in questions concerning the Turks and Islām, because all Europe trembled before the onrush of the Turks in his time. He preached against the Turks, and asked for special prayers and supplications that God might spare Christendom from that scourge. In 1542 he wrote a preface and an epilogue to the Qur'ān [Koran] translation of Brother Richard, a Dominican friar, which was made about 1300. In that he states that he formerly could hardly believe that reasonable beings on earth could be induced by the devil to accept and believe such horrible things as are found in the Qur'ān. He also remarks that he thought the whole Qur'ān was an invention of some Italian writer in order to glorify the pope all the more. But now after he had seen the Qur'ān in Latin, he was sure that it was no fiction.[4] And then he states, 'I do not consider Muhammad to be the Antichrist. He is too unrefined. He has a clearly perceivable black devil who is unable to deceive neither reason nor faith ... but the Pope in our lands, he is the real Antichrist, because he has a subtle, sly, and glamorous devil.'[5]

Melanchthon sees in Muhammad the politician who used religion only to further Arab nationalism and to build an Arab empire; therefore his religion is simple and fitted to accommodate soldiers.[6] Concerning his religion he said, 'Now came Muhammad and threw all the former heresies in one pot, and boils them up, declaring deceitfully that he wants to create unity.'[7] To Melanchthon the Qur'ān is a monstrosity; in it, not a human or divine voice speaks, but a beastly voice, and it has the devil as originator.[8] Like many of the reformers, Melanchthon believed that he saw in Muhammad and the power of Islām all the indications of the little horn of Daniel 7.[9]

Since the nineteenth century, commentators are less outspoken, although hardly less uncomplimentary. They consider Muhammad to be an epileptic, or a victim of hallucinations, living under a heavy emotional strain.[10] Others again see in him a shrewd and cunning politician, a statesman.[11] Carlyle assigned him a place among the heroes of mankind. The Muslims consider him to be the wisest of all men, the kindest of all mankind, the seal of the prophets,[12] and the light of the world.

What, then, was Muhammad in reality? Was he a prophet or a charlatan, a saint or a devil?

MUHAMMAD'S EARLY LIFE

In the following we shall try to piece together an unbiased picture of Muhammad, as far as we can gather it from the most authentic source we possess, the Qur'ān itself. In this I am greatly indebted to Tor Andræ's excellent study, *Mohammed, the Man, and His Faith*. Using the Qur'ān as a basis, Muhammad's biography should really begin with his fortieth year, that is, the time when he received his first revelation. Muhammad lived the ordinary life of a citizen of Makka. He was considered to be a friendly, amiable, and trustworthy man, and was known under the name of Al-Amīn (The Trustworthy). The date of his birth is not quite fixed, either A.D. 570 or A.D. 571.

His father, 'Abdallah, belonged to the well-known, although not very wealthy, family of Hāshim, a branch of the Quraysh, the ruling clan of Makka. His father died before Muhammad's birth, and the orphan was cared for by 'Abd-al-Muttalib, his grandfather. As a young boy, he spent a number of years in the desert with the Beduins—a time-honoured custom, which even today is considered favourably, and practised by some of the old families who have settled in towns, but whose roots go back to the desert. When his grandfather died, he was cared for by Abu Tālib, his uncle; and as a young man entered the caravan business of Khadīja, a wealthy widow of Makka. His first trip, according to tradition, was so successful that she offered him her hand. He accepted gladly, although she was fifteen years his senior. He lived the life of a devoted husband, and had no wife besides her as long as she lived. Four daughters and two sons were the fruit of this marriage, but the sons, unfortunately, died in infancy.

Here, perhaps, is the right place to make an observation on

the often-debated question as to whether Muhammad was illiterate or not. In order to enhance the value of the Qur'ān, the orthodox tradition makes a big point of the prophet's illiteracy ('ammi). More modern biographers and Western scholars are inclined to credit him with possessing the knowledge of reading and writing. In reality it does not matter much either way, in view of the fact that thousands of Arabs today have a wonderful command of the Arabic language, and are able to recite 10,000 verses and compose poetry without knowing how to read or write.

On the other hand, Muhammad, belonging to a better-class family in Makka, might easily have acquired this knowledge, and his acceptance by Khadīja as business manager would also rather prove the latter position. That, of course, does not imply that he was a scholar. Nowhere does the Qur'ān give the impression that Muhammad was a man of scholarly disposition, who arrived at his conclusions by patient research. But it reveals that Muhammad was certainly of a contemplative nature. Although he was inclined to meditation, he combined with it a keen sense of the need of the hour, and was able to come to practical decisions. In the tradition we read that he often spent long periods in the solitude of the desert, around Mount Hirā. What kind of development and change a soul undergoes during such periods of loneliness, of solitude, and of meditation, no outsider will ever be able to tell.

MUHAMMAD'S REVELATIONS

Muhammad had certainly come in contact with Christians and Jews during his travels. He had received many new ideas and conceptions by these contacts. Tor Andræ even considers it highly probable that he might have heard once or perhaps several times some Nestorian missionary preacher.[13] Those sermons or contacts must have sunk deep into his consciousness. He displays in his later period a considerable knowledge of Christian ideas and usages. According to this evidence he failed to grasp the most vital points of Christian teaching, either because he was unable to comprehend them, or they were not correctly presented to him. The greater unity among

ISLĀM, ITS FOUNDER AND HIS MESSAGE

Jews, their belief as it appeared to him, in one God, one Book, one Prophet—that is, Jehovah, the Torah, and Moses; and the deeper spiritual outlook among Christians, who also believed in one God, one Book, one Prophet—Jehovah, the injīl (Gospel) and 'Isa (Jesus)—were in sharp contrast with the disunity of the Arabs. Their lack of understanding of the deeper problems of life, their laxity in morals, their indifference to spiritual things must have deeply perturbed and depressed him. And, seeker after truth as he was, the idea might have crossed his mind: perhaps he, Muhammad, would be the instrument in the hand of the All-powerful, and be the leader of His people.

Then one day, while again in the solitude of the desert, he received a revelation. A voice called him and demanded, 'Recite in the name of thy Lord who created.'[14] It is said that he was greatly agitated by it, and that grievous doubts oppressed him whether this was a genuine call from God or not. He related this strange experience to his wife Khadīja. She, however, believed in him and strengthened him in his conviction that it was a divine call. But in spite of that assurance, the revelation was suspended for a considerable period; no other such experience occurred. Muhammad suffered periods of deep despondency. This period is called *fatra* by the Arab biographers, and continued, according to different traditions, for six months to three years. Muir says: 'The accounts, however, are throughout confused and sometimes contradictory; and we can only gather with certainty that there was a time during which the mind of Muhammad hung in suspense, and doubted the reality of a heavenly mission.'[15]

After that period of doubt and suspense, the voice came again to him, probably after he had seen Gabriel in a tremendous vision. He himself describes this experience in the Qur'ān at a later period.

'The Qur'ān is nothing less than a revelation revealed to him. One terrible in power[16] taught it him. Endued with wisdom. With even balance stood he. In the highest part of the horizon: Then came he nearer and approached, and was at the distance of two bows, or even closer. And he revealed to his servant what he revealed.'[17]

From then on, it is said, the stream of revelation flowed steadily, with only minor interruptions occurring from time to time. In general, it is accepted that the first part of Sūra 96 was his first revelation, which was followed by Sūra 74. But this is in no way certain. As Andræ remarks: 'Which was the first Sūra was actually as little known to the earliest theologians of Islām as it is to us. There are many opinions, and several of them are much better substantiated than the opinion that it was Sūra 96.'[18]

There is, of course, another possibility which should not be lightly rejected, as a friend suggested to me, and which could have been of great influence in shaping Muhammad's character and career. It can be conceived that Muhammad obtained through his various contacts with Christians sufficient information about the basic points of Christianity, such as the sinful state of man, salvation from sin, redemption through Christ, etc., and that he understood these points. But he, however, rejected them. Now, rejecting a truth, on whatsoever level, is a fatal decision which can lead man to extreme positions; then, having embarked on a wrong line and committed himself to any degree, man's pride in most cases, forbids him to retrace his steps. He follows his chosen course logically to the end. He is true to his decision, and, in time, the knowledge of having wilfully rejected a truth is by the multiple requirements of everyday life practically crowded out of his consciousness. This also might have been the cause of the development of Muhammad's career. Who is able to give final judgment upon the motives of a man's heart?

Let us return to the study of the revelations which Muhammad received. All of them were of the auditory type except three: the aforementioned vision, and a second vision of the Mighty in Power near the Sidra tree, which is the outer boundary in heaven beyond which neither men nor angels can pass,[19] and third, the famous night journey through the seven heavens, which is considered by most orthodox Muhammadans as a real physical occurrence, but by the modern group just as a vision. But most likely it was only a dream.[20] Muhammad heard sounds and voices, and his revelations were dictated to him.[21]

According to tradition, he himself is reported to have said:

'The revelation comes to me in two ways: Sometimes Gabriel comes to me and tells it to me, as a man speaks to another; but that slips away from me. But sometimes it comes to me like the voice of a bell, and that blends with my heart and it never slips away from me.'[22] Sometimes the revelation came with such force upon him that the sweat dropped from him even on cold days.[23]

We may well ask if Muhammad acted in good faith when he recited his revelations. All that has been said so far regarding the period of doubt, his uncertainty as to whether he should take up the call at once, and his behaviour after he began to proclaim his message, as we shall presently learn, can be taken as a proof that Muhammad, at least in the earlier period of his career, acted absolutely in good faith. He himself certainly was convinced that he acted as an instrument of divine power, and was influenced by that conviction greatly.

THE JUDGMENT MESSAGE

We may further ask: Did he have a message, or were his sayings only the ramblings of a morbid mind—senseless, disconnected hallucinations? We should do the greatest injustice to ourselves if we should discuss the sayings of Muhammad casually, thinking it is not worth while to give them serious consideration, or regard them merely as the writings of a deceiver who went out to deceive. If we take time to study the sayings of Muhammad, we shall soon find that he had a message —a most important message—the message of the coming judgment of God. He felt the urge to carry this message to his people, the Arabs in Makka, in order to warn them and to arouse them to the fear of God, because the judgment drew nigh. With passionate fervour and in impressive poetical language, he began to proclaim that one great subject. He painted it in all colours, describing the awfulness of this coming day, the distress and despair of the evildoers, the joy and exaltation of the blessed ones. He unfolded hell with its terrors, heaven with its bliss, and then sounded the warning that none will escape that day; every one has to stand before his Judge alone, and none will intercede. Not all the passages can be quoted in this work, but a few samples may suffice to show the fervency of his style:

'When the heaven is cleft asunder
And when the stars are scattered
And when the seas gush together,
And when the graves are turned upside down,

Each soul shall know what it has accomplished or kept back.
O man! what hath misled thee against thy generous Lord,
Who has created thee and moulded thee, and shaped thee
    aright?'[24]
'When the sun shall be folded up,
And when the stars shall fall,
And when the mountains shall be set in motion,
And when the she-camels shall be abandoned,
And when the wild beasts shall be gathered together,
And when the seas shall boil,
And when souls shall be paired *with their bodies*,
And when the female child which has been buried alive
    shall be asked
For what crime she was put to death,[25]
And when the leaves of the Book shall be spread out,
And when the Heaven shall be stripped away,
And when Hell shall be made to blaze,
And when Paradise shall be brought near,
Every soul shall know what it has produced.'[26]

'Hath the tidings of the day that shall overshadow reached
    thee?
Downcast on that day shall be the countenances of some,
Travailing and worn,
Burnt at a scorching fire,
Made to drink from a fountain fiercely boiling.
No food shall they have but the fruit of *Dari*[27]
Which shall not fatten nor appease their hunger.
Joyous too, on that day the countenances [of others],
Well pleased with their labours past,
In a lofty garden:
No vain discourse shalt thou hear therein:

Therein shall be a gushing fountain.
Therein shall be raised couches,
And goblets ready placed,
And cushions laid in order
And carpets spread forth.'[28]

'But when one blast shall be blown on the horn
And the earth and the mountains shall be upheaved and crushed into dust in one single crushing,
On that day the resurrection shall take place.
And the heavens shall cleave asunder, for on that day it shall be fragile;
And the angels on its sides, eight of them shall bear the throne of the Lord above them on that day.
On that day ye shall be brought before Him: none of
Your hidden deeds shall remain hidden.'[29]

And then he continues, stating that to every one will be given a book in which the deeds he did are written. Those who receive it in their right hand shall rejoice, but upon all who receive it in their left hand will fall eternal gloom. Fear the Lord, the day of judgment, and the day of resurrection, was his theme. This he proclaimed over and over again in the market place of Makka. But what impression did it make upon the people of Makka? How was he received?

He was laughed at, ridiculed, derided—a crazy poet was he, telling fables, fables of the Ancients. 'What! When we shall have died, and become dust and bones, shall we indeed be judged?'[30] As the agnostic Sadducees of old—or as the Athenians when Paul spoke about the resurrection—laughed and mocked, likewise the Makkahs of Muhammad's time heaped ridicule upon his head.

But Muḥammad did not belong to those who are easily discouraged. In ever-fresh variations he preached the same theme:

'It needeth not that I swear by the day of Resurrection,
Or that I swear by the self-accusing soul.
Thinketh man that we shall not reunite his bones?
Aye! his very finger tips are we able evenly to replace.

But man chooseth to contradict what is before him.
He asketh, Whence this day of Resurrection?
But when the eye shall be dazzled,[31]
And when the moon shall be eclipsed,
And the sun and the moon shall be united,
On that day man shall cry, "Where is there a place to flee to?"
But in vain; there is no refuge.
With thy Lord on that day shall be the resting place.
On that day shall man be told of all that he has done, first and last.
Yea, a man shall be the eyewitness against himself.'[32]

'Aye, but ye love the transitory,
And ye neglect the life to come.
On that day shall faces beam with light,
Looking up towards their Lord;
and faces on that day shall be dismayed,
As if they thought that some great calamity would befall them.'[33]

MUHAMMAD ON THE STATE OF THE DEAD

At first Muhammad may have thought that this day was immediately at hand, and he may have proclaimed it so. However, when it was delayed, then he said:

'They will ask thee of "the Hour," when will be its fixed time?
But what knowledge hast thou of it?
Its period is known only to thy Lord;
And thou art only charged with the warning of those who fear it.'[34]

And then follows a most interesting verse:

'On the day when they shall see it, it shall seem to them as though they had not tarried [in the tomb] longer than its evening or its morn.'[35]

In other words, Muhammad here makes a statement on the complete unconsciousness of the soul after death. There is no intermediate state between the day of death and the day of resurrection—no purgatory, no heavenly abode, where the soul leads a separate existence. No, the moment an individual dies, he becomes completely unaware of the lapse of time. When the day of resurrection comes, it appears to him that he has passed just a single night's quiet, peaceful rest.

Andræ takes due notice of this point, and he considers it a strong argument for the theory that Muḥammad must have had contact with the Nestorians, because at that time they were the only sect of the Christian church who held that doctrine.[36] There are other verses in the Qur'ān, however, which leave the question somewhat open. At least commentators are not agreed upon their explanation. For instance, speaking about hypocrites and other Arabs who have turned away again, the statement is made: 'Twice we shall chastise them: then they shall be given over to a great chastisement.'[37] The tradition takes hold of these verses, and asserts that Muhammad was convinced about a chastisement in the grave. When 'Ā'isha asked him about it, he confirmed it and said: 'Certainly the chastisement in the grave is a reality.'[38]

MUHAMMAD AND THE PEOPLE OF MAKKA

As previously mentioned, the people of Makka did not heed Muhammad's warnings. He could gather but few followers, and those mostly from the unskilled labourers and the slaves. Very few from the aristocracy of Makka were won to his views. However, among these was Abu Bakr, a most sincere man, who became his truest friend, and after his death became his immediate successor. Some time later 'Umar ibn al Khaṭṭāb, one of his fiercest opponents, was won, to become in time the second caliph, and one of the most distinguished men in Islām. But besides these two rather exceptional conversions, Muḥammad's ardent invocations to repent did not achieve any results. He found it necessary to change his method of approach. He began to prove that he was neither a mad poet nor an innovator, but that he was only one in the great line of warners who are sent by God to call their countrymen to repentance. From time immemorial, God has spoken through such men—the prophets. If the people heeded the warnings, God's bounties would again be showered upon them; if not, sure destruction would befall them. He now began to cite Noah, Abraham, Moses, Aaron,

David, Jesus, and other men of more local importance. Therefore, the Sūras of the later Makkan period lost much of that soul-stirring appeal. Their style changed. They compare somewhat with the apologetic sermons of a revivalist.

But in doing so, Muhammad laid, perhaps quite unintentionally, the foundation for the historical outlook of Islām. He widened the horizon of the Arabs, made them history conscious, and moored them firmly to Abraham, the founder of this race. Therewith he gave them an antiquity and a place among the nations of old. In addition, in putting himself in line with the great prophets and seers of old, like Moses, David, and Jesus, he laid the ground work for that highly developed superiority complex which every Muslim has, stemming from the belief that Muhammad is the highest of all prophets. Being the latest, they regard him as superseding all others, either annulling or perfecting their messages.

In spite of these earnest endeavours on Muhammad's part, the situation in Makka did not improve to any degree. On the contrary, his followers were persecuted until they found it wiser to take refuge in Abyssinia for a time. They returned and the number of Muhammad's followers increased from the lower classes. The rich merchants of the town and the nobility considered him a nuisance, and prohibited him from speaking publicly. Then they boycotted him and his family and his clan, the Hāshimīs. They could not buy or sell; only in the sacred months of truce could they intermingle freely with the rest of the people. Starvation set in, and would have taken severe toll if some friends, working stealthily at night, had not driven a camel laden with food into their quarter at various times during the more than two years of boycott.[39] Yet, in spite of all these setbacks, Muhammad was still determined to deliver his message. If the people of Makka would not accept it, perhaps the people of another town would be willing to do so. Thereupon he went to al Tā'if, a town in the hills east of Makka, to preach Islām, the surrender to God. The people of Makka, however, had passed on a warning to this town, and when Muhammad started to preach, such an uproar arose that he had to flee for his life.

ISLĀM, ITS FOUNDER AND HIS MESSAGE

Perhaps after this experience, or about this time, a gradual change took place in his thinking. As often happens, a tragedy was enacted, from which there seems to be no escape in this world. Whenever a new idea or an ideal threatens to take shape in a material form, the inherent resistive power of matter and its own law of causality, or circumstances as they in reality exist, mould this idea into a far-different design from what was originally intended. Therefore, idealists and reformers, after being opposed by brutal force, often fall back upon the same means, employing force against force, cunning against cunning, terror against terror, thereby destroying their own lofty ideals.

MUHAMMAD IN MADĪNA

From now on we see Muhammad in negotiation with certain factions of the people from Yathrib, later Madīna,[40] first secretly, afterwards more openly. This culminated in the gradual emigration of all his followers from Makka, and eventually to his own flight with Abu Bakr to Madīna in A.D. 622, after narrowly escaping his persecutors who wanted his blood. This flight is called Al Hijra. The year of the Hijra has become the starting year of the Islāmic calendar; therefore A.D. 622 equals 1 A.H. The Muhammadan year is an uncorrected lunar year with 354 days.

The moment Muhammad arrived at Madīna, his position changed fundamentally. He was not any longer the preacher, the warner, the prophet in the true sense of the word. He could not be such any longer. He was called to be the arbiter between two warring factions in the town. Besides these two factions, there was a large, rather influential Jewish community in Yathrib. Furthermore, he had brought his own followers to this place. These were fanatically attached to him; with the fervent zeal of a newly found faith, they constituted a foreign element in the town. Muhammad had to deal with these differing elements, and tried to smooth out their differences so as to satisfy them all. The result was that he made himself obnoxious either to one faction or the other. But the decisions he made were considered final, and thereby he gradually abolished the customary law and established a divine law in its stead. He was personally fully convinced that his judicial decisions were the verdict of Allah himself.

Through this new development, former loyalties were severed. Formerly a man was expected to be loyal to those of his own blood, to his clan or tribe. Now, a new loyalty was established—the loyalty to those of like faith. From this time on, Muhammad begins to speak with authority; and again and again we find, in the Sūras of the Madīna period, statements of the following nature: 'And it is not for a believer, man or woman, to have any choice in their affairs, when God and His Apostle have decreed a matter; and whoever disobeyeth God and His Apostle erreth with palpable error.'[41] Muḥammad's words became law—a law not to be questioned but to be obeyed.

Not long after their settling in Yathrib, a serious problem arose. Through the influx of the immigrants the population had increased considerably, and provisions ran short. There is no way of raising larger crops in an oasis, and even if that had been possible, it would not have relieved the immediate pressure. There is only one way of getting the necessary food in such a country—by robbing others, an age-honoured custom in the desert. Muhammad could not devise another way, and resorted to the same method, with the innovation, however, that he did not even consider himself bound by the months of truce, during which the Arabs abstained from waylaying one another.

THE BATTLE OF BADR

Soon the relations between the new community in Madīna, led by Muhammad, and Makka, his home town, deteriorated to such an extent that open hostilities developed. The first and most important battle in Islāmic history was fought at Badr. Today, of course, we would call it a minor clash, an insignificant skirmish, hardly worth mentioning. The dead on the Makkan side were forty-nine, and on Muhammad's side, fourteen.[42]

But this battle of Badr had the most far-reaching consequences. It was not only a great psychological uplift for the severely harassed followers of Muhammad in Madīna, but it gave birth to the religion of the sword. It was taken as a sign that God had blessed their weapons.

'Ye have already had a sign in the meeting of the two hosts. The one has fought in the cause of God, and the other was infidel. To their own eyesight the infidels saw you twice as many as themselves.[43] And God aided with His succour whom He would. And in this truly was a lesson for men endued with discernment.'[44]

And in another Sūra, which also dwells rather lengthily upon the victory at Badr and upon the division of the spoils accrued through that victory, the following conclusion is reached:

'Say to the infidels: if they desist from their unbelief, what is now past shall be forgiven them; but if they return to it, they have already before them the doom of the ancients.

'Fight then against them till strife be at an end, and the religion be all of God's.

'If they desist, verily God beholdeth what they do.'[45]

Herewith the sword as a legitimate means for spreading the faith was installed. Every participant in the battle of Badr became a venerated fighter, belonging from now on to the elite of the new society. Ibn Sa'd gives a detailed biography of each one of them.[46] The victory at Badr means a turning point in the life of the new religion.

THE POSITION OF WOMEN

Much has been written about the lasciviousness of the prophet in his later years—a point on which Christian polemics in former times dwelt at length. Therewith they tried to prove that Muhammad is to blame for polygamy and the degradation of women in general in Eastern countries. However, this point easily backfires. In order to arrive at a just evaluation of the facts, we have to take into consideration the time in which Muhammad lived. His legislation concerning marriage limited the number of legal wives to four, with the condition attached that the husband must deal equitably with them, otherwise he should take only one wife.[47] This law laid considerable restriction upon the Arab, who was accustomed to indulge in an unlimited number. Furthermore, Muhammad's insistence upon giving women their rightful dowry made polygamy an expensive luxury. The dowry which has to be given to the father or brother of every free-born woman is often considered the price of purchase. From one point of view this could be considered true, but in reality it is a kind of safeguard for the woman. After the father has deducted his expenses for the trousseau or the outfit of the new home, the rest of the amount becomes the sole property of the wife, over which she has full legal rights. She may dispose of it in any way she pleases without consulting her husband, as he has no legal claim upon it. That in reality put the married woman on a more independent basis than women in Christian lands had been, where until the emancipation movement of the nineteenth century and the beginning of this century married women had no right to hold separate property, and were not allowed to transact business on their own. We should not forget that equality of status between men and women cannot be hailed as a virtue which was observed in Christian lands because of their Christian attitude, but that it is a development of our modern age for which women had to fight hard. On the other hand it must be acknowledged that the better comprehension of Christ's principles of what constitutes the right human attitude made it possible that in Christian lands women could first reach a status of equal rights in every respect. An exception, of course, are those countries in which the matriarchial form of society was the established custom.

The one aspect which puts women at a great disadvantage, accentuates their inferiority, and makes family life rather unstable in Islām, is that divorce or repudiation of the marriage is the sole right of the man, a right which he can exercise out of a whim, and for which he is not bound to give the least explanation. On the other hand, whenever the wife has given birth to a son, her position is pretty well established in the family.

The veiling of women also is by no means an invention of Muhammad, but was practised long before his time by the Greeks. The strict purdah system was established later in Islāmic history because of developments in towns. The women of the Arabs in the desert up to the present day are practically always unveiled.

The regrettable fact in the life of Muhammad was that he did not feel himself bound by his own regulations, which restricted the number of legal wives to four, but that he claimed exemption for himself for further indulgence.

MUHAMMAD'S INNER DEVELOPMENT

But the question which interests us most is, what is Muhammad's inner relationship to the changed conditions in Madīna? We have seen him as an ardent proclaimer of a most unpopular message. We have seen him continuing his work under most trying circumstances, under ridicule, persecution, boycott, and very meagre success. For twelve years he was plodding along. Now, coming to Madīna, is it possible that he turned into a deceiver and scoundrel overnight, as so many assert? If not, how then is it possible to explain the rather lengthy revelations which he now received, and which often came at the precise moment when a decision had to be made or to be confirmed? On this point Andræ observes:

'However, it is a natural enough process, that an originally spontaneous inspiration should be transformed more and more into an inspiration of ideas, becoming increasingly subject to the control of the conscious will. We see how the prophet gradually grew accustomed to think of ideas that emerged in his consciousness and decisions that matured in his soul as direct expressions of the divine will. As far as I can see, such a development must be regarded as psychologically normal. In such circumstances we must beware of speaking of the conscious misuse of falsification of revelation.[48]

I should like to add that Muhammad and persons under like circumstances can hardly escape the belief that they are instruments of divine providence, if every word they utter is immediately taken up by their followers and admirers as a sign of supernatural wisdom and divine volition. And this tendency is strengthened even when it is clear to their own conscience that these thoughts are their own private ideas, yet as soon as the words fall from their lips their followers hasten to announce a new revelation. Very few find the courage to call a halt to this; the majority probably continue to play the role which is forced upon them until they have finally fully identified themselves with it.

Furthermore, another factor enters into the picture—the intoxicating influence of power. No greater danger exists for a human being than getting power into his hands. His moral fibre is not usually strong enough to resist the vehement demand of the temptation to wield power for his own benefit. Power can have the most devastating influence upon the soul, and is able to change a saint into a devil. To me, as a believing Christian, the most remarkable fact in Christ's life is not the deeds He did, but the deeds He refrained from doing. Consider that with all the divine power at His command, He never misused power. He never used it for His own benefit or for His own glorification.

Muhammad, human as we all are, succumbed to this temptation. This can hardly be denied in his actions in the affair with the wife of his adopted slave Zayd and his part in the slaying of the poet Ka'b ibn al Ashraf,[49] and in other instances. But considering the power Muhammad wielded in later years, we have to admit that he acted with great wisdom and self-restraint. He never claimed to be more than the apostle, or messenger, of God; he never considered himself sinless; he never proclaimed, like Jesus, that he was the Way, the Truth, and the Life, but rather, like David or other prophets of old, he felt the need of the benevolent clemency of God and His forgiving mercies. 'Know, then, [O Muhammad] that there is no god but God, and ask pardon for thy sin, and for believers, both men and women. God knoweth your busy movements, and your final resting place.'[50] A somewhat similar expression is found in Sūra 40: 57 (56).[51] This is the picture we gain from the Qur'ān. Is that the picture which the common believer among the Muslims has of his prophet? Is that the way the zealous modern young Muslim looks at Muhammad? This will be considered in the following chapter.

---

[1] J. P. Migne, *Patrologiæ, Cursus Completus*, Series Graeca, Vol. XCIV, cols. 763-766.

² Dante Alighieri, *Divine Comedy of Dante Alighieri*, translated by Melville B. Anderson, p. 151.

³ In Bibliander, '*Mahumetanorum sectam omni ratione carere, commentationcula lecto dignissima,*' quoted from Manfred Koehler, *Melanchthon und der Islam*, p. 32.

⁴ Dr. Martin Luther's *Sämmtliche Schriften*, Walch ed. Vol. XX, col. 2218.

⁵ *Ibid.*, col. 2282.

⁶ Koehler, *op. cit.*, p. 32.

⁷ *Ibid.*, p. 35.

⁸ *Ibid.*, p. 47.

⁹ *Ibid.*, p. 63, citing *Corpus Reformatorum* 13. 860, 861.

¹⁰ See A. Sprenger, *Das Leben und die Lehre des Mohammed*.

¹¹ See D. S. Margoliouth, *Mohammed and the Rise of Islam*.

¹² That is, he was the instrument of God's final revelations to mankind.

¹³ Tor Andræ, *Mohammed, the Man and His Faith*, p. 126.

¹⁴ *Qur'ān*, Sūra 96: 1. Note: The English text follows in general J. M. Rodwell's translation; if it varies, the writer gives his own rendering based on the Arabic edition of the Qur'ān, as published by the Government Press, Būlāq, Egypt, 1344 A.H. (A.D. 1925). First numbers indicate the verses in the English edition, in parentheses those of the Arabic edition if they differ.

¹⁵ W. Muir, *The Life of Mohammed*, ed. 1912, p. 51.

¹⁶ Allusion to the angel Gabriel.

¹⁷ Sūra 53: 4-10.

¹⁸ Andræ, *op. cit.*, p. 62.

¹⁹ Sūra 53: 13, 14.

²⁰ Sūra 17; Al Baydāwī, Tafsīr, Commentary to Sūra 17. See also Ibn Sa'd, *Kitāb al Ṭabaqāt al Kibīra*, vol. 1¹, pp. 143, 144.

²¹ Sūra 75: 16-19.

²² Ibn Sa'd, *op. cit.*, 1¹, pp. 131, 132.

²³ *Ibid.*, p. 132.

²⁴ Sūra 82: 1-7.

²⁵ It was a custom among the Arabs prior to Muhammad's time to bury surplus female children alive. This custom was abolished by Muhammad.

²⁶ Sūra 81: 1-14.

²⁷ The name of a bitter, thorny shrub.

²⁸ Sūra 88: 1-16.

²⁹ Sūra 69: 13-18.

³⁰ Sūra 37: 51 (53).

³¹ By the loss of light; Baydāwī.

³² Sūra 75: 1-14.

³³ Sūra 75: 20-25.

³⁴ Sūra 79: 42-45.

³⁵ Sūra 79: 46.

³⁶ Andræ, *op. cit.*, pp. 123, 124.

³⁷ Sūra 9: 102 (101).

³⁸ Al Bukhārī, *Kitāb al Jāmi' al Ṣaḥīḥ*, Bāb Al Jana'iz, Vol. I, p. 345 (French ed. El-Bokhārī, *Les Traditions Islamiques*, Vol. I, p. 443).

[39] Muir, *op. cit.*, pp. 94, 95, 104.
[40] Madīna is an abbreviation of Madīnat-al-nabī which means the town of the prophet.
[41] Sūra 33: 36.
[42] Andræ, *op. cit.*, pp. 205, 206.
[43] At Badr Muḥammad, with 319 followers, routed 1,000 Makkans, 2 A.H.
[44] Sūra 3: 11 (13).
[45] Sūra 8: 39, 40 (38, 39).
[46] See Ibn Sa'd, *op. cit.*, volumes 3^1 and 3^2.
[47] Sūra 4: 3.
[48] Andræ, *op. cit.*, p. 69.
[49] Muir, *op. cit.*, p. 245.
[50] Sūra 47: 21 (19).
[51] The doctrine of the sinlessness of all prophets is a later development.

CHAPTER THREE

HOW MUSLIMS PICTURE MUHAMMAD TODAY

ALTHOUGH the sketch given in the previous chapter represents a fair evaluation of the historical facts regarding the prophet Muhammad, it is by far not the picture which the common Muslim has in mind. Nor is it the conception of the modern educated youth in Eastern lands. Each group of Muslims holds a picture of Muhammad which, while radically different from each other, also differs fundamentally from the conception which even the considerate and kindly disposed Westerner has of the prophethood of Muhammad.

Muhammad is to the Muslim not a prophet in the sense that Isaiah and Daniel are prophets to the Jewish or Christian believers, namely holy men of God who spoke as they were moved by the Holy Ghost. His prophethood is by no means connected with the idea of his personal holiness nor with that of predicting future events, or giving an insight into God's plan. It means merely that he was instrumental in delivering a message from God to the people. This is what Muhammad emphasized again and again. He stated that he was only an instrument, a tool, in the hand of God in bringing the Qur'ān to the people. He did not claim to have anything to do with the diction of the Holy Book. He never claimed what many of his followers later attributed to him—to be an intercessor, to possess miraculous qualities, or to have had prenatal connections with the heavenly world. Orthodox theologians of Islām will always defend the simple historical point of view, free of all supernatural trimmings, except those which are mentioned in the Qur'ān.

TRADITIONS AROUND MUHAMMAD

But, alas, frequently the thinking of the theologians does not correspond to that of the people. That is only too true in Islām.

To the people in general Muhammad means much more. Already in the later years of his life, his actions, his daily routine down to the minutest detail were carefully observed. How he washed his hands, how he combed his beard, his likes and dislikes—all were considered important and became a pattern for the life of the faithful Muslim. To imitate the prophet was the highest goal piety could aim at.[1] Ibn Sa'd reserves long paragraphs describing the eating habits of the prophet, the manner of his gait, his hair, his dress, his shirt, his comb, and so forth.[2] Soon after Muhammad's death his followers took the greatest care to legitimize all their actions by referring to precedents in the prophet's life. A whole system of thought sprang up, known as the *Sunna*: the way of life of the prophet which became the life of Islām. It is evident that no precedent in the life of the prophet could be found for many intricate problems arising in connection with the rapidly growing empire. Caliphs and judges in order to give weight to their decisions had to refer to some precept in the life of the prophet. No wonder that many incidents were antedated or even fabricated as having occurred during the lifetime of Muhammad in order to satisfy public clamour.

Traditions and legendary tales grew around Muhammad and his life so that two hundred years later learned men made it their lifework to sift the genuine from the false. A new science was developed, the science of Hadīth or Tradition.[3] That in itself would be nothing extraordinary. Legends and tales grow around every great man in history, but in Muhammad's case a most significant change took place. The whole original aspect of Islām was changed. The accent shifted to a great extent from the 'Revelation of the Book' to the 'Person of Muhammad.' Muhammad was not any longer an accidental instrument in the hand of God to deliver a message of warning, but his person and his life became the centre of interest.

MIRACLES ATTRIBUTED TO HIM

Soon still another development set in. In their newly conquered territories the Muslims came into contact with older civilizations far superior to their own. After the first heat of conquest had passed, discussions between Muslim Arabs and learned men of other faiths, especially Christians, took place. In these debates, the Arab, to his great embarrassment, discovered that the Christian produced very powerful arguments to disclaim the authenticity of Muhammad as a true prophet. Did your prophet perform miracles? Did he walk on the sea? Did he heal the sick? Did he raise the dead? Was he born in a miraculous way? Did he exist before his birth? The Muslim was speechless; he had no answer for all these unheard-of claims. The only miracle to which he could point was the Qur'ān; but that this was the greatest miracle was his firm conviction.

Naturally, in the long run, the situation became unbearable, and soon—perhaps at first by wandering storytellers, but then crystallizing quickly into an authentic tradition—Muhammad's life became filled with miracles from his birth to his last breath. One or two examples may suffice: When he was born, Āmine, his mother, said that a light went forth from him that illuminated the castles of Syria, and that she could see the necks of the camels in Busra. Another tradition asserts that a light shone forth from the East to the West, the moment he was born. This illuminated the whole world. He fell on the ground at his birth, but sat upright at once, gaping towards heaven.[4] Once in later years, when he was out with four hundred men on a *ghazu* (a foraging expedition), they were in the desert and had no water and nothing to eat. The prophet sat down, and the others followed his example. Suddenly a goat appeared, walked up to the prophet, and he milked it, thus quenching the thirst of the four hundred with him.[5]

PRE-EXISTENCE OF MUHAMMAD

Still another development set in. The Near East is the age-old melting pot of ideas and philosophies, of mysticism and strange cosmologies. And it is astonishing what a vitality some of these ideas possess, and how they crop up at different ages under different cloaks. Therefore we find, barely a hundred years after Muhammad's death, in the cosmogony of al Mughīra, a Shī'ī,[6] the old gnostic ideas of the pre-existence of a prophet—

here the pre-existence of Muhammad, of course. Briefly, this may be illustrated as follows: After God had created the two seas, the sea of light and the sea of darkness, He created the shadows of men, and the first two were those of Muhammad and 'Alī.[7] The teaching spread that the prophet already before creation knew the pious of the Shī'a by name and asked the Lord to pardon their sins.[8]

The teaching of the pre-existence of Muhammad was readily accepted by the Sūfīs, the mystics of Islām. They were not satisfied with the conceptions of inspiration held by the orthodox: that Gabriel transmitted all knowledge to Muhammad, and that before that period Muhammad was just as ignorant as all other men. They believed, on the contrary, that God puts into the hearts of His elect special wisdom and knowledge of some of His secrets. To Muhammad, however, He gave all wisdom and all knowledge, long before the creation of this world; it became part of his being long before he was sent to men.[9]

The Sūfīs distinguished between three grades of faith: believing first, that Muhammad was a prophet among the prophets; second, that he united in himself all characteristics of prophets and became the prophet to the prophets; finally, the highest grade of faith, Muhammad, when he received the revelation from God, received a part of God's being, and things were made known to him which remained secrets to the angels and even to Gabriel, the faithful spirit. The strength of faith in Muhammad became the measuring rod for the strength of faith in God, because there is no other way to God except through his intercession.[10] Thus Muhammad became the intercessor, and the mediator. This, in short, is the development of the idea of Muhammad's mediatorship.

MAULID AL NABĪ

Here perhaps some may object, and say the Sūfīs form only a small minority in Islām, and do not represent the whole of Islāmic thought. That is correct, but the tremendous influence which the teachings of the Sūfīs had upon the masses through the different dervish orders should never be underestimated.

HOW MUSLIMS PICTURE MUHAMMAD TODAY

Although the masses do not understand the underlying esoteric meaning of the sayings of the Ṣūfīs, they have used their vocabulary and interpreted it to their own simple understanding. No one who ever witnessed or participated in the *maulid al nabī* celebrations, the festivities on the prophet's birthday (12 Rabīʿ al Awwal of the Muḥammadan year), and heard the hymns and eulogies lavished upon Muhammad, will ever deny that Muhammad has taken the same place in the hearts of the Muslims that Christ has in the hearts of the Christians. In these eulogies we read that he is the light of all light; he is the loveliest of all men; like a rose in the garden, like a pearl in the shell; through him all blessings flow.[11]

The orthodox theologians at first fumed against this cult of Muhammad, and called it *bidʿa* (innovation), but soon they had to give way to popular feelings. Then they called it *bidʿa hasana*[12] (a good innovation). In this way Muhammad became the helper of the faithful during their lifetime and their intercessor on the day of judgment. No one who dies with the confession of faith and the name of Muhammad on his lips will be lost, regardless of what his character has been. On the other hand, no one, regardless of the purity of his character, will enter Paradise if, in his last hour, he does not call upon Muhammad. This is the general conception of the masses, and expresses what Muhammad means to them.

THE MODERNLY EDUCATED AND MUHAMMAD

The modern Muslim educated on Western lines will, of course, smile at these crude notions. But even to him Muhammad means much more than only the messenger, who transmitted a message from God. The message itself is reinterpreted. Attempts are made to explain mystical passages or those which were acceptable for medieval minds but which are no longer acceptable to those who deal in scientific terms. So, for instance, *jinn* are not imps or evil spirits, but they are microbes, and so forth.[13] But vastly more important is the attitude of the modern Muslim toward Muhammad. To him Muhammad is the embodiment of enlightenment (*Aufklärung*). He is the educator, the liberator, the genius. One quotation will illustrate this fact.

Muhammad is 'a social mentor and lawgiver by whose code today one fifth of the human race is governed; a prophet who led human souls from idolatry and paganism into the simplest and clearest conception of the Creator and His worship; rational and humane, he struck at all fetters and brought forth the first true reformation by faith and reason; he opposed slavery and abolished caste, class, colour, and race distinction; he encouraged learning and mercy, taught charity and good will.'[14]

Or here are a few lines written by an Indian Muslim:

'His life is the noblest record of a work nobly and faithfully performed. He infused vitality into a dormant people; he consolidated a congeries of warring tribes into a nation inspired into action with the hope of everlasting life; he concentrated into a focus all the fragmentary and broken lights which had ever fallen on the heart of man. . . . Such was his work, and he performed it with an enthusiasm and fervour which admitted no compromise, conceiving no halting; with indomitable courage which brooked no resistance, and allowed no fear of consequences; with a singleness of purpose which thought of no self.'[15]

This is certainly an amazing development. Muhammad, the instrument of God, has become the centre of interest, the miracle worker, the pre-existing Muhammad as the first of creation, the mediator, the helper of the common people and their intercessor—the most advanced sociologist and benefactor of mankind.

---

[1] Ignaz Goldziher, *Mohammed and Islam*, pp. 31, 32.

[2] Ibn Sa'd, *Kitāb al Tabaqat al Kibīra*, vol. 2.

[3] The most important and authentic collections of the Sunnīs are those of Al Bukhārī; Muslim; and Baghawī, Mishkāt al Masabīh; of the Shī'īs: *Al Kāfī* of Muhammad ibn Ya'qūb al Kūlīnī, and *Al Istibsār fī ma khtalafa fihī lakhbār* of Muhammad al Tūsī.

[4] Ibn Sa'd, *op. cit.*, vol. 1^1, p. 63.

[5] *Ibid.*, vol. 1^1, pp. 118, 119.

[6] The Shī'a form a large group of Muhammadans which separated from the Sunna, the orthodox followers, originally on account of the succession of the caliph. They claimed that the caliph should be a descendant of Muhammad. But later many divergent theological conceptions were developed among the Shī'īs.

[7] Tor Andræ, *Die Person Muhammeds in Lehre und Glauben seiner Gemeinde*, p. 314, translated from Shahrastānī, I, p. 204.
[8] *Ibid.*, p. 310, translated from Kūlīnī, folio 139a.
[9] *Ibid.*, p. 308.
[10] *Ibid.*, pp. 311, 312.
[11] Al Būsīrī, *Al Burda*.
[12] Goldziher, *op. cit.*, o. 298.
[13] H. A. R. Gibb, *Modern Trends in Islam*, p. 72.
[14] G. D. Kheirallah, *Islam and the Arabian Prophet*, preface, unpaged.
[15] Syed Ameer Ali, *The Spirit of Islām*, p. 112.

CHAPTER FOUR

FUNDAMENTALS OF ISLĀM

Having sketched the life of the founder of Islām and the progressive stages of his metamorphosis in the hearts and minds of the believers, we now turn our attention to the great work of his life, the Qur'ān. We shall consider how it came into being, what is its position in Islām, and some of its theological concepts.

QUR'ĀN AND BIBLE; DIFFERENCE IN CONCEPTION OF INSPIRATION

Many assume that the Qur'ān and the Bible occupy similar positions in their respective spheres. That is true in some respects: the one is the Book of the Muslims; the other, the Book of the Christians. Both books are considered by their respective believers to be of God, to be holy and infallible. There is no doubt that many similarities can be found in their subject matter, especially when dealing with certain historical topics. But there are, on the other hand, just as many divergencies, and certainly many of the most vital character.

The Bible was written by many different authors, who lived at different times and under different circumstances. Each writer had his own particular background—historical, educational, ethical—racial as well as geographical, whereas the Qur'ān is unique in the sense that it is the product of one man, Muhammad. The Christian believes men inspired by the divine Spirit wrote under divine guidance, but expressed the thoughts in their own style and language. The Muslim is taught that Muhammad had no part in composing the book, but that it was transmitted to him by Gabriel as it is in heaven on the preserved tablet. 'Yet it is a glorious Qur'ān written on the preserved tablet.'[1]

The Qur'ān, therefore, becomes an absolutely rigid unit. There is no possibility of the slightest change, nor is there possibility of an authorized translation. It is more rigid than the Bible in the hands of even the strictest defenders of verbal inspiration. The latter, at least, although perhaps inconsistently, admit the possibility of a mistake in translation.

Yet in spite of accepting such an unpliant form of revelation, the Muslim has no exact idea of the sequence in which the different parts of the Qur'ān were revealed. The Qur'ān as it is today is compiled by the simple expedient of putting the longest sūras[2] at the beginning of the book and the shortest at the end. But even this practice is not consistently followed. By applying this method in the compilation of the book, the chronological sequence has often been reversed, as the longer sūras contain to a great extent revelations which took place during the Madīna period. The shorter ones fall mostly into the earlier period before the Hijra. Muslims are perfectly aware of this fact, and their commentaries give verse by verse explanation as to when and where and under which circumstances each particular verse was revealed.

The English translation by Rodwell[3] is an attempt to bring the sūras into chronological order. The most exhaustive work in this respect has been done by T. Noldeke as well as more recently by Dr. A. Jeffery.[4]

RECENSION AND INFLUENCE OF THE QUR'AN

When Muhammad died, the Qur'ān was not completed in its written form. It certainly was not arranged. It was more or less in the hearts of the believers. The texts were written on whatever material was handy—palm branches, white stones, leather, shoulder bones of animals, and the memory of men. At first, little attention was paid to get all the revelations properly collected. But when, during the first wars of conquest, many of the old companions who had the Qur'ān in their hearts, died in battle, apprehension was felt that some of the precious knowledge might be lost. Thereupon, according to the best traditions, Zayd ibn Thābit was charged by the caliph Abu

Bakr, to make a collection of all the material in order to bring it into book form.[5] A number of years later certain discrepancies were noticed between the readings of the Qur'ān in large centres, like Kūfa, Damascus, and Madīna. The third caliph, 'Uthmān, charged Zayd ibn Thābit to make a recension, which, when completed, was sent to every great centre of Islām. All the former copies were withdrawn and destroyed. This second version, which was published under the caliphate of 'Uthmān, is the standard version of the Qur'ān in the Muslim world to the present day.[6]

The Qur'ān is certainly the mainspring of all Islāmic thinking, but it is by far not its only source. A good knowledge of the Qur'ān, essential as it is, does not yet help one to achieve a perfect understanding of Islām. Islām is not simply a theology; it is a form of life. Many other streams and streamlets of thought, many habits and customs of different races and peoples in its vast domain have contributed to building the House of Islām as we find it today.

The Qur'ān has certainly exercised an enormous religious influence over the thinking of millions, but in another line its influence has been perhaps equally important: the Qur'ān has formed and stabilized the Arabic language. Arabic became the language of Islām, and thereby the *lingua franca* of all the people from the shores of the Atlantic in Morocco to the Persian Gulf and the Indian Ocean. Arabic became the Latin of the East, the language of religion, of philosophy, and of science. And today it is not a dead language like Latin, but a living language used by over sixty million people. Furthermore, it serves as a most useful key to languages as far apart as Turkish, Persian, Urdu, Swahili, and even Malay. Arabic is the key which opens to the student a vast treasure house of poetry, philosophy, and mysticism. It has been, and still is, the language of the poets and thinkers of those countries, and of all truly educated in the Islāmic world. After this short excursion into the realm of the 'angelic language' of Arabic, let us briefly consider some of the chief points of Qur'ānic teaching.

It has always been stressed that Islām rests on five pillars. These are: faith, prayer, alms, fasting, and the pilgrimage.

What do these five pillars mean? Do these terms convey the same idea to the believing Muslim that they do to the Christian?

THE CONCEPTION OF GOD IN ISLĀM

Faith consists primarily in the *shahāda*; that is, in the public testimony that there is no God besides Allah, and that Muhammad is the Apostle of Allah.

There is no God besides God. Islām, like Judaism and Christianity, is strictly monotheistic. All three religions recognize only one God, but in each of them a different aspect of God is stressed. This results in a different conception of life, which again leads to an entirely different approach to daily tasks and problems.

In Judaism the holiness of God is placed in the foreground; in Christianity the love of God is the centre of all thought; but in Islām, the chief emphasis is on the omnipotence of God and His absolute free will. In Judaism God is jealously watching that His holiness be not infringed upon, and people and prophets stand in awe and holy fear before the throne of the Almighty. In Christianity the accent is shifted from the holiness of God to the love of God. Love is the ultimate motive of all the actions of God. God has limited Himself in His dealings with mankind by the Law of Love. Islām, however, stresses neither the holiness nor the love of God, but the free will of God, unhampered and unrestrained by any limitation. Therefore God can be inconsistent—such it appears at least to human thinking; what He does today, He may recall tomorrow. And even if He had wished, He could have recalled the Qur'ān and blotted it out. This, in fact, happened with certain verses. 'Verses which we [God] abrogate or cause them to be forgotten. We bring a better [in its stead] or a similar one. Knowest thou not that God is able to do all things?'[7] This idea is inconceivable to the Christian mind, but fully acceptable to that of the Muslim in his thinking about God.

That means, of course, that Muslims have a fundamentally different conception of God. To a Muslim, God can only be described by negatives. He is neither this nor that. He is not in any way like man. He is utterly different from man in form and essence; He is completely incomprehensible. To a Christian the highest conception of God is expressed in Christ's words: 'God is a Spirit: and they that worship Him must worship Him in spirit and in truth.' John 4: 24. To the Muslim that very thought is repugnant, because he does not understand the term 'spiritual' in the same way as Christians do.

When the Qur'ān states, 'I, God, breathed into him from my spirit,' it in no way implies that God gives of His own Spirit to man or that He imparts His own essence. This simply means that the spirit in man is likewise God's creation, and for that very reason is God's possession. The spirit is a created thing, like all other created things; perhaps invisible and mysterious like those spirits who rule in the unseen worlds, but decidedly not of the essence of God. Herein lies the basic difference. To a Muslim, God and man are essentially different; there can be no kinship whatsoever between them. To a Christian, man is essentially a spiritual being; he is essentially a child of God. Even if he has estranged himself from God, he is akin to God, called to fellowship with God, called to the high destiny of becoming one with Him even as Christ and the Father are one. In their essence God and man are not two opposites. And though God is not man nor man God, nevertheless God and man can be spiritually one. That is the essential meaning of the Christian faith in incarnation. God and man have thus become one. Heaven and earth have joined hands. Man has the possibility of coming into direct communion with God. As Paul expressed it so clearly, 'I live, yet not I, but Christ liveth in me.' Galatians 2:20.

Such a conception of the relationship between man and God is utterly foreign to the orthodox Muslim. In Sūfī circles, however, it can be found. This radical difference in the conception of the 'spiritual' between Christianity and Islām must always be borne in mind in order to understand the latter faith, as well as to appreciate the difficulties the Muslim has in understanding Christianity. To him there is no kinship whatsoever between God and man; they are different in essence. Whereas the Christian can easily accept God as the leading spiritual force in the universe, a force which acts according to a guiding principle, the Muslim accepts only an omnipotent force—a concept which naturally must lead him to fatalism.

This attitude benumbs all individual endeavour and leads man only too easily to mental and spiritual inertia. It is true that the Christian conception of God also leaves many points unexplained. However, it gives man the certainty that he is not dealing with an arbitrary force, but with a God whose guiding motives are truth, righteousness, and love. That basic difference has always to be borne in mind. The use of the word 'God' before a Muslim audience does not create the same mental picture, nor produce the same reaction as it does before a Christian audience.

THE PRINCIPAL OBLIGATIONS OF A MUSLIM

The second pillar of Islām is *salāt* (prayer). Here again the essential difference becomes clear. Prayer is a solemn obligation upon every believer. It should be performed five times a day—at dawn, at noon, about three o'clock in the afternoon, at sunset, and one and a half or two hours after sunset. Preceding each prayer, ablutions have to be performed according to standing rules. Prayer without these ablutions is void, even sinful. Physical uncleanliness pollutes the spirit; conversely the spirit can be purified by physical cleanliness. The Muslim finds it most difficult to understand how a Christian can ever worship without bodily purification. Such a prayer is no prayer at all to him. After the ablution the faithful has to face Makka and then begin his invocations, standing, kneeling, and prostrating himself before God. Every movement and every genuflection is exactly regulated. If the exact positions are not observed, the prayer is void. Prayer can be performed anywhere, yet preferably near running water in order to comply with the command of ablutions. It can be performed alone or in a small company, or in a mosque. The Arabic world for mosque is *masjid*, meaning the place of prostrating oneself before God.

If prayer is performed in a mosque, the believers stand shoulder to shoulder, rich and poor, educated and uneducated, side by side in long rows. Before them stands the Imām, who leads the worshipers in prayer. Anyone can be the Imām. It is a most impressive sight when hundreds of worshippers perform the different phases of prayer in complete rhythm and unity. Prayer has become a duty, and has taken the form of adoration, or worship, or self-surrender to the will of the Omnipotent. It is evident that it cannot be anything else in Islām, holding the conception of God that Islām does. It cannot be a spiritual intercourse between man and his Creator, as prayer really should be. There is no possibility of a heart-to-heart talk with a Being who is utterly different and whose attitude is unpredictable. It must necessarily become a form of worship which has to be dutifully performed.

In no way, of course, should we underestimate the value of such a regular performance. It has a sobering effect on the heart to be conscious of standing before one's Creator. It safeguards man on his perilous journey over this earth; it helps him to keep in bounds. It tends also to make him a strict formalist; it hardens him to self-righteousness, from which it is only one step to fanaticism. And that is just the opposite of what prayer at its best should accomplish. It should not strengthen our ego, increase our self-centredness; but on the contrary, it should open the horizon, give us wider vistas into the realm of the spirit, and thereby give us a deeper understanding of the needs of our fellow men.

The third pillar of Islām is almsgiving—*zakāt*.[8] The alms-tax, or *sadaqa*,[9] is a freewill offering to the poor. But it is difficult to differentiate correctly between these two terms, because even in the Qur'ān they are sometimes used interchangeably, and in later theological writings they often became synonymous.

Almsgiving has been considered a meritorious act since time immemorial, and Muhammad did not institute anything new by making almsgiving obligatory in Islām. He states that Ismā'īl enjoined almsgiving on his people,[10] and makes Jesus speak from the cradle that almsgiving will be a part of His service.[11] No definite amount or percentage which should be given is stated in the Qur'ān. On the contrary, we find statements like the following: 'If you lend God a generous loan, He will double it to you, and will forgive you, for God is grateful and long suffering.'[12] The doctors of the law in later times worked out an exact scheme of how much the *zakāt* should be under different circumstances. In most cases it is much less than the Biblical tithe, and also debts had to be paid first before the *zakāt* could be deducted. The recipients of the *zakāt* were not the clergy, because there is no clergy in Islām, but the poor and needy, Muslim captives in enemy lands, those engaged in holy war, wayfarers, and travellers.

The fourth pillar of Islām is 'fasting.' The month of fasting, Ramadān,[13] is mentioned in Sūra 2: 179-183 (183-188), which describes in detail how the fast should be performed, and lists the actions permitted or prohibited during this sacred month. According to tradition, Muhammad himself fasted three days every month, long before the month of fasting was instituted in the later Madīnian period. Many scholars suggest that Muhammad conceived the idea of a month of fasting after having had contact with the Jews in Madīna. Others think that Ramadān is comparable to the Christian Lent. But the Muhammadan fast differs widely from its Jewish and Christian predecessors. It is not an abstinence from certain kinds of food, but a complete abstinence from any food or drink, including water, from smoking, or any other stimulant during the daytime; or, more exactly speaking, from the moment a white thread can be distinguished from a black one in the early twilight of the morning till sunset sharp. From sunset to that early morning hour, eating and drinking are permitted. Often Ramadān becomes a month of feasts. Special food is prepared, families join together, the Qur'ān is chanted by special singers, religious plays are enacted, and the *Dhikr*[14] performed.

It is interesting to note how conceptions about Ramadān have changed. Modern writers practically always emphasize that the great value of fasting lies in gaining control over most unpleasant sensations, like hunger and thirst, in strengthening the will power, in preparing man to endure hardships, and in evoking compassion for the poor, who so often experience the pangs of hunger.[15] These modern conceptions were, of course, not at all the motivating power in instituting Ramadān, nor were they prevalent in early Islām. Fasting was considered to be a most suitable means of gaining favour with God. It was considered as a most fitting atonement for transgressions committed. A few statements may suffice:

'The scent of the breath of a fasting man is pleasanter to God than the scent of musk. The one who forsakes his eating and drinking and his lust for My sake I shall recompense tenfold.'[16] In heaven is a special gate called Bāb-al Rayyān, through which the faster will enter Paradise.[17] Further, when Ramaḍān begins, the gates of heaven will be opened, the gates of hell closed, and the devils chained.[18] And Abu Hurayra reports that the prophet said, 'Who fasts in Ramadān with faith and hope of recompense will receive forgiveness of his previous sins.'[19]

But whatever the conceptions and arguments are, which are brought forth to defend Ramadān, it does not matter. The practical results of Ramadān are much more important, and these are undoubtedly a close knitting together of all the followers of Islām, because nothing binds men more strongly together than privations and hardships suffered in common. Many egos with as many wills unite together in one common aim with one common goal, therewith creating a community spirit. This imparts its strength again to the individual ego, gives him a feeling of elation, and creates in him the spirit of fidelity to this community.

The fifth and last pillar of Islām is the pilgrimage, *al ḥajj*. The pilgrimage is obligatory on every adult Muslim of either sex. Only sickness, want of subsistence, or being in a state of servitude may relieve the individual from fulfilling this pious duty. Many rites connected with the pilgrimage were in well-established usage among Arabs long before Muhammad came. All these rites have to be observed on certain days, on the last of which a sacrificial animal is slain. Participants have to be in a state of ritual purity.

Muhammad himself never mentioned the pilgrimage in his early preaching as long as he was in Makka. But after he had migrated to Madīna, and his hopes of winning the Jews of Madīna to his cause were shattered, he began to turn his attention again to Makka, the old and most important centre

FUNDAMENTALS OF ISLĀM

of Western Arabia. He changed the '*qibla*,' the direction of prayer, from Jerusalem back to Makka, to the old house of worship of the Arabs, the Ka'ba, which contained within its walls the sacred black meteorite.[20] Finally he incorporated the pilgrimage to this holy shrine into Islām as one of the most meritorious works.[21] But even older rites, as the visiting of al Safā and al Marwa, the real meaning of which had long been lost, but which were still practiced in Muhammad's time, were sanctified.[22] Makka therewith was raised from a centre of pagan Arabia to the religious centre of the Muslim world. Makka became enshrined in all Muslim hearts. It became the city toward which all their yearnings flowed.

With this step, the strangest contradiction became reality. Islām, the most outspoken monotheistic religion, which confesses that God is one, and that God, the one supreme Being beyond time and space, can be worshipped anywhere, has as the centre of its worship a black meteorite, toward which the faithful bow five times a day. That is just one of the inscrutable oddities of human nature. It is capable of accepting and holding at the same time two or more convictions which logically exclude each other.

The practical result of the pilgrimage, however, can scarcely be overestimated. There is hardly anything in Christianity which can match it. In a time when travel was an adventure, and was seldom indulged in by a European Christian of the common rank and file, Muslims became the greatest travellers of the world. *Al hajj* brought together the sturdy tribesmen of the Iranian highlands and the Afghan mountains with the fierce warriors of Morocco and Algeria, the Indian prince and merchant with the aristocratic Arab of Damascus, the Turk from the Golden Horn with the Malay from the Spice Islands. It kindled as nothing else the bond of Islām between peoples, races, and colours, and made every pilgrim realize the vastness of the Dār al-Islām in which Allah ruled supreme.

---

[1] Sūra 85: 21, 22.
[2] Sūra = chapter, revealed unit, although a good number are composites.

BRIDGE TO ISLĀM

Each Sūra has a special heading, for instance, Cow, Ant, The Inevitable, or just simple letters, as Ta, Ha, etc.

³ *The Koran*, translated from the Arabic by J. M. Rodwell. Everyman's Library, 1945.

⁴ See Th. Nöldeke, *Geschichte des Qurāns* (3 vols. in 1; A. Jeffery, *Materials for the History of the Text of the Qur'ān*.

⁵ Noldeke, *op. cit.*, vol. 2, pp. 11-15.

⁶ *Ibid.*, pp. 48, 49.

⁷ Sūra 2: 100 (106).

⁸ Joseph Schacht, 'Zakāt,' in *The Encyclopædia of Islam*, Vol. IV, pp. 1202-1205.

⁹ T. H. Weir, 'Sadaqa,' in the same volume, pp. 33-35.

¹⁰ Sūra 19: 56 (55).

¹¹ Sūra 19: 32 (31).

¹² Sūra 64: 17.

¹³ Ramadān is the ninth month in the Arabian calendar. As the Muhammadan year is a lunar year, it wanders through all the seasons of the year. The names of the months of the Muhammadan year are the following: Muharram, Safar, Rabī' I, Rabī' II, Jumāda I, Jumāda II, Rajab, Ramadān, Shawwāl, Dhu'l Qa'da, Dhu'l Hijja.

¹⁴ *Dhikr* in this connection means 'Remembering of the Name of God.' It is a ceremony in which a limited number of men take part. They stand in two rows facing each other and repeating the formula of faith, simultaneously swinging their bodies from left to right and from right to left, until they frequently reach a state of ecstasy or are exhausted.

¹⁵ Maulana Muhammad 'Ali, *The Religion of Islām*, pp. 482-484.

¹⁶ Al Bukhārī, *Al Jāmi' al Sahīh*, Vol. I, p. 473 (in French translation, El Bokhārī, *Les Traditions Islamiques*, Vol. I, p. 607.)

¹⁷ *Ibid.*, Arabic, p. 473; French, p. 608.

¹⁸ *Ibid.*, Arabic, p. 474; French, p. 609.

¹⁹ *Ibid.*, Arabic, pp. 474, 475; French, p. 609.

²⁰ Sūra 2: 137-145 (143-150).

²¹ Sūra 3: 91 (97); 5:2; 2: 192-196 (196-200).

²² Sūra 2: 153 (158).

CHAPTER FIVE

JESUS IN ISLĀM

THE five pillars of Islām—confession of faith, prayer, alms, fasting, and the pilgrimage—are of course, not the only subjects covered in the Qur'ān. Many historical figures known from the Old Testament pass before our eyes, clothed in a somewhat different garb, yet easily discernible. It would lead us too far afield if we should mention them all, but one figure holds our interest. That is Jesus, or 'Isa, as He is called in the House of Islām. What does the Muslim know about Jesus? What picture of Him has he in his mind? What does he learn of Jesus from the Qur'ān?

In the following the Qur'ān may speak for itself. Only here and there a remark is interwoven in order to explain some otherwise unintelligible passage.

JESUS AS PICTURED IN THE QUR'ĀN

The wife of 'Imrān made a vow to her Lord that she would dedicate her child to the service of the Lord if He would grant her that happiness. The child was born, but she was somewhat disappointed when she saw that it was a girl. But, resigned to the will of God, she exclaimed: 'God knows about it.' She called the child Maryam (Mary) and asked the Lord to protect the girl from Satan the stoned,[1] which request God granted.[2] This protection from Satan has a special significance, because, according to a well-established tradition, every newborn child was touched by Satan, except Maryam and her son.[3] That is the idea of the Immaculate Conception, in a slightly different form. At the same time it shows that the Muslims do not accept the doctrine of original sin.

Maryam was reared in the temple under the guardianship of Zacharias. Whenever he came into her room, he found her supplied with food. When he expressed surprise about it,

Maryam told him that God cared for her.⁴ Then the narrative continues:

'Remember when the angels said: "O Maryam, verily God has chosen thee, and purified thee and has chosen thee above the women of the world. O Maryam, be humble to your Lord, and prostrate yourself, and bow down with those who bow." '⁵

Thereupon follows the Lord's announcement to Mary:

' "O Maryam, verily God brings good news to thee, a word from Him. His name shall be Messiah 'Isa, son of Maryam, illustrious in this world and in the next, and he will be one of those who are close to God [*al muqarrabīn*—cherubs]. And he shall speak to men alike when in the cradle and when grown up, and will be one of the righteous."

'She said: "O Lord, how shall I have a son, when man has not touched me?" He said: "So it will be; God will create what He will; when He decrees a thing, He says to it, 'Be,' and it is.

' "And He will teach him the Book, and the Wisdom, and the Torah, and the Injīl [Gospel, New Testament], and he will be an Apostle to the Children of Israel." '⁶

In another Sūra, which bears the title 'Maryam' a detailed description of the birth of Jesus is given.

'And mention in the Book, Maryam, when she separated from her family to a place eastward.

'And she took a veil [to shroud herself] from them: and we [God] sent our spirit [Gabriel], and he appeared before her in the form of a perfect man.

'She said: "I fly for refuge from thee to the Rahmān [the God of Mercy]. If you are pious [go away]."

'He said: "Verily, I am a messenger of thy Lord, that I shall bestow upon thee a pure [holy] son."

'She said: "How shall I have a son, when man has not touched me? And I am not unchaste?"

'He said: "Thus shall it be, Thy Lord has said; 'This is an easy matter with Me.' And we will make him a sign to the people, a mercy from us. And that is a thing decreed."

'And she conceived him and retired with him to a far-off place."⁷

Baydāwī remarks about this verse, that Gabriel breathed at

her and it entered her rib. He describes the far-off place as behind the mountain of her home town, probably.

'And the pangs of birth came upon her near the trunk of a palm, and she cried: "Oh, that I would have died before this, and would have been altogether forgotten."

'Then he called from below her [either the infant Jesus or Gabriel], "Grieve not. Thy Lord has provided a streamlet at your feet.

' "And shake the trunk of the palm-tree towards thee, and fresh, ripe dates will drop upon thee.

' "Eat and drink and be of cheerful eye, and if thou shouldst see anyone, say to him,

' " 'I have vowed a fast to the Rahmān—to no one will I speak today.' "

'And she came to her people with the babe, carrying him. They said: "O Maryam, you have done a strange thing!

' "O Sister of Aaron, your father was not a wicked man, nor was your mother unchaste."

'And she pointed at him [made signs unto the child to answer them], and they said: "How can we speak with one who is an infant in the cradle?"

'And he [the babe] said: "Verily, I am the servant of God. He has given me the Book, and has made me a prophet.

' "And He has made me blessed, wherever I may be, and has ordered me [to observe] prayer and almsgiving;

' "And to be respectful to my mother, and has not made me a tyrant nor a vicious man.

' "And the peace of God was upon me the day I was born and will be the day I shall die, and the day I shall be raised to life."

'This is 'Isa, the son of Maryam. This is a statement of truth, about which they doubt [quarrel among themselves].'[8]

On His early development and His manhood, we have the following statements:

'He [Jesus] will say: "I have come to you with a sign from your Lord. I shall form out of clay the figure of a bird for you, then I will breathe into it, and with the permission of God, it will become a bird. I will heal the blind and the leper and, with the permission of God, I shall bring the dead to life again, and I shall tell you what you eat and what you store up in your houses. Verily in this will be a sign for you, if you are believers.

' "And I have come to approve of what is between my hands of the Torah and to allow you part, what was forbidden to you; and I have come with a sign from your Lord. Therefore fear God and obey. Verily, God is my Lord and your Lord, so worship Him, this is the straight path."

'And when Jesus felt their unbelief, he said: "Who are my helpers with God?" Then said the Hawārī [disciples?]: "We are the helpers of God. We believe in God and bear witness that we are Muslims." '[9]

In the fifth Sūra, the foregoing is repeated in similar words, but then Muhammad describes his conception of the Lord's supper:

'When the Hawārīs said: "O 'Isa, son of Maryam, is your Lord able to send a Table [with food upon it] down from heaven?" he said: "Trust God, if ye be believers."

'They said, "We want to eat from it and to have our hearts assured and know that thou hast spoken the truth to us, and we shall be witnesses thereof."

'Thereupon 'Isa, the son of Maryam, said: "O god, our Lord, send to us a table from heaven, which will become a recurring festival to the first and last of us, a sign from you to provide for us, and you are the best provider."

'And God said: "I shall make it descend upon you, but whoever among you shall disbelieve hereafter, I shall chastise him with a chastisement wherewith I shall not punish any other creature in the worlds." '[10]

Then God questions 'Isa about his teachings while he was on earth:

' "O 'Isa, son of Maryam, hast Thou said to mankind, 'Take me and my mother as two Gods besides God?' "

'He said: "Glory be unto Thee. It is not to me to say what I know is not the truth. If I had said it, Thou wouldest have known it. Thou knowest what is in me, but I do not know what is in Thee. Thou well knowest things unseen.

' "I did not say to them except that which Thou ordered

me: 'Worship God, my Lord and your Lord.' And I was a witness of their actions while I stayed among them, and since Thou hast taken me to Thyself. Thou hast observed them and Thou art a witness of all things, if Thou punish them, they are Thy servants, and if Thou forgive them, Thou art mighty and wise." '[11]

The next verses explain what the Qur'ān teaches about the relationship between God and the Messiah.

'Infidels are those who say that God is the Messiah, son of Maryam. The Messsiah said: "O children of Israel, worship God, my Lord and your Lord!" Verily who joins other gods with God, God will forbid him Paradise; his abode will be the Fire, and the wicked shall have no helper.

'Infidels are those who say that God is the third of three. There is no God but one God, and if they refrain not from what they say, a severe punishment will befall the unbelievers among them. . . .

'The Messiah, Son of Maryam, is but an Apostle; other Apostles have flourished before him; and his mother was a just person, they both ate food.'[12]

'Verily infidels are those, who say that God is the Messiah, the son of Maryam. Say, Who rules over God, if He chose to destroy the Messiah, the son of Maryam, and his mother and all mankind?'[13]

On the death of Jesus and his ascent to heaven, the statements which we find are not consistent. We have already mentioned the text of Sūra 19: 34, which states that 'Isa spoke from the cradle, and that he prophetically emphasized that the peace of God rested upon him on the day of his birth, and would rest upon him on the day of his death and on the day of his resurrection. But there are verses, the explanation of which either is doubtful or emphatically denies his death. First, Sūra 3: 48 (46):

'O 'Isa, verily I will cause thee to die (*mutawaffīka*), and I shall take thee up to Me and cleanse thee [deliver thee] from those who believe not.'

Baydāwī, however, explains that *mutawaffīka* has here the meaning of *mustaufa ajlaka*, which is, 'I shall complete thy years.'

Naturally after the completion of the life span death follows, but in a case like 'Isa's not necessarily so. And to 'I shall take thee up' Baydāwī adds, 'to a place of my honour and to the abode of the angels.'

But second, the most definite statement is the following:

'And for their saying: "Verily we have slain the Messiah, 'Isa the son of Maryam, the Apostle of God." Yet they slew him not, and they crucified him not, but one was made to appear to them like 'Isa (*shubbiha lahu*). And they who differed about him and were in doubt had no real knowledge but followed only an opinion; and they certainly did not kill him, but God took him to Himself, and God is mighty and wise.'[14]

THE RETURN OF JESUS

According to the Muhammadan view, 'Isa is now in heaven as one who has access to the throne of God. And according to tradition, Muhammad, on his night journey to the seventh heaven, met 'Isa in the second heaven and was introduced to him by Gabriel; whereas others of the fathers were in a higher place, for instance, Joseph in the third heaven, Aaron in the fifth, Moses in the sixth, and Abraham in the seventh heaven.[15]

Jesus is expected to return to this world shortly before the day of judgment, and a number of remarkable happenings will occur in connection with this event. This is a firm belief among Muslims, although there is only one verse in the Qur'ān with rather obscure wording that has a reference to the second coming of Jesus. 'Verily, he ['Isa] is only a servant whom we favoured and made him an example to the children of Israel and if we pleased we could have given you angels as offspring. And verily, he ['Isa] is the knowledge of the last hour';[16] that means, by his coming the nearness of the 'Hour' will be known. Others read it, 'He is a sign of the last hour.'

Around this verse tradition has built a whole eschatological structure with some rather remarkable features. Baydāwī, the famous commentator on the Qur'ān, summarizes the wealth of material found in the collections of traditions compiled by the two, Muslim and al Bukhārī, in the following manner:

'His ['Isa's] coming is one of the conditions to be fulfilled before the break of the Judgment Hour, for by this, we shall know the close approach of that Hour. . . . It is mentioned in the Hadīth that 'Isa will descend on a mountain path in the Holy Land, probably near Afiq, carrying in his hand a spear, wherewith he will kill the *al dajjāl* [the great deceiver, the Antichrist]; then he will enter the Holy Mosque at the time of the morning worship. The Imām will step back to make room for 'Isa, but the latter will fall into line and pray behind the Imām according to the rites of Muhammad. Then he is going to kill the swine and break the cross and destroy all synagogues and churches and will kill all those Christians who have not accepted him.'[17]

So far Baydāwī. Others often go further, stating that 'Isa will also slay the monkeys (meaning that the Hindu religion as well as the Jewish and Christian will be abolished). From that time on there will be only one faith on earth. 'Isa will reign for forty years and then die and be buried in Madīna between Muhammad and Abu Bakr. In the tomb of the prophet there is now a spare place for only a single grave, which is reserved for 'Isa ibn Maryam after his second coming.[18] Others connect him with the Mahdi (the one who is guided by God) who will come before the end and restore the faith in its pristine purity. After 'Isa has fulfilled his mission and is laid to rest, the sound of the trumpet will be heard, and the great Day of Judgment will dawn.

This is the picture of Jesus which the Muslim gains from his own sources. Every time the name of Jesus is mentioned this picture flashes through his mind. It is not an altogether bad picture, but, alas, how different from the one Christians have in their minds! It pictures Jesus as a highly exalted being, having entered this world in an exceptional and miraculous way, having been protected from the touch of Satan and endowed with powers not granted to other human beings, even prophets. After having fulfilled His prophetic mission, He was permitted to leave this world in a similar miraculous manner, in order to live in a quasiangelic state until a time when He has to return to this earth to complete His tasks, and to die like other human beings. It is true, as the Qur'ān puts it: 'Exalted in this world and in the next,' but it lacks all the essential elements which make Jesus the Christ, the Anointed of the Father, Immanuel, God with us, the Healer of our souls, the Saviour; the Inborn of the Father, the Son of man, who brings us close to the heart of God.

It would be easy to point out to the Muslim the different heretical elements which contributed to the distorted picture of Jesus which Muhammad received. It would be easy to lay the finger upon the Ebionites or the Docetists or upon the apocryphal Gospel of Thomas, all of which are rejected by official Christendom, but that would not change an iota of the fact that the above description remains the authentic picture of Jesus for every Muslim. On the contrary, it would strengthen his belief, that the Christians themselves are disunited and do not know what they are talking about. Only by patiently presenting the real picture of Jesus, with all its spiritual implications, will it be possible to lay the foundation of the bridge which will finally span the gulf.

THE HOLY SPIRIT AND THE QUR'ĀN

Here is perhaps the right place to mention two other conceptions in Islām, which often are the cause of serious misunderstanding. Already in the previous chapter we have pointed out the great difficulties which the Muslim has in understanding spiritual things. Here is another example. The term 'Holy Spirit' is mentioned in the Qur'ān. 'Say, the Holy Spirit [*rūḥ al qudus*] brought it down from thy Lord in truth.'[19] But the Muslim understands that the Holy Spirit is Gabriel, the Faithful Spirit (messenger) of God. When, therefore, Christians refer to the Holy Spirit, as they often do, as the third person of the Godhead, it is perfectly obnoxious and revolting to the ears of the Muslim believers, as to them it means the placing of an angel, Gabriel, on the same level and with many of the same attributes with God.

SATAN IN THE QUR'ĀN

Another interesting point is that the Qur'ān gives us a full description of the fall of Satan. Whereas the Bible speaks only in metaphors on this point (Isaiah 14: 12-14 and Ezekiel 28: 12-15), and in no way explains the reason for his fall, the Qur'ān explains it in full detail. Nevertheless, it does not mean an explanation of evil, as the Muslim is not in need of solving this problem which causes so much distress to the Western mind. Allah is the cause of everything, of Evil as well as Good.

'He created you, then fashioned you, then said He to the angels, "Prostrate yourselves unto Adam": and they prostrated themselves all in worship, save Iblīs [Satan]: he was not among those who prostrated themselves.

'To him said God: "What hath hindered thee from prostrating thyself in worship at My bidding?" He said, "Nobler am I than he: me hath thou created of fire; of clay hast thou created him."

'He said, "Get thee down hence: Paradise is no place for thy pride: get thee gone then; one of the despised shalt thou be."

'He said, "Respite me till the day when mankind shall be raised from the dead."

'He said, "One of the despised shalt thou be."

'He said, "Now, for that Thou hast caused me to err, surely in Thy straight path will I lay wait for them: Then will I surely come upon them from before, and from behind, and from their right hand, and from their left and Thou shalt not find the greater part of them to be thankful!"

'He said, "Go forth from it, a scorned, a banished one! Whoever of them shall follow thee, I will surely fill hell with you altogether." '[20]

---

[1] An attribute of Satan; it is a common expression among Muslims: 'I take refuge with God from Satan the stoned.'
[2] Sūra 3: 31, 32 (35-37).
[3] Baydāwī to Sūra 3: 36.
[4] Sūra 3: 32, 33 (37).
[5] Sūra 3: 37, 38 (42, 43).
[6] Sūra 3: 40-43 (45-49).
[7] Sūra 19: 16-23 (16-22).
[8] Sūra 19: 24-35 (23-34).
[9] Sūra 3: 43-45 (49-52).
[10] Sūra 5: 112-115.

[11] Sūra 5: 116-118 (115-118).
[12] Sūra 5: 76, 77, 79 (72, 73, 75).
[13] Sūra 5: 19 (17).
[14] Sūra 4: 156 (157).
[15] Bukhārī, *Kitāb al Jāmi' al Sahīh*, Vol. III, pp. 29, 30; French trans., Vol. III, pp. 38, 39.
[16] Sūra 43: 59-61.
[17] Baydāwī, Commentary on Sūra 43: 61.
[18] R. F. Burton, *Personal Narrative of a Pilgrimage to El-Medinah and Meccah*, Vol. II, pp. 86, 87.
[19] Sūra 16: 104 (102).
[20] Sūra 7: 10-17 (11-18).

CHAPTER SIX

IDEAS REGARDING PREDESTINATION AND SIN

MUHAMMAD was a preacher, not a theologian; and, as is often the case, preachers who possess originality are seldom good theologians. They feel the need of the hour and find the right word at the right moment to inspire and satisfy their audiences. But when their sermons or speeches are recorded for posterity, theologians later encounter great difficulties in bringing the heterogeneous elements of their utterances into a harmonious system. The same problem confronted the Muhammadan theologians when they approached the Qur'ān in order to formulate a clear and well-balanced dogma. It took about three hundred years for a dogma to crystallize which finally became the generally accepted view of Islām. That does not mean, of course, that the problems were solved therewith. It means only that certain groups were strong enough to impose their ideas upon the rest of the believers.

On the question of predestination, for instance, we find a great number of passages in the Qur'ān which leave not the least doubt that man's course of life is mapped out beforehand. That in itself would be acceptable as long as it would refer to circumstances connected with man's outer life. But the moment it is linked with the complete arbitrariness of God's dealing with man on a spiritual level, it becomes highly objectionable from the Christian point of view. Here follow some of these more representative passages:

'No one can die except by God's order, according to the book that fixeth the term of life.'[1]

'No people can forestall or retard its destiny.'[2]

In a planned universe the idea is conceivable that people and nations have their fixed time. But the Qur'ān goes further and proclaims: 'Had God pleased, they had not joined other gods with Him.'[3] 'And whom God shall please to guide, that man's breast will be open to Islām, but whom He shall please to mislead, straight and narrow will He make his breast. . . . '[4] 'Say, God's is the east and the west; He guideth whom He will into the right path.'[5] 'To God belongs what is in the heavens and on earth. He forgives whom He pleases and punishes whom He pleases, for God is forgiving and merciful.[6]

With statements like these, of course, all moral initiative, all striving to achieve higher goals, all endeavours to improve character are nullified. There is no room for personal responsibility, no possibility for success or failure with the accompanying emotions of elation or distress, no healthful striving. Striving for perfection alone means a better life.

It is evident that such ideas followed logically to their end would take out all force from a preacher's message. Muhammad would have dug his own grave. Therefore we can find in the Qur'ān just as many passages which stress the personal responsibility of accepting God's message, the value of righteous living and its reward, and the punishment for trespassing God's demands. For example:

'And say the truth is from your Lord: let him who will, believe; and let him who will, disbelieve. But for the evildoers we have got ready the fire whose smoke shall enwrap them; and if they implore help, helped they shall be, with water like molten metal, which shall scald the faces. Wretched the drink! and an unhappy couch!

'Verily, those who have believed and done the things that are right, verily we will not waste the reward of him, whose works were good.

'For them, are the gardens of Eden, under whose shades shall rivers flow: decked shall they be therein with bracelets of gold, and green robes of silk and rich brocade shall they wear, reclining upon thrones therein. Blissful the reward! And a goodly couch!'[7]

'To those who respond to their Lord shall be an excellent reward, but to those who respond not, had they all what the earth containeth twice over, and they surely would give it for ransom, their account will be evil and hell will be their home! An evil bed will it be!'[8]

IDEAS REGARDING PREDESTINATION AND SIN

'And those who keep the pact of God and break not the covenant, and who unite that what God has commanded to be joined, and fear their Lord and dread a woeful reckoning, and those who persevere in seeking their Lord's countenance, and observe prayer and give alms, secretly and openly, and overcome evil with good, to them is the recompense of that abode, gardens of Eden.'[9]

It is evident that these last-quoted passages are diametrically opposed to the aforementioned, because they presuppose the element of free choice in accepting or rejecting the messages sent by God. They require a conscious acceptance of principles and precepts, and a life which is based on following such principles meticulously. Muhammadan theologians were painfully aware of these contradictory elements in the Qur'ān, and different schools of thought were disputing on these and similar subjects, until Al Ash'arī (260-327 A.H.; A.D. 873-935) settled the question. He maintained the absolute, eternal, free will of God, including His power to will evil and to do evil. But he allowed man certain powers. This he called *kasb* or *iktisāb*, which as a theological term has the meaning of acquisition. That means, if God wills a thing, He creates in man the power to acquire it. The acquiring of the thing willed by God is man's own act, and thereby his responsibility is established. So taught Al Ash'arī.

That this is no real solution is very apparent. It is just a make-believe scheme that man has his own choice in determining his fate while in reality he cannot acquire any object, good or evil, except God creates in him the power to acquire it. It is fatalism somewhat camouflaged. This view has become the accepted philosophy of the masses in Islām. It is a most convenient and satisfactory mode of thought for the Muslim, because God, having decreed for him to be born a Muslim, has placed him on the safe side anyway, and to consider the situation of the non-Muslim, even speculatively, is of no concern to the believer.

What is the practical result of this fatalistic attitude in daily life? Does it mean that the Muslim will fold his hands, settling down to await the raven of Allah to feed him? Does it mean that he will live a life of inactivity, completely neglecting all duties of life? Not at all. Everyone who has come in contact with Muslims will testify that they can be very active in trying to achieve their aims; he will have observed that the common man toils from morn to night to make an honest living. Fatalism does not mean inactivity or laziness, as it is often pictured by Western tourists. It is rather an unconcern over the final outcome, an unconcern borne by the keen sense of God's absolute sovereignty and man's complete dependence upon God. This attitude prevents the Muslim from despairing in times of adversity and misfortune. It prevents him from indulging in self-accusations and useless regrets over things past, while Westerners often make their lives miserable by self-reproach, and suffer nervous breakdowns, ulcers, and other disorders of this modern age.

THE CONCEPTION OF SIN IN ISLĀM

This fatalistic concept prevents him also from feeling guilt or remorse, an element of basic importance in the Christian religion. Out of it grows the longing for a new and better life, a life on a purer spiritual level. Herewith we have touched the very centre of the problem—the problem of sin. Sin and its redemption is the pivotal point in all religious thinking. All other subjects dealt with in religion are of secondary nature, so that one may dare the somewhat bold statement: If it were not for sin, and this unfathomable feeling of guilt in the human heart, no religion would ever have been conceived. Therefore a religion which loses sight of this, its prime object, namely, sin and its removal, or sin and its redemption, is fast becoming a philosophy or merely an ethical code. Should not then the question be raised, What position does sin occupy in Islām? What position can it occupy?

Reviewing the first part of the chapter in our minds, we certainly would come to the conclusion that there is not much room for sin in a predestined system of life, because according to the Christian conception, sin presupposes the possibility of man's choosing wilfully to do wrong. And yet Islām speaks of sin, even of an unpardonable sin. What, then, does Islām understand by sin?

IDEAS REGARDING PREDESTINATION AND SIN

In Islām, God is supreme. He is different in essence and form from men, He is incomprehensible. In Him everything has its existence, and through Him every action is caused. To conceive, therefore, another god besides God, to put another being at the side of this Supreme Being, is the most abominable wickedness man can fall into. It is *shirk*, the unpardonable sin.

'Verily, God will not forgive the union of other gods with Himself! But other than this will He forgive to whom He pleaseth. And he who uniteth gods with God hath devised a great wickedness.'[10]

Christians are often accused of practising *shirk*, because of a misunderstanding of the Christian doctrine of the Trinity. However, the Muslims are not altogether to blame for that. Muhammad himself seemed to have had the notion that Christians believed in three gods, God the Father, God the Son, and Mary, the Mother of God. It is, of course, easy to repudiate this wrong concept of the Trinity. This Christian doctrine is often represented by theological writers, especially from the West, in a way, that it appears as if Christians did believe in a kind of tritheism, of three divinities in heaven. Such a teaching would destroy the unity of God. Such a thought is unbearable to a Muslim; it is an abomination; it is a *shirk*. Therefore whatever good deeds a Christian may perform, and however noble his character may be, he is despicable, because he is perpetually committing the unpardonable sin, he is practising *shirk*.

Otherwise, sin in Islām is simply that which Allah forbids. There are certain things *halāl* (permitted), and others *harām* (forbidden). These may be on an ethical or a ritual level; there is no difference between the two. There are certain obligations which man has to fulfil towards his Creator; they are called *fard* or *wājib*. But life is so diversified that not all actions could be classified as religiously permitted or forbidden; hence the Muhammadan moralist has invented two other terms. There exist actions which are *mubāh* or *jāiz* that means actions which are neither recommended nor forbidden, and neither reward nor punishment is expected for doing them. And there are others which are *makrūh* (disproved, hateful), but they do not lead to the loss of paradise, and are not punishable. They, however, could not be recommended from a religious point of view.[11]

Moreover, God is compassionate and merciful. He desires to make your burden light, because man was created weak.[12] There is nothing in Islām which resembles the Christian conception of sin as a fall from grace, a falling away from God and His holy law, an alienation from God, resulting in the corruption of the human heart and the total depravity of human nature in making its own ego instead of God the centre of interest, affection, and worship. Naturally, as there is no deep conviction of sin in Islām, no feeling of an estrangement between God and man, there is no need for reconciliation, no need for redemption, nor for a Saviour from sin, no need for a complete turn in life, nor for being born again in the likeness of the Spirit. And here lies the deepest gulf which separates Christianity from Islām.

---

[1] Sūra 3: 139 (145).
[2] Sūra 15: 5.
[3] Sūra 6: 107.
[4] Sūra 6: 125.
[5] Sūra 2: 136 (142).
[6] Sūra 3: 124 (129).
[7] Sūra 18: 28-30 (29-31).
[8] Sūra 13: 18.
[9] Sūra 13: 20-22.
[10] Sūra 4: 51 (48).
[11] Th. Juynboll, *Handbuch des islamischen Gesetzes*, pp. 59, 60.
[12] Sūra 4: 32 (28).

CHAPTER SEVEN

RELIGIOUS LIBERTY IN ISLĀM

To speak of religious liberty in Islām—many will say—is a mockery. Is not Islām the religion of the sword, the religion which put before the conquered the alternative either to accept Islām or be killed? Does there not slumber in the mind of every European the horror of the Turks beleaguering Vienna, and the atrocities of the fierce corsairs all around the Mediterranean? Do we not all remember the massacres of the Armenians? Is it not frivolous to speak of religious liberty in Islām? There is no religious liberty in Islām.

On the other hand, we hear modern commentators praising Islām as the most lenient and tolerant of all religions. Then, books like T. W. Arnold's *The Preaching of Islām* tend to ascribe the success of this religion largely to the missionary activities of its members. Furthermore, we should never forget that for centuries large non-Muslim minorities have lived under the banner of Islām. What, then, is the truth? Does religious liberty exist in Islām or not?

The difficulty seems to lie in the definition of 'religious liberty'. In the democratic nations of the West these words mean the full freedom of the individual to worship God or any other being in whatever form he deems best, as well as the right to propagate his particular belief in order to win others. There can be no control or dictation from the state. This conception of religious rights can almost be called new. It was expressed by some early Christian writers as Tertullian[1] and Lactantius,[2] but was lost sight of after Christianity became the religion of the Roman state. The concept in its present form is the outcome of the rationalism of the eighteenth century which found its expression in a separation of church and state, in dividing life's interests into two separate spheres—a material, or secular, sphere and a spiritual sphere. The secular sphere comprises all of man's daily occupations and necessities; the spiritual sphere governs his relationship to the Unseen. In the field of education these two spheres overlap and often cause friction.

During the ages preceding our time life was considered an absolute unity. This division into separate spheres of interests and activities did not exist. Hence, a social order disconnected from religion was inconceivable. Religion meant spiritual force, and was the dominating or even the moving factor of all of man's dealing in this world. Life in itself had no value except in its relationship to the respective religion. Political power also found its only moral justification in defending the faith. It had no right in itself. Rulers starting out for conquest had to find a religious motive for doing so. Even discoveries were not made for purely geographical reasons as men today, for instance, try to discover the secrets of the Antarctic. The ultimate goal in those days was always the glorification of God, and the conversion of the world to Christianity. This becomes eminently clear in the writings of Columbus.[3]

Life was considered to be a short, transitory state which found its ultimate goal in the eternal union of the individual with his Maker and a life of bliss; or if the individual did not live up to the standard required, in his eternal rejection and doom. This was the conception of life in the Roman and Byzantine empires during the early centuries of the Christian era and the Middle Ages, and this is likewise the conception of life in Islām till the present day. Life presents a completely religious aspect. Under such a spiritual totalitarianism, to use a modern phrase, there remains no possibility for a dissenting group to exist. It has no place in the whole scheme; it does not fit in. It is like a thorn in the flesh which should be eliminated. Of course, there is one other possibility—even if it is not quite logical—and that is to tolerate such groups. But there definitely cannot be any possibility of giving liberty to groups which endanger the safety of the whole structure. Which of the two possibilities did Islām adopt in regard to dissenting groups—extermination or tolerance?

Theoretically, both ways are possible in Islām: The elimination of the unbeliever, or tolerating him. We read:

RELIGIOUS LIBERTY IN ISLĀM

'And when the sacred months[4] are passed, kill those who join other gods with God wherever ye shall find them; and seize them, besiege them, and lay wait for them with every kind of ambush: but if they shall convert, and observe prayer and pay the obligatory alms, then let them go their way, for God is Gracious, Merciful.'[5]

That is the classical passage which is always quoted to show that Islām is the religion of the sword. Surrender and become a Muslim, or you will be killed. Yet this command to kill refers only to idolaters, to those who join other gods with God; there is no other choice for them.

TOLERATION AS IT WAS PRACTISED

A few verses further on in the same Sūra we read:

'Make war upon those who believe not in God and in the last day and who forbid not what God and his apostle have forbidden and who do not practise the religion of the truth from amongst those to whom the Book has been brought until they pay tribute readily and be humbled.'[6]

In this passage nothing is said of being killed or of accepting Islām after being defeated in battle; but it speaks of paying tribute to the conqueror without the necessity of changing the religion. To whom does this verse refer? To the *ahl al kitāb*, the people of the Book. That means the Jews and Christians, because Muhammad regarded the Torah, the Psalms, and the Gospel as messages sent from God, and considered those people to whom they were sent on a much higher level than the idolaters. The Sabians, who according to Muslim commentators are considered to be the Zoroastrians, were also included. Muhammad even conceded that if they would only follow the guidance given to them, they would be richly blessed.

'But if the people of the Book believe and have the fear of God, we will surely put away their sins from them and will bring them into gardens of delight; and if that they observe the law and the Evangel, what has been sent down to them from their Lord, they shall surely have their fill of good things from above them and from beneath their feet.'[7]

The first great waves of Arab conquest principally overran

Christian or Zoroastrian territory; hence, the latter principle was always adhered to. The inhabitants of these countries were not forced to forswear their faith nor were they killed, but when subjugated they had to pay the *jizya*, the poll tax. They were classified as *dhimmī* or *ahl al dhimma*, meaning the protected people, the people of the covenant. The Islāmic state guaranteed them protection of life and property as well as freedom and protection in the exercise of their religion.[8] This tax, together with the land tax, *kharaj*, was in the beginning often not more than the people were accustomed to pay to their former rulers. At the same time they were protected and did not have to perform military service. Or, to be more specific, they were not allowed to perform military service or to carry arms.

And here lies the crux of the whole problem. If a man is not allowed to carry arms, if he is not allowed to defend himself, he is not free; he is subjugated, an inferior being, always at the mercy of his master. And that is what the status of the *dhimmī* amounted to. He did not enjoy full civil rights. His testimony in court was not considered equal to that of the Muslim. According to the *fiqh*[9] the *dhimmī* was without legal rights, considered as a minor. According to Abū Hanīfa and Ibn Hanbal, the leaders of two important schools of religious law, the life of a *dhimmī* was evaluated like that of a Muslim. This means that if a *dhimmī* was murdered the same amount of blood money had to be paid. The other two important schools, however, considered the life of a *dhimmī* less valuable. According to the school of Mālik, only half the amount should be paid, and according to the school of Shāfi'ī only a third. For a Zoroastrian, only one-fifteenth should be paid.[10]

Furthermore, other rather humiliating conditions were imposed upon them. The caliph 'Umar wrote to 'Amr ibn al 'Ās, the conqueror and first governor of Egypt, that the *dhimmī* must show their belts, shave their beards, ride their mounts aside—they are not allowed to dress themselves in the same manner as Muslims. They were prohibited from attempting the conversion of a Muslim or obstructing the embracing of Islām by a Christian.[11] It is interesting to note the conclusion at which a modern Muslim, a former member of the Egyptian Bar, and

Assistant Departmental Secretary of the Minister of the Interior, arrived. He writes:

'Nevertheless, the situation of the Zimmis . . . was always inferior in Muslim states from the social point of view; it resembled, in many points, the situation of the Jews in European countries in the Middle Ages. . . . The Zimmis were, moreover, the object of suspicion and apprehension to the authorities; the early Muslim governments rarely allowed them to occupy official posts other than those of accountants and tax gatherers, in which they excelled. . . .

'It is not amazing therefore that the Zimmis, in those times, were anxious to liberate themselves from the chains and humiliations of this régime, that their intelligent and ambitious elements preferred to earn for themselves by embracing Islām, all the social and economical privileges enjoyed by the Muslims.'[12]

This statement represents a true picture of the situation. There is no religious liberty in Islām, but there is toleration. Toleration, however, means the granting of a privilege, whereas 'religious liberty' is the recognition of a right. Moreover, the religious toleration in Islām is tinged with social discrimination. And social humiliations are in the long run often harder to bear than religious persecution. On the other hand, it always should be emphasized that as long as the Arabs wielded the sceptre of Islām, a tolerance towards the unbeliever, especially the *ahl al kitāb* prevailed in the vast domain of Islām such as was impossible to imagine in contemporary Christendom. In this early period there is no question of any religious fanaticism towards unbelievers.[13]

The official church in the Byzantine Empire treated its fellow Christians who did not conform in all points to the accepted dogma in far worse manner than the Muslims ever treated their *dhimmī*. The following incident may serve as an illustration:

'When Melitene was recaptured by the Byzantines, the Jacobite patriarch together with seven prominent theologians was brought to Constantinople and put into prison. The large church in Melitene was confiscated for the Orthodox church. The patriarch died in exile near the Bulgarian border, one of his co-workers in prison, another was stoned to death outside the gate of the imperial palace, three abjured their faith and returned to orthodoxy, were rebaptized but found no rest of their souls and became the laughing stock of the devils. Finally the elders of the Syrian church could not bear the liberation any longer in the now again Christian territory and changed the seat of the Patriarchate to Amida, back into the territory of the more tolerant unbelievers [Muslims].'[14]

Another interesting sidelight which illuminates the situation is the fact that the Crusaders who came with the purpose of liberating the holy shrines of Christendom from the hand of the infidels did not themselves have the least understanding of the spirit of tolerance. Here is a statement:

'The Coptic Church too had little cause for complaint under Saladin's strong government, and during the time of the earlier Mamlūk sultans who succeeded him the Copts experienced more enlightened justice than they had hitherto known. The only effect of the Crusades upon Egyptian Christians was to keep them for a while from pilgrimage to Jerusalem, for as long as the Franks were in charge, heretics were forbidden access to the shrines. Not until the Moslem victories could they enjoy their rights as Christians.'[15]

The age of 'religious liberty' had not yet dawned. And yet the Arab, although he felt himself always far superior to all the other races, being the conqueror and having been honoured to receive the last and final revelation from God, was the most lenient conqueror of all so long as his prerogatives were not infringed upon.

TREATMENT OF BACKSLIDERS

One other point must be mentioned in this connection, and that concerns the treatment of backsliders or apostates from Islām. There is no direct statement in the Qur'ān that the death penalty should be inflicted upon them, unless we take Sūra 4: 90, 91 (88, 89). However, according to Bayḍāwī this refers to members of an Arab clan who left Madīna and went back into the desert and entered the ranks of the hostile Arabs. Therefore, the same treatment as that given to the unbelievers should be meted out to them. On the other hand, the strongest curse is pronounced upon those who turn away from Islām after being enlightened by the true religion. The wrath of God shall fall upon them, and they shall be ostracized and outlawed by man.

'How shall God guide a people who, after they had believed and bore witness that the apostle was true, and after that clear proofs had reached them, disbelieved? God guideth not the people who transgress. To those the punishment is, that the curse of God, and of the angels, and of all men, is upon them! Under it they shall abide for ever; their torment shall not be assuaged! Nor shall God even look upon them.'[16]

Soon after Muhammad's death, in the earliest tradition the death penalty for apostasy is mentioned, and the *fiqh*, science of Muslim law, is unanimous that the male apostate who has reached the age of maturity must be put to death, and a woman must be imprisoned until she recants. In general, execution was by the sword, and sometimes torture must have been used, because Bājūrī expressly forbids tortures in any form like burning, drowning, strangling, impaling, and flaying, But according to him Sultan Baybars, 708, 709 A.H. (A.D. 1308, 1309), was the first to introduce torture.[17]

Furthermore, the marriage of an apostate is invalid, and all his property is held under guardianship until he dies, and then it will be disposed of. According to other teachers of *fiqh* it should be disposed of the moment his apostasy has been established. The matter is summed up very briefly in the famous book *Al Madkhal*, of Muhammad al Abdarī ibn Hajj, Vol. II, p. 181 (Cairo Edition), where we read:

'As for apostates, it is permitted to kill them by facing them or coming upon them from behind, just as in the case of polytheists. Secondly, their blood if shed brings no vengeance. Thirdly, their property is the spoil of true believers. Fourthly, their marriage ties become null and void.'[18]

This is the law that is in force at present in all Muhammadan countries where the Sharī'a Law is recognized. It is somewhat mitigated, however, by western influence or by the interference of a dominating western power. For this reason the convert to Christianity finds a certain measure of protection. But even in those countries this law has never been annulled or abrogated. This way of thinking has, of course, nothing in common with the Western conception of religious freedom, but it is logical on the basis of the previously mentioned idea of the unity of life. It corresponds exactly with the idea held by the Roman Catholic Church, which she put into practice during the Middle Ages, and which likewise has never been repudiated. At the present time, because of Western influence, secularism has made deep inroads into Islām, and this, one would think, would lead to a loosing of the tight grip of religious law, ushering in a period of freedom for the individual and of greater liberty of conscience. But alas, the blossom of liberty seems to wither already, as a new tyrant strides upon the scene. Hand in hand with secularism marches nationalism, which in those countries means a rejuvenated Islām on a national basis; and now an apostate from Islām is frequently looked upon as a traitor deserving the treatment of traitors in war.

ISLĀM'S POSITION ON ALCOHOL

As a little sidelight. I would like to mention that all countries under Muslim rule are officially 'dry.' This has been achieved by the simple admonition in the Qur'ān which, of course, has the same force as a command. 'O believers! surely wine and games of chance, and statues and the *divining* arrows, are an abomination of Satan's work! Avoid them, that ye may prosper.'[19] Therefore, wherever in Muslim countries shops are found which sell alcoholic beverages, they are owned by either Christians or Jews. The Wahhābīs, the puritans of Islām, even laid a ban upon smoking and upon every kind of love and dance music.

Concerning food the following regulation is given:

'But that which dieth of itself, and blood, and swine's flesh, and that over which any other name than that of God hath been invoked, is forbidden to you. But he who shall partake of them by constraint, without lust or willfulness, no sin shall be upon him. Verily God is Indulgent, Merciful.'[20]

While holding closely to the Qur'ān in this chapter as elsewhere it is manifestly impossible to give an adequate picture of present-day Islām without reference to other sources. It cannot be over-emphasized that even the best knowledge of the Qur'ān would not give an adequate picture of present-day Islām. Islām is not an abstract intellectual structure. It is a form of life, based on very deep religious convictions. As life is ever changing and never at a standstill, Islām could not escape undergoing many changes and adopting many customs and habits foreign to itself, but which were imposed upon it by the overwhelming influence of circumstances. In spite of having assimilated many different customs and ideas of people and races so far apart as those of a West African negro from those of a cultured aristocrat of Damascus, it has succeeded remarkably well in preserving the integrity of its basic beliefs. It has welded a bond of unity between all its followers till the present day. This bond is so strong that whenever one member of the Muslim family of nations is attacked or mistreated by an outsider, it resounds in the whole 'House of Islām' and has repercussions in the far corners of the earth.

---

[1] To Scapula, chap. 2, in Ante-Nicene Fathers, Vol. 3, p. 105.
[2] Epitome to the Divine Institutes, chap. 54, in Ante-Nicene Fathers, Vol. 7, p. 244.
[3] First Letter of Christopher Columbus to the Noble Lord Raphael Sanchez, dated Lisbon, March 14, 1493.
[4] The four holy months of truce between the pre-Islāmic Arabs.
[5] Sūra 9: 5.
[6] Sūra 9: 29.
[7] Sūra 5: 70 (65, 66).
[8] A. J. Wensinck, *Handwörterbuch des Islam*, p. 96.
[9] *Fiqh* = Science of Islāmic law.
[10] A. Mez, *Die Renaissance des Islāms*, p. 36.
[11] Muhammed Enan, *Decisive Moments in the History of Islam*, p. 18.
[12] *Ibid.*, p. 19.
[13] W. Björkman, 'Kāfir,' in *The Encyclopædia of Islam*, Vol. II, p. 619.
[14] A. Mez, *op. cit.*, pp. 37, 38, citing *Barhebræus Chronic, ecclesiast*, Vol. I, p. 432 ff. Translated by the author.
[15] James T. Addison, *The Christian Approach to the Moslem*, p. 35.
[16] Sūra 3: 80-82 (86-88).
[17] W. Heffening, 'Murtadd,' in *Encyclopædia of Islam*, Vol. III, p. 737.
[18] S. M. Zwemer, *The Law of Apostasy in Islam*, p. 50.
[19] Sūra 5: 92 (90).
[20] Sūra 2: 168 (173).

CHAPTER EIGHT

INTERRELATIONSHIP BETWEEN ISLĀM AND CHRISTIANITY

ISLĀM is the one great non-Christian religion of the world which knows of Christ, recognizes Christ, and venerates Christ. Confucianism is a moral philosophy. Hinduism has developed many aspects, and has figures like Krishna which are able to inspire lofty ideals. Buddhism has its own way to overcome the wheel of fate. But all three know nothing of Christ. Judaism sullenly refuses to recognize the Messiah in the person of Jesus. But Islām accepts Christ, accepts His supernatural birth, His ability to work miracles, His flawless life; but at the same time it denies His eternal relationship to God, His death, and His resurrection, and therewith rejects just those essential factors which make Jesus the Christ.

Muhammad had come in contact with Christians and had learned a number of Christian ideas, but unfortunately at second hand. In his time an Arabic translation of the Bible from which he and the Arabs could have learned the truth about Christ at first hand did not exist. The lack of any authentic religious book in Arabic on the one hand, and the revelation of the Qur'ān in Arabic on the other, make the overwhelming success and veneration of the latter among the Arabs understandable. Muhammad incorporated into his holy book the ideas about Christ which he had gained from various sources. He put himself in line with Jesus and the previous prophets. Being convinced that he was the chosen instrument of God at a period when the teachings of Jesus had already become corrupted, he and his followers quite naturally gave to his revelation a higher position and regarded it as superseding all previous revelations given to prophets of earlier ages.

Christianity stood at the cradle of Islām, or more exactly, it constituted one of the components of Islām. Yet that was not all. When the dynamic of this new faith caught hold of the

ISLĀM AND CHRISTIANITY

Arabs, and drove them out of the barren wastes of their peninsula on the road of conquest, they invaded and overran at the first, principally Christian territories—lands such as Mesopotamia,[1] Syria, Palestine, and Egypt, which for centuries had been under the rule of the Eastern Church. Soon afterwards they conquered countries such as the whole of North Africa and Spain, in which the Latin Church was established. The inhabitants of those vast territories sooner or later changed their allegiance from Christianity to Islām. Thereby a large percentage of Muslims, at times perhaps even the largest percentage, were of Christian origin. These brought, of course, their Christian traditions with them, also their customs, superstitions, and their whole Christian background. The result was that the connection between Islām and Christianity became more and more intertwined, and that these two great religions have passed through all phases of human relations—through aggression and defence, through respect and toleration, enmity and friendship. In modern times this interrelationship has become closer than ever before although by no means less turbulent or less problematic.

At this point of the study, it might be well to give a short historical sketch of the extraordinarily rapid expansion of Islām. Muhammad closed his eyes in 632, ten years after his flight from Makka to Madīna. During these ten years the whole of the Arabian peninsula was subdued and nominally accepted Islām. But all was not well with the Beduins. Fickle as the shifting sand, they easily might have thrown off the yoke of Madīna, together with the newly acquired faith. Thereby the whole structure of Islām would have fallen to pieces. The death of Muhammad could have been the signal for such a move, and unified Arabia would have been a beautiful but short dream. Fortunately for Islām, Muḥammad was followed by two most able and powerful personalities, Abu Bakr and 'Umar ibn al Khattāb.

At the most crucial moment of Islām's history, when the news of Muhammad's death spread consternation among the Arabs, when unrest and revolt were in the air, and the fate of the new faith hung in the balance, Abu Bakr stepped forward and proclaimed solemnly to the seething crowd: 'O Muslims, Muhammad has left this world. Whosoever has followed Muhammad, Muhammad is dead, but whosoever has followed Allah, Allah lives and will never die.'[2] With these stirring words, the crisis was past; the balance had swung in favour of Islām. Abu Bakr ordered that preparations for the Syrian expedition, which Muhammad had arranged, should be continued. After subduing some of the tribes in the south who had revolted, Abu Bakr placed the gathering armies in the hands of most capable leaders, and ordered them to march towards the east and the north. The expedition was set in motion, the Arabs had started on their victorious career. It would not come to a halt until the waves of the Atlantic on the western shores of Europe lapped at the hoofs of their horses, until they had carried the banner of Islām eastward over the mountains of Irān to the steppes of the Tartars, and unfurled it on the heights of the Khyber Pass and in the land of Sind. All were now under the shadow of the crescent.

THE EARLY SPREAD OF ISLĀM

Some dates may illustrate their very rapid progress:

634, Basra was captured.

635, a great victory over the Persians was won in the battle of Qadasiyya.

636, the Byzantine forces were decisively beaten at the Yarmuk, an eastern tributary to the Jordan, and Palestine and Syria lay wide open to the conqueror.

637, 'Umar, the second caliph, entered Jerusalem, and this ancient city changed masters to become one of the great centres of Islām.

638, Mesopotamia was conquered.

639, Egypt was entered by an amazingly small force and soon lay prostrate before the Arabs.

641, the greatest victory over the Persians was gained at Nehavend, which shattered forever the glory of the Sassanids, and all the wealth and splendour of ancient Persia lay spread before the wondering eyes of the dauntless sons of the desert.

647, North Africa was invaded for the first time.

ISLĀM AND CHRISTIANITY

667, Sicily was invaded.

670, Kairowān in North Africa was founded to become the fourth most holy city of Sunnī Islām.

674-679, Constantinople was besieged unsuccessfully, thanks to the employment of the Greek fire[3] by the defenders.

697-698, the last remnants of the Roman Empire disappeared from the southern shore of the Mediterranean.

711, the narrows between Africa and Europe were crossed by Ṭāriq.[4]

711, 712, Sind and Transoxiana [Uzbek] were conquered.

732, exactly 100 years after the death of Muhammad, the first decisive defeat was encountered by the Muslim armies on the battlefields in central France at Tours and Poitiers, which finally brought the waves of conquest to a standstill.

In one hundred years Islām had carved out for itself an empire of parts of Western Rome, Eastern Rome, and Persia, reaching from the Atlantic to the steppes of Central Asia, and the Hindu Kush. In one hundred years Islām as a religion had grown more rapidly than any previous religion during a comparable length of time. And what is all the more remarkable, Islām had been able to maintain its gain in spite of mass conversions and this mushroom growth—a method which often has been the undoing of others. Islām, on the contrary, succeeded marvellously in uniting all these different tribes and peoples with their different languages, habits, and backgrounds. It was able to use them all and infuse into them the spirit of one supreme loyalty—the loyalty to Islām. What is the secret of this success? What is the secret of former Christians becoming the stoutest defenders of Islām? Certainly not the sword. It is true that the sword carved out that empire, but the sword alone could never have kept the people loyal to Islām. The sword was not even able to preserve the political unity of the empire.

Certainly many factors worked together to bring about the tremendous initial success of the Arabs. Armed with enthusiasm, zeal, and even fanaticism alone, the ill-equipped Arab horsemen could never have inflicted such decisive defeats upon the two greatest military powers of their time. What were they compared with the Byzantine Empire and Persia, the two powers which divided the world between themselves? As military strategists the Arabs were hardly worth a moment's consideration. Yet here again, history teaches us that numbers and equipment alone are not decisive. Muḥammad had come and given the Arabs a national and religious impetus for the first time in their history. He had given them an ideal and had pointed to a goal which filled them with enthusiasm and zeal, and had released in them forces which nobody had foreseen or even deemed possible. All this took place at a most propitious moment, at an hour when the two great world powers, Eastern Rome and Persia, had exhausted themselves by incessant and devastating wars.

Moreover, the Byzantine Empire was divided into many religious factions. The great dogmatic controversies had raged in the East with far greater violence than in the West, and had led to the formation of large separate churches, as, for instance, the Nestorians. These rejected the idea that Mary, the mother of Jesus, should be called *theotokos*—God-bearer—or *meter theou*, mother of God. They allowed her, however, the title *christotokos* —Christ-bearer. They disapproved of the worship of saints, images, and relics, as well as of the practice of celibacy. The other great separatist group, the Monophysites, held that Jesus, even after having come in the flesh, had only one nature, the divine. In the valley of the Nile, the Copts, the Nubians, and the Abyssinians, and in Syria and Mesopotamia a large group, the so-called Jacobites, and a large part of the Armenians, accepted this doctrine.

All these groups resented to the utmost the pressure which the Greek Orthodox Church exercised with the help of imperial authority. Being themselves not of Greek stock, they began to look upon everything Greek as a hateful foreign intrusion. Therefore, when the Arabs came to the tribes and to the people of the northern borderlands of Arabia, who were of the same Semitic stock, they were welcomed as liberators from the hated Byzantine yoke. Their strange new belief was considered by many as a new brand of unitarian Christianity, a kind of Arianism. This was a view which was shared for a long time by the theologians of the East and the West. Even Luther con-

ISLĀM AND CHRISTIANITY

sidered Islām as a new offspring of the rejected doctrine of Arianism.[5] It is true the people were not quite sure what the doctrines of these men from the desert were, but at least they were refreshingly simple. They cleared the air of all the inexplicable and abstruse reasonings of the theologians and their never-ending disputes, excommunications, and anathemas. Moreover, when the Arabs came, they did not force the Christians to accept Islām. On the contrary, whole tribes embraced Islām voluntarily, and many individuals, seeing the enormous benefits accruing to those who became Muslims, joined the Muslim army to live a life of adventure and conquest.

THE INFLUENCE OF THE MOSQUE

But all these reasons are not enough to explain the enduring influence of Islām. These extraordinarily fortunate circumstances explain the initial success, but these gains would have been just as easily lost if Islām had lacked a positive and stabilizing element in itself. Where does it lie? Cash in his *Christendom and Islam* points in the right direction:

'Wherever a group of Moslems settled, their first duty was to erect a place of worship. The strength of Islām has not been the sword or army nearly so much as the mosque and school.'[6]

The primary function of the mosque is, of course, religious, 'but it serves also to house religious schools of an advanced type and occasionally even primary Koran schools. It is also an inn where any belated traveller may rest for the night, where the poor who must beg for their living can sleep, and where any man who is sick may rest till he recovers, if he has no better place to go. . . . This function of the mosques as philanthropic institutions is very important. No beggar, no traveller, no stranded sick man need lack of shelter, at least, in any Mohammedan city.'[7]

The mosque has become the centre of community life. And here probably lies the secret of that marvellous influence of Islām. The mosque, the place of worship, where the faithful join in prayer five times a day, and the simple 'Kuttāb' school attached to every mosque, where the Qur'ān was taught exclusively, have welded the heterogeneous elements of so many alien nations into one big fraternity—the fraternity of Islām.

CULTURAL DEVELOPMENTS

The Arabs, although living in primitive surroundings, were a very gifted and capable race, and when the doors to the wide world were suddenly thrust open to them, they acted with sagacity. They did not destroy in blind fanaticism whatever they found, as did the Mongols later, who butchered millions for the sake of destruction. On the contrary, the Arabs were very careful not to inflict unnecessary harm.

Most instructive, and at the same time showing clearly the tendency, are the orders which the first caliph Abu Bakr gave to the army commanders before they set out for the first great campaign:

' "Men, I have ten orders to give you, which you must observe loyally: Deceive none and steal from none; betray none and mutilate none; kill no child, nor woman, nor aged man; neither bark nor burn the date palms; cut not down fruit trees nor destroy crops; slaughter not flocks, cattle, nor camels except for food. You will fall in with some men with shaven crowns; smite them thereon with the sword. You will also meet with men living in cells; leave them alone in that to which they have devoted themselves." '[8]

The Arabs with their alert minds assimilated whatever was possible to assimilate of the higher Greek and Persian culture, and therewith they laid the foundation of the famous Islāmic culture of the East and of Spain. Arabic became the leading language—the language of culture and science—and many a famous man in the field of literature, philosophy, medicine, and physics of that period, although not Arab by race, wrote and taught in Arabic, contributing thereby to the fame and glory of the Arabs.

A large part of the financial administration of the empire remained in Christian hands. Many professions, for example that of the physician, were largely filled by Christians; most of the translators of Greek philosophical works were Christians.[9] During the eighth century the Nestorian patriarch Timothy I

ISLĀM AND CHRISTIANITY

of modern Baghdad (A.D. 779-823) conducted a large mission work, and bishops were appointed for Afghanistan, Tibet, India, China, and central Asian districts.[10]

There was no deep-seated animosity between Muslims and Christians in those early centuries in the East. As long as the Christians accepted their status as a protected minority group under the rule of Islām, all was well. Under such circumstances a cultural progress was made in the East which cannot be matched with anything in the West in the same period.

Schools of higher learning were established and endowed with large benefices. Students came from far and near and flocked around famous teachers. In many of these institutions education was free, and the students were well cared for. Hospitals were established. Medicine made considerable progress. Rhazes, Abu Bakr Muhammad Zakariyya, or Razi (ca. 865-925) wrote a compendium of medicine, which was used in the universities of Europe till the seventeenth century. He wrote about smallpox and measles, knew about vaccination, located the retina as the seat of vision, urged that chemistry should be brought into the service of medicine, and knew how to produce artificial ice.[11] And he was not alone in these endeavours. Many other interesting developments could be mentioned if space would permit.

All this progress and development were made at a time when in Europe, except for a handful of monks and laymen, nearly everybody was illiterate, when schools of higher learning did not exist, when cities were unpaved, soap was unknown, and baths a rarity. During that same period Baghdad, Damascus, and Cōrdōba were great cities. Cōrdōba in the tenth century was the most civilized city in Muslim Spain.

'Travellers from the north heard with something like fear of the city which contained 70 libraries and 900 public baths; yet whenever the rulers of Leōn, Navarre or Barcelona needed such things as a surgeon, an architect, a dressmaker or a singing-master, it was to Cōrdōba that they applied.'[12]

Also the art of paper making came to Europe through the Arabs. They had learned it from the Chinese when Samarkand was captured in 704, and they were the first to establish paper mills in Syria and later in Spain and Sicily.[13] During this golden age of Islām the relationship between the two faiths was most cordial except perhaps at the borderlands in Asia Minor and in Northern Spain, where political rivalries were cloaked, as usual in a religious garb. This agreeable relationship would soon undergo a definite change caused by two unforeseen factors.

While learning and culture flourished, and life was filled with pleasure and ease in the vast domain of Islām, the political power was being undermined by internecine strife. The caliphs who were sitting on the throne in Baghdad were not any longer of the calibre of those powerful empire builders like 'Umar ibn al Khaṭṭāb, or Mu'āwiya of the house of Umayya, or Al Manṣūr and Al Ma'mūm of the house of 'Abbās. They did not have such able generals and governors by their side, as Khālid or Muthanna or Al Hajjāj. They were weaklings, subjected to court intrigues, instruments in the hands of unscrupulous officers of foreign breed. They had become pawns in the hands of their Turkish bodyguard. Storm clouds gathered in the north-east and out of the great steppes of Central Asia emerged another people, the Turks. They had accepted Islām and began to overrun that beautiful empire.

In wild ferocity they sacked many a large city, and put to the sword Muslim and Christian alike. They were a warrior race like the Arabs, but not talented and gifted like the latter with the graces of art and poetry, nor with an indwelling sense of curiosity which finds delight in intellectual pursuits and leans to toleration. On the contrary, the Turks were rather a stern, disciplined, military people with a single-track mind. In their hands Islām became rigid and hard. Divisions could not be tolerated, and regulations were more strictly enforced. This naturally had its effect upon the relationship between the Muslim and Christian communities and left its indelible mark. The gulf widened between the two religious groups; their differences rather than their similarities were accentuated.

THE HOLY WARS OF THE CHRISTIANS

About the same period a development began in Europe which soon would cast its shadows over the East. The power of the pope in Rome had slowly but surely increased till the day when Hildebrand (Gregory VII) proudly proclaimed that all kingdoms of the earth were under the dominion of the Holy See, and that its authority ought to be as universal as the church it represented. This conception of the supreme authority of the Church of Rome was not accepted willingly. It resulted in a violent conflict with the Emperor of Germany. A counterpope was chosen, and after Gregory's death in 1085 two popes were contending for power to rule the world through the Church of Rome. When Urban II was elected (1088) he had a precarious position. His powerful rival, Clement III, resided in Rome and was supported by the imperial party. Only some bold move could gain Urban the power desired. He must find some means to unite the disintegrating forces.

Further, he must find a way to solve one of the most urgent problems of his time. He must find a means of stopping the incessant feuds, pillaging, and robberies of the feudal lords and barons. He must give these counts and knights a new vision. Summoning a council at Clermont, he invited the knighthood of France to attend. He himself crossed the Alps, and after having attended the other business of the council, climbed a specially erected platform on the tenth day of the council and made the following solemn proclamation:

'Christian warriors, who seek without end for vain pretexts for war, rejoice, for you have today found true ones. You who have been so often the terror of your fellow citizens, go and fight against the barbarians, go and fight for the deliverance of the holy places; you who sell for vile pay the strength of your arms to the fury of others, armed with the sword of the Maccabees, go and merit an eternal reward. If you triumph over your enemies, the kingdoms of the East will be your heritage; if you are conquered, you will have the glory of dying in the very same place as Jesus Christ, and God will not forget that He shall have found you in His holy ranks. This is the moment to prove that you are animated by a true courage; this is the moment in which you may expiate so many violences committed in the bosom of peace, so many victories purchased at the expense of justice and humanity. If you must have blood, bathe your hands in the blood of the infidels. I speak to you with harshness, because my ministry obliges me to do so: soldiers of hell, become soldiers of the living God! When Jesus Christ summons you to His defence, let no base affections detain you in your homes; see nothing but the shame and the evils of the Christians; listen to nothing but the groans of Jerusalem, and remember well what the Lord has said to you: "He who loves his father and his mother more than Me, is not worthy of Me; whoever shall abandon his house, or his father, or his mother, or his wife, or his children, or his inheritance for the sake of My name shall be recompensed a hundredfold and possess life eternal." '[14]

At first the large assembly of princes and barons and knights were stunned. Then a solitary voice cried, '*Dieu le volt*,' and soon the whole assembly joined in the shout, 'It is the will of God.' The Holy War was declared. Christendom had its jihād.

Urban II had not been sure of success when he went to Clermont, but he had to play his last card against his rival. When he saw the response, he himself was overwhelmed, although he did not know what an avalanche he had set in motion. Europe went into a frenzy. For more than a hundred years Europe thought only about the Holy War and how to wipe out those devils, the Turks and the Saracens. Emperors and kings, princes, knights, and yeomen, the flower of Europe went East to fight for God.

The impact of the Crusades was not very profound on the empire of Islām as a whole. It just dented some of its fringes. Islām did not need to muster all its strength and marshal all of its forces to repulse the invaders. It is true that the Crusaders were able to establish the Kingdom of Jerusalem and to occupy a narrow coastal strip of Palestine and Syria. The sheer weight of the vast Arab hinterland, however, was sure to smother sooner or later the tiny foothold of the West on these eastern shores. The Crusaders did not cause any dislocation in the *Dār al-Islām*; their inroads were like pin pricks compared with the terrible scourge which was soon to fall upon this vast domain and leave it shattered and in ruins, devastated and in desolation. When Genghis Khan's hordes swept down from Central Asia, the whole Islāmic East was destroyed and has never recovered.

After that catastrophe Islām never again reached the height of its early glory. Hence, the Crusades could really have been treated as a minor episode from the Muslim point of view if they had not caused untold damage in other respects. They convinced Islām of the aggressive qualities and potent danger of European Christianity, and of the hate and hostility of the Christians towards them. The gulf between the two faiths widened, and the possibility of bridging it became more and more remote.

At that time only one lonely voice in Europe rose in warning. It was the voice of the great Catalan scholar and poet, Raymond Lull. He promulgated the idea of a peaceful crusade. He selected groups of monks for the study of the Arabic language, and prepared them for the work of preaching and martyrdom among the Saracens.[15] He wrote: 'Whence it seems to me that the conquest of the Holy Land ought not to be attempted except in the way in which Thou and Thine apostles acquired it, namely, by love and prayers, and the pouring out of tears and blood.'[16] He himself, when advanced in age, went to North Africa and died preaching as a Christian martyr, stoned to death by an angry crowd (A.D. 1315).[17]

The strength of the Crusades spent itself. The East was again sealed for Europe. Then the East began to gather its forces for a counter-attack. The Osmanli Turks had settled in Asia Minor. They had reduced the Byzantine Empire to a pitiful state, robbed her of all her Asiatic as well as of most of her European possessions, besieged Constantinople, the pearl of the Bosporus, and stormed its apparently impregnable walls. In 1453 the bulwark of Eastern Christendom came down with a crash. Nothing now stood in the way of the Turks to prevent them from overrunning Eastern Europe and pressing into its heart. The ships of the Turks, and pirates operating in their own behalf, were harassing the coasts of Italy and Spain, and finally with an enormous flanking movement the Osmanlis tried to subdue Europe from the East.

How did this situation, on the other hand, appear to the eyes of the Europeans? Europe was hemmed in from all sides. There was no outlet to the south. The Islāmic empire lay like a huge barrier between her and the unknown regions of Africa. There was no connection with the southeast. There, too, Islām stood in the way. India and China were shrouded in mists, in fable, and legend. When the two intrepid travellers, Marco Polo and his brother, returned from their perilous journey and reported of the wonders of Cathay, they were ridiculed and considered to be mountebanks and liars. There was no outlet to the East. In the wide plains of Russia roamed the wild Tartars, and they too had become Muslims. To the West stretched the unconquered ocean, the great sea, which meant the end of the world. Did not these waters encircle the disc of the earth?

EUROPE DISCOVERS THE SEA ROUTES

Can you imagine today what it meant for the people of Europe in those days when Christopher Columbus and Vasco da Gama ventured into the wide, unknown, and uncharted sea? Can you imagine what it meant to Europe when the news came that the ocean had been conquered and that beyond the sea there was new land? Can you imagine what it meant to have found an outlet and to have outflanked Islām by finding a way around Africa and a way to the fabulous land of Hind? That huge barrier, which had towered like an insurmountable obstacle between Europe and the East, was finally circumvented.

With all their pent-up energies the European nations took to the sea and discovered the world for themselves. In wonderment the white man looked upon a world which had lived thousands of years, which had built up systems of thought and developed forms of life quite foreign to his own, which had lived in luxury and ease, and had not even taken notice of him, so insignificant was he. These new vistas, however, filled him with greed, and he grasped and grasped and tried to dominate the East. Yet he was chasing a phantom, for the East was stronger in spirit.

By the discovery of the sea routes, a window to the wide world had been opened, but not all European nations comprehended its significance. The great majority were still land minded. At this moment the Turk launched his powerful attack on Central Europe. One of the eastern bastions, Budapest, was already in his hand. The next, Vienna, was to follow, and then the road to the heart of the German Empire would be open. In this hour of deadly peril the princes of Europe united to stay the attack. Vienna was saved, and the Turk was forced to retreat. Incidentally, Protestantism was saved by this attack of the Turk on Vienna, for the forces of the Catholic princes, which were in the process of being assembled in order to give Protestantism the deathblow, were diverted by the common danger of the infidels.

LUTHER AND IGNATIUS OF LOYOLA

Luther was as good a preacher as any in arousing the people to join the war and fight against the Turk. He considered the Turks to be the last wrath of the devil before the fast-approaching end of the world. Nor did he consider the killing of a Turk a sin. 'Your fist and your spear, O warrior, are the fist and spear of God. If you should die on the battlefield, you cannot die a more honourable death than in defence of your faith.'[18] He also advocated a 'scorched earth' policy if the warriors had to retreat.[19]

Luther was deeply interested in developments connected with Islām, but he cherished no hopes for its reformation, nor did he envisage the idea of mission work among Muslims. The first Protestant to undertake such a step was the Swiss theologian Bibliander, but he was discouraged from doing so by Bullinger. He had translated the Qur'ān and written an up-to-date history of Islām, but he and the printer encountered endless trouble because the city councillors of Basel, where the book was to be printed, considered it a danger to the faith, and a smear on their good Christian reputation, that such a 'hellish law' should be printed inside the walls of their city. The type was confiscated and the printer had to flee. Luther was compelled to interfere and to throw his weight into the scale in order that the book could finally be published.[20]

Among the Catholics we have Ignatius of Loyola. After having made a pilgrimage to Jerusalem, he conceived the idea of starting a holy order with the express purpose of doing mission work among the Muslims, so deeply was he impressed by the situation he saw in the East. But when he laid his plan before the pope, the latter discouraged him because circumstances did not seem to favour it. Thereupon Ignatius put his band of enthusiastic missionary volunteers at the disposal of the pope, and out of this grew the Jesuit Order.[21]

CHRISTIAN MINORITIES IN THE DĀR AL-ISLĀM

As already remarked, Islām was not any longer under the guiding hands of the Arabs who, with their open minds, had been eager to absorb whatever seemed to be of value. Islām had now passed into the hands of the Turks, who, mainly interested in military achievements, and stern, vigorous, and unbending in their character, reduced it to a harsh legal code and discouraged all intellectual pursuits outside the framework of the precepts of Islām, as can be seen by a law of Sulaymān the Magnificent, who forbade by the penalty of death the study of books of any other religion than that of Islām.

The Christian minorities in the realm were, of course, protected according to canon law. But the relationship between the two communities had taken a turn for the worse. There existed no longer a spiritual or even intellectual exchange. And should we be astonished at this? As early as the late fourteenth century, the Turks had begun to raise a levy of 1,000 young, strong Christian boys every year. They were snatched away from their parents, forced to accept Islām, and after undergoing a period of apprenticeship, were enrolled as *yeni chéri* (new troops), later known as the famous and notorious Janissaries. Can we expect that Christian mothers looked forward with hope to the day on which the Muslim recruiting officers came around to look for their boys? Can we imagine that any sympathy for such a system was left in their hearts, or anything except dread, horror, and hatred, even though in later years it was regarded as a privilege to belong to the Janissaries? This system was not abolished until 1826.

Through discovering the sea routes, Western Europe grew stronger year after year, and Russia, under the leadership of Peter the Great, who had spent a number of years in the West, was able to free herself from the shackles of Tartar rule and began to pursue for the first time an active foreign policy. Her

ISLĀM AND CHRISTIANITY

most powerful neighbour to the south and south-east was the Turkish Empire. At that time all the countries bordering the Black Sea including Bulgaria, Rumania, Bessarabia, large parts of the Ukraine, the Crimea, and the whole of the Caucasus were under the sceptre of the Ottomans. With changing fortunes, intermittent warfare started between Russia and Turkey. Slowly the scales tipped to the advantage of the Russians, and in 1774 the Treaty of Kutchuck Kainardji was signed, which contained the famous Article 7.

'The Sublime Porte promises constantly to protect the Christian Religion in all its Churches, and also agrees that the Ministers of the Imperial Court of Russia make representations in favour of the Church to be erected at Constantinople, as well as those officiating therein, and promises to receive these remonstrances as coming from a trustworthy person in the name of a sincerely friendly neighbouring Power.'[22]

This article was construed as granting to Russia the protection of all the Orthodox Christians in the Ottoman Empire, and henceforward Russia entered the scene and greatly influenced the decline of the Ottoman Empire as a dominant and dictatorial power.[23]

From this moment the situation of the Christian minorities underwent a gradual but radical change. The Serbs, Bulgars, and Greeks on the Balkan peninsula began to look towards the north to the big Christian brother who would come to their help in delivering them from the yoke of their oppressors. Russia, on the other hand, found in them a willing fifth column, ready to undermine the strength of the Turk from within. And it did not take very long until the fruits of her policy began to appear. In 1805 a revolt broke out in Serbia, in 1807 a convention between Russia and Serbia was signed, and in 1830 Serbia became an autonomous state. In 1821 the fires of revolution were kindled in Greece and after many ups and downs, after the population of many towns had been massacred, and after the intervention of practically all important Western powers, the revolution was crowned with the independence of Greece in 1833.

In the same manner, the Christian minorities farther east,

the Armenians, Assyrians, and the Maronites in the Lebanon, began to look towards the Christian powers of Europe as their coming liberators. They entertained high hopes that these Christian powers, impelled by Christian motives, would speed their deliverance, not comprehending, unfortunately, that politics knows nothing of morals. Too late, and to their detriment, they discovered that they were used as pawns in the vile game of power politics.

To the Turks, however, it became exceedingly clear that these Christian minorities constituted a potential danger from within, that Christians could not be trusted, and that their priests and religious and educational leaders were a most dangerous element. These formed the connecting link between the foreign powers and their local communities. These considerations and fears were not imaginative or chimerical, but very well founded as later events proved. The result, especially among the educated class, was a very genuine hatred against everything Christian. Christian meant anti-Turkish and antinational; and since nothing is easier to fan than the baser instincts of the masses, sporadic but most violent persecutions and massacres followed. These massacres—of the Armenians, for instance—were religious in nature and appearance, but in reality they were directed against groups which were no longer considered loyal to the state. The massacres had deep repercussions in the Christian West, and were followed by an outcry again these barbarians, the Turks, who were regarded a disgrace to humanity. This again strengthened the conviction of the Turks, and of Muslims in general, that the Christian nations were united in a conspiracy against the world of Islām. To the Muslims it was not an issue of secularized power politics; it was an issue between Christianity and Islām. Some dates may tell the tale of how far the evidence justifies the apprehensions of the Turks.

1812, Bessarabia annexed by Russia.

1830, Serbia autonomous.

1830, Algeria occupied by France.

1832, Greece declared to be an independent state. (In London.)

1854, 1855, Crimean War.
1878, Bulgaria created as an autonomous principality. The provinces of Ardahan and Kars, and the oil district of Batum, given to Russia. Cyprus annexed by England.
1879, Rumania independent.
1881, Tunis occupied by France.
1882, British intervention in Egypt. Egypt under British influence.
1897, Crete autonomous.
1908, Bosnia and Herzegovina annexed by Austria.
1911, Tripolitania and Lybia annexed by Italy.
1911-13, Balkan wars with further loss of territory in Europe.
1919, the final amputation: Turkey was reduced to Asia Minor and a small bridgehead west of the Bosporus in Europe. In the east the Kingdom of 'Irāq was established in the valleys of the Euphrates and Tigris. On the eastern shores of the Mediterranean, the Western powers created interest spheres for themselves, the so-called mandates. Syria and Lebanon became French mandates, and Palestine and Transjordan fell under British administration. All around the coasts of Arabia small imāmates and sultanates were recognized, which, however, were soon to be overshadowed by a powerful figure arising from the central parts of Arabia.

Is it any wonder that the Turk, and the Muslims in general, look somewhat apprehensively and suspiciously upon any endeavours of the European and American in his land, no matter how well meant these activities may be?

THE NEW WESTERN CONCEPT OF LIFE

During the nineteenth century another development took place that far outstripped any religious consideration. Beginning with the Renaissance in Italy, strengthened by the deep influence of the humanists like Erasmus and Reuchlin, helped by the basic concepts of Protestantism, but finally brought about by the eighteenth century natural philosophers in England such as Newton, Locke, and Hume, a new approach to life was discovered. Life itself became of major importance, not only life in its relationship to the hereafter. Science was no longer pursued for the sake of religion or to substantiate religious dogma. Man now began to engage in science for the sake of science. His attention became focused upon everything perceivable by his senses, be it the smallest particles in his close vicinity or the remotest bodies in the faraway heavens. The universe suddenly expanded in both directions. Man became aware of a marvellous microcosm around him and of a universe of such dimensions that his own little abode became a minor speck among the starry galaxies. His inquisitive disposition urged him on from discovery to discovery, from experiment to experiment in his quest to unveil the secrets of nature. It inspired him to inventions in all lines of human endeavour. The understanding of an increasing number of laws of nature and the harnessing of some of its forces provided him with powers which he has not even yet learned to master. The sum total of this profound change in the thinking of man resulted in our modern industrial age and materialistic civilization.

The homeland of this extraordinary development was Western Europe. These revolutionary changes took place north of the Mediterranean. Islām remained static. It never experienced a renaissance or anything which could be compared to the Reformation. Life in that vast empire continued in the same way and under the same conditions as life had flourished in the Middle Ages in Europe. Life had to be lived under a solemn obligation to God, and its earthly requirements could be fulfilled by following the hereditary calling. The son followed his father. If the latter was a farmer, he became a farmer; if the father was a craftsman, the son practised the same craft and handed down the secrets of his craftsmanship to his son. The ultimate motive for work was not gain and prosperity or a desire for improvement, for a better and more comfortable living, but to fulfil the call which the incomprehensible will of God had placed upon him. The competitive principle which permeates Western economic thinking was virtually absent in this form of society.

Islām did not care for this new form of Western life. It tried to close its doors as long as possible, because it felt instinctively that this new Western way would ultimately destroy all its ideals. But modern Europe did not care to take notice of closed doors; it just banged them open. It threw its cheap goods on the markets of the East, paralyzing and often destroying therewith the old crafts. It cut the Suez Canal through Islāmic territory to connect its own points of interest. It laid railways, and in recent times air lines, across these countries. It behaved as if these countries were part of its own domain. At the same time the West advertised that the white man's civilization is the highest and best ever achieved by human beings.

CHRISTIAN MISSIONARIES

Into this highly complex picture, full of dynamic forces, stepped another figure, that of the Christian missionary. Protestant missionary societies, mostly sponsored by British-, American-, or German-sending organizations, entered the countries of Islām. Many of the men and women who followed the mission call were inspired by the highest ideals, and were willing to lay their lives on the altar in order to bring the Christian message to their Muslim brothers. But often their idealism outstripped their knowledge of the actual facts of the situation. This is not a slur. They had to break ground. They had to blaze a trail into unknown territory. The world of Islām had to be rediscovered and their devoted work and studies on the spot have largely contributed to our present-day knowledge of Islām.

They found themselves confronted with the utterly foreign world of Islām, but as if that were not enough, the overbearing influence of Western materialism made itself felt in an increasing measure. They did not approve of it, but being sons of their time they often could not escape the atmosphere which pervaded the whole thinking of the age, and which made material progress, material benefits, and material happiness the measuring rod. Observing the tremendous difference between the living conditions of their home countries and the countries of their adoption, they often threw themselves with all their inborn vigour and energy into philanthropic work. They built schools, hospitals, started rural uplift plans, and tried to clean up the territory. They fought a valiant battle against ignorance, superstition, and disease. And they certainly can book to their credit the fact that many ideas and many of their plans were taken up later by the respective governments of these countries. Government institutions, being largely subsidized, have now far outgrown the old mission schools and institutions. In all these manifold activities missionaries frequently forgot that their prime purpose in coming to the East was to preach Christ and bring a knowledge of Him to the regions where He is unknown.

On the other hand, the missionary force was always absolutely inadequate to counterbalance the general impact of the West, to outweigh the tremendous influence of commerce and industry and the mad scramble of the West for the wealth of the earth and its resources. And often, unfortunately, the missionary in laying stress upon civilization's progress, in pointing proudly to these modern achievements, in teaching them these very things, has helped to confuse the issue between Christianity and modern civilization, at least in the minds of his Muslim observers.

No wonder that missionaries were considered with the greatest distrust by the Muslim authorities and that they were under suspicion from the moment they set their feet on land in any of these countries. They were looked upon as the vanguard of imperialism, as spies of the oil-hungry foreign powers, who garbed themselves in the raiment of a hypocritical religion. The integrity of character of the individual missionary could not blot out this generally accepted conception and deep-lying suspicion. Was not the missionary a foreigner protected by his foreign power? Did he not enjoy special rights and privileges? Did he not always make use of these rights when the opportunity was favourable? Certainly, he must be an envoy of these domineering forces.

The dominating influence of the so-called Christian powers of the West was till the present time the greatest handicap to a friendly exchange of religious thoughts and values, and to presenting Christ as a purely spiritual force. World War II with the resulting decline of foreign interference and the reaching of independence of the countries of the East, as India for instance, has put the representatives of Christ on an equal footing with their Muslim and Hindu brothers, and will certainly clear the way to a more spiritual and truly religious approach.

This is a general outline of the forces which have helped to shape the destiny of the Near East, and which are still at work.

In the following chapters we shall deal in a more specific way, country by country, with the problems which they present. The vast territory of Islām is by no means homogeneous, but contains many diverging factors, which make it one of the most interesting regions on the globe.

---

[1] Mesopotamia in early Islāmic history comprised only the northern part of modern 'Irāq and the north-eastern part of modern Syria, the country between the two great rivers, the Euphrates and the Tigris. The part, roughly speaking, from Baghdad south to the Persian Gulf is always referred to as 'Irāq. The modern country of 'Irāq comprises the eastern part of the former Mesopotamia, 'Irāq, and part of Kurdistan.

[2] Tabari, *Chronique* (Fr. trans.), Vol. III, p. 218.

[3] *Pyr thalassion*, a sea fire, a mixture of sulphur, naphtha, and quicklime which took fire spontaneously when wetted, and which was hurled against the enemy's ships, a secret well guarded by the Byzantines.

[4] Gibraltar = Gabal Tāriq—the mountain of Tāriq carries till the present day the name of the victorious Arabian general.

[5] M. Luther, *Sammtliche Schriften*, Vol. 16, col. 2214. Walch ed. St. Louis, Mo., 1907.

[6] W. W. Cash, *Christendom and Islam*, p. 45.

[7] Paul W. Harrison, *The Arab at Home*, p. 236.

[8] W. Muir, *The Caliphate, Its Rise, Decline and Fall* (1924 ed.), p. 65.

[9] T. Arnold, *The Legacy of Islam*, pp. 315-317.

[10] John Stewart, *Nestorian Missionary Enterprise*, pp. 82-84, 90.

[11] W. Gorlitz, *Wachter der Glaubigen*, pp. 42 ff.

[12] Arnold, *op. cit.*, p. 9.

[13] *Ibid.*, pp. 144, 145.

[14] *The Historians' History of the World*, Vol. VIII, p. 333.

[15] Adam Gottron, *Ramon Lulls Kreuzzugsideen*, p. 14.

[16] S. M. Zwemer, *Raymond Lull*, p. 53.

[17] *Ibid.*, p. 143.

[18] Martin Luther, *Sämmtliche Schriften*, Walch ed., Vol. XX, cols. 2160 ff.

[19] *Ibid.*, cols. 2167 ff.

[20] C. Pestalozzi, *Heinrich Bullinger*, p. 311.

[21] A. H. Newman, art. 'Ignatius of Loyola,' in *The New Schaff-Herzog Encyclopedia of Religious Knowledge*, Vol. V. pp. 447, 448.

[22] Wilbur W. White, *The Process of Change in the Ottoman Empire*, pp. 29, 30.

[23] *Ibid.*, p. 30.

CHAPTER NINE

ARABIA

IN THE second half of this study an attempt will be made to survey briefly the countries of the Near and Middle East. Here again the attention is not so much directed towards the material progress those countries have made, but mainly to their spiritual developments and attitudes. Physical features and descriptions will be considered only in so far as they contribute to make the latter more intelligible. More and more we learn that many of our ideas and conceptions are influenced by our environment, and that physical conditions and spiritual reactions are often interdependent.

In arranging this book many probably would have chosen the opposite method of approach. They would have given a description of the countries of Islām first, and then proceeded with Islām as a religion. But the author thought it more profitable to reverse this process, and to acquaint the reader first with the fundamental facts of this great religious power, in order to pave the way for an understanding of the many variations of the general concept. Thus it would be possible to help him to appreciate the different shades and hues which blend into the multi-coloured picture of present-day Islām. We, therefore, shall begin with a sketch of the heart land of Islām, Arabia proper, and, in widening circles, travel through the countries of the Near East.

The peninsula of Arabia is in many respects unique. It is a vast expanse of land, of about 1,000,000 square miles, or about two-thirds the size of India. From the northern point at the gulf of 'Aqaba to the southernmost point in al Yaman (Yemen), the distance is about 1,800 miles. About 600 miles of desert and sand separate the Red Sea from the Persian Gulf. But while India supports a population of close to 400,000,000, the population of Arabia has been variously estimated as between

ARABIA

7,500,000 and 12,000,000. The *World Almanac* for 1948 gives it as 'estimated 10,000,000.'

Neither forests nor rivers enliven this vast territory. It is a dry and desolate country with steppes which blossom in spring, and deserts where nothing will grow at any time. In regions where the water is near the surface and wells can be dug, oases, small and large, have grown up, and a luxuriant growth provides restful shade for the sun-blurred eye. Here also a typical civilization has been developed, the civilization of the oasis dweller, which is in striking contrast to that of the wandering Beduin.[1]

Geographically Arabia can be divided roughly into three rings. An inner ring comprises the central tableland with wide beds of former rivers and with many an oasis. A second ring of complete desert surrounds the inner circle on three sides—the Great Nufūd to the north, the Dahnā' to the east, and to the south-east the fearful Rub' al Khālī, the empty quarter, into which even Arabs do not like to venture.[2] The third outer ring is high and mountainous in the west and flat and rather low in the east, with two towering bastions on each side. In the southwest there is the mountain mass of al-Yaman rising to a height of 12,000 feet, and the Jabal Akhdar in the south-east corner in 'Omān with elevations up to 9,000 feet. These mountainous districts have rainfall sufficient to sustain regular crops, because these regions belong to the monsoon belt of India.

CHRISTIANS IN ARABIA

Arabia is often called the cradle of Islām, and rightly so, but it is often forgotten that large Christian communities existed in Arabia before the days of Islām. We have no definite records which prove how and when Christianity entered Arabia. The apostle Paul says of himself that he went to Arabia.[3] How far he entered and to which district he went cannot be determined. Probably he went to some border tribes just east or south of Damascus where the power of the Roman Empire, and where also the arm of the Jews, could not reach him. From later records we learn that in the north and north-east whole tribes embraced Christianity, for instance, the Bani Ghassān around

Damascus and the eastern part of what we call Transjordan today, and the kingdom of Ḥīra in the region of Karbalā near the Euphrates valley. Christianity had gained a permanent foothold during the fourth and fifth centuries in those parts of Arabia and was quite popular.

Not only in these borderlands were Christian communities found, but also in the south-west corner of Arabia in the ancient land of Himyār, in al Yaman and Najrān. We hear of large Christian communities in those parts and of wars of extermination and periods of recovery. A Jew, Dhu Nawās (d. 525), who ruled over Himyār, marched against Najrān with its predominantly Christian population. All who refused to abjure their faith were thrown into large pits filled with burning fuel. When this fiendish act became known, it created a mighty stir in the whole Christian East, and prayers were offered in many churches for the afflicted brethren in Najrān. The Abyssinian king came with an army to avenge this massacre; Dhu Nawās was defeated and his army routed. Abraha, the Abyssinian governor, ruled over South Arabia, and was praised for his justice and moderation.[4] Under his rule the great cathedral of Sanʻāʼ was built, the ruins of which bear witness, until the present day, of that ancient Christian community.

But soon Islām arose and united the Arabs under its banner. At the beginning the Christians in Najrān were tolerated, but under ʻUmar they had the alternative put before them either to accept Islām or to emigrate. The majority preferred the latter course, and settled in Syria or in Mesopotamia in the vicinity of al Kūfa, where the colony of Najrāniyya long maintained the memory of their expatriation.[5] Arabia, the heart of Islām, became a closed land to the unbeliever; it became the home of the faithful, where the faith could be preserved in its primitive purity.[6] And Arabia has remained a closed land ever since. Few Christian explorers have ventured to travel in Arabia, and even today nobody of any other faith is permitted to enter Makka and Madīna under penalty of death. Only in disguise as Muslim pilgrims have some European scholars been able to visit the holy places of Islām, and they have furnished us with voluminous information. A detailed description of all explorers

ARABIA

who helped to lift the veil of secrecy which hung so long over Arabia is found in R. H. Kiernan's book, *The Unveiling of Arabia*.

THE WAHHĀBĪS

Arabia had accepted Islām. It became the religious sanctuary, but it could not keep the political supremacy. Soon the political centre of the empire shifted to more convenient places like Damascus under the Umayyads, Baghdad under the 'Abbāsids, and to Cairo under the Fāṭimids. Losing its political influence Arabia fell back into its old tribal rivalries, now, however, under the auspices of Islām. Nothing of importance seems to have happened until the middle of the eighteenth century, when a reformer arose, Muhammad 'Abd al Wahhāb (ca. 1703-1787), with the intention of restoring Islām to its original purity. His followers are called the Wahhābīs. Their doctrines can be summed up in the following points:

Reasoning has no place in religious questions. They must be settled solely according to the test of 'the book.'

Consensus of the theologians, *igmā'*, is rejected.

Analogy, *qias*, is rejected. That means, it is not allowed to judge cases or permit usages on the basis of a precedent; the Qur'ān should be the only basis.

Opinions of compilers of codes are void of authority.

Neither the prophet nor any saint may serve as intercessor.

Visits to tombs are forbidden.

Oaths are forbidden, except by the name of God.

No drinking, smoking (placed under the category of greater sins), dancing, or music, no wearing of silk or ornaments, as gold, silver, and gems, are allowed.

Mosques are to be of the greatest simplicity.

The jihād (holy war) is one of the main points stressed.

These Wahhābīs are the puritans among Islām. Not long after they had established themselves in Inner Arabia, they were on the warpath against the Sunnī Muslims, whom they considered to be backslidden idolaters and tomb worshippers. Their political fortunes, however, after a brilliant start soon declined. Their present ruler Ibn Su'ūd (Ibn Saud, or his full name, 'Abd al 'Azīz, ibn 'Abd al Rahmān ibn Fayṣal ibn Su'ūd) lived as a fugitive in Kuwayt in his youth. Ambitious and purposeful, he, with a very small force, seized Riād, the ancient capital of his ancestors, and established himself there as its legitimate ruler. Soon his power began to be felt over the whole of Central Arabia. In 1926, after a short war with King Husayn of Hijaz, he entered Makka and became thereby the guardian of the holy places of Islām. With marvellous ability and great sagacity, he was able to direct the fanaticism of his Wahhābī brethren into useful channels and to introduce far-reaching reforms.[7]

Many regard Ibn Su'ūd as the greatest Arab ruler since Muhammad's time, and certainly Arabia has never been so united as she is under his able hands today. He possesses all the qualities which the Arabs expect a leader to have, and he enforces in his dominion the stern Qur'ānic law, which, for instance, prescribes that a thief should be punished by cutting off his right hand. He has thereby made Arabia the most secure spot in the East and perhaps in the world. Recently, however, in places where Western oil companies have obtained concessions, this stern law cannot be enforced, with the result that thefts and burglaries have become common again.

OIL AND MODERN IDEAS

Incidentally, very rich deposits of oil have been found in the Ḥasa district near the Persian Gulf, which has brought Arabia to the forefront of world interest. In Zahrān, where oil refineries have been built, and a whole city has sprung up in the most forbidding surroundings, hundreds of Americans are living today. A regular air service has been established between Zahrān and Jidda across the deserts of Arabia, which carries passengers in six to eight hours from the Persian Gulf to the Red Sea, a journey which a few years ago was seldom undertaken and for which a caravan needed about a month.

It is difficult to evaluate the influence which these changes will have upon the Arab. But that they make deep impressions is easily noted when we scan articles appearing in the newspapers of Su'ūdī Arabia. For instance, in the *Al Bilād al Su'ūdiyya* a daily which appears in Makka, we find an article in the issue for January 27, 1947, which makes a strong appeal for modern education, and stresses the necessity of creating a new generation of Arabian youth, a generation which will have the educational tools in its hands to join in the awakening of the Arab world. And in the issue of February 24, 1947, another article is printed entitled 'No Life Except by Knowledge.' In this the writer stresses the following points:

'No real knowledge exists except in revealed religion [Islām]. But since God has permitted various useful although secondary branches of knowledge, as for instance the science of agriculture, the dyeing of wool, the manufacturing of various tools, therefore it is also permissible to engage in various branches of modern science, as biology, chemistry, physics, and so on.'

Here we see that the Arab still feels that he is in need of a religious sanction before embarking in scientific investigations, a notion which the Western world has discarded long ago.

Su'ūdī Arabia, which is going to play an increasingly important role in the future, and which is exposed as never before to the modern spirit of the West, does not have in its borders a single representative of the best which the West can offer. There does not exist a single mission station of any mission group in Su'ūdī Arabia. The only missionaries who have entered Central Arabia were physicians of the Arabian Mission of the Reformed Churches of America who went on special invitation of King Ibn Su'ūd to treat him and members of his household, and who on their expeditions to and from the king's capital gave medical treatments and some Bible lectures. Lately they have received permission to make regular visits. One of these successful itineraries of Dr. Storm of the Arabian Mission, covering eight months, is reported in *The Muslim World*.[8]

These visits are the first visits of Christian representatives on Central Arabian soil since the time when the Christians of Najrān had to leave Arabia in the seventh century. On the other hand, the Shaykh Ḥamīd of Qaṭar has built for the mission a good little hospital in his territory. That is certainly an encouraging sign that prejudice is breaking down even in the cradle of Islām. But except for these itinerant journeys of recent years, Arabia is untouched by the Christian message of the redeeming Saviour. What a challenge to all who believe that every nation, people and tongue are to hear the gospel before the second coming of Christ!

---

[1] See C. M. Doughty, *Travels in Arabia Deserta*, Vol. I, chaps. 8, 9, 12, 19, 22; Vol. II, chaps. 1, 2; P. W. Harrison, *The Arab at Home*, chaps. 2, 3.
[2] See H. St. Philby, *The Empty Quarter*.
[3] Galatians 1: 17.
[4] For a fuller description of this episode see A. Moberg, *The Book of the Himyarites*, pp. ci-cxlv.; or J. Stewart, *Nestorian Missionary Enterprise*, pp. 55-63.
[5] W. Muir, *The Caliphate, Its Rise, Decline and Fall*, p. 146.
[6] W. Cash, *Christendom and Islam*, p. 32.
[7] See H. C. Armstrong, *Lord of Arabia, Ibn Saud*.
[8] *The Muslim World*, Vol. 38, No. 2, April, 1948, p. 146.

CHAPTER TEN

AL YAMAN, ADEN AND HADRAMAUT

WHEN speaking about Arabia, we think most naturally of Suʻūdī Arabia, as it is at present, the most powerful state of the Arabian peninsula. But there exist a number of smaller independent or semi-independent states which, although Arab and Muslim states, have yet developed their own characteristic features; have, so to speak, their own physiognomy.

In the south-west corner of the peninsula lies the country of al Yaman (Yemen), the Arabia Felix of the ancients, the land of frankincense, of myrrh, of gold and onyx and carnelians—a country of high mountains and deep valleys, a country where flowers grow and fruits are plentiful, a country unlike the rest of the peninsula, not a howling wilderness or a land of wandering tribes but a country of a settled population of small farmers or farm hands, who cultivate every available fertile spot on the mountain slopes by carefully terracing the ground. It is the country where the famous Arabian coffee, the Mocha, grows, and where, paradoxically enough, not much coffee is drunk, but only a brew is made from the husks of the coffee berry spiced with ginger or cardamom. Here a stimulant, Qat, is chewed by rich and poor. Qat or Ghat (*Catha edulis*) is a shrub, the tender leaves of which when chewed produce a hilarity of spirits and an agreeable state of wakefulness.[1] Al Yaman is besides a narrow, flat, desert-like and extremely hot coastal strip, the most alpine country of Arabia with much grandeur and beauty. It is no wonder that the ancients called it Arabia Felix, the happy Arabia.

No wonder that civilizations flourished here which left some records to later generations. Here we find the traces of the ancient Minæan kingdom, which must have been established around 1500 B.C. and held its own until around 750 B.C. Then it was followed by the Sabæans, of whom an inscription of Sargon, the great Assyrian monarch (715 B.C.), makes mention. Later the Sabæans were superseded by the Himyarites (about 115 B.C.), who left us a wealth of rock inscriptions and inscriptions of other nature in many places scattered all over South Arabia.[2] It is in all probability the country from which the queen of Sheba came, who visited Solomon to vie with his glory. In ancient times the boundaries of these different kingdoms expanded at times towards the east of al Yaman's present borders and included the districts of Hadramaut or even faraway 'Omān where the Persian Gulf enters the Indian Ocean. The western part of the latter is called by the Easterners the Arabian Sea.

Arabia Felix obtained its prosperity not only by its own favoured climatic conditions, but from the fact that it constituted an important link in the great trade route from India and the Spice Islands to Egypt and to ancient Rome. Rome even set out to subdue and conquer South Arabia during the reign of Augustus in order to exclude the Arabs from the trade and make the profits for herself. The military expedition for this purpose, led by Elius Gallus (24 B.C.), proved to be a complete failure.[3]

When in later times other trade routes were opened, Arabia Felix lost its importance and fell back into a lethargic slumber. The peoples of South Arabia were known as expert stonecutters, and Arab tales of lofty houses with windows of translucent stone are not much exaggerated.

Another exceptional feature found in al Yaman is the large settlement of Jews in this country. According to tradition 75,000 are said to have left their homeland under Jeremiah and settled there. The real immigration, however, seems to have taken place in the second century since Christ. They enjoyed a large measure of prosperity until the sixth century, but later, especially under the jurisdiction of the Imāms, their situation deteriorated considerably. They were forbidden to wear good or new clothes, nor were they permitted to ride even an ass or a mule. But more important than these humiliating conditions was the stipulation that they were not permitted to engage in any money transaction. Therefore, practically all the Jews in al Yaman became very efficient in handicrafts. They numbered at the beginning of the nineteenth century about 30,000.[4] Since 1909 many have emigrated to Palestine although the Imām tried by all possible means to prevent this emigration.

Al Yaman at present covers a territory of about 75,000 square miles with a population estimated as low as 1,600,000 and as high as 4,000,000. The true figure will probably be somewhere in the middle. The inhabitants of al Yaman accepted Islām very early in its history, and never changed their fidelity, although a majority adopted a special brand of Shī'a teaching, the teaching of the Zaydites to which they adhere until the present day. The Zaydites go back to Zayd ibn 'Alī, the grandson of Husayn (died about 122 A.H.; A.D. 740). They formed during a later period a state near the Caspian Sea, but were unable to keep true to their tenets and soon disintegrated. Only in al Yaman they overcame the vicissitudes of centuries, and at times were in full control of the country, at others subdued.[5]

The late Imām Yahya (d. 1368 A.H.; A.D. 1948), was continually in rebellion again the Turks who had held sway over the country since the sixteenth century. In 1911, finally, a Turko-Imāmic pact was signed by which the ruler, or Imām, of al Yaman became semi-independent. The Imām Yahya remained neutral during World War I but continued friendly relations with Turkey. After the war the Turks evacuated the country and the Imām became the undisputed ruler. In 1934 a conflict with Su'ūdī Arabia broke out during which the Imām lost part of his northern territory but was left nominally autonomous. In the same year the British recognized for the first time the independence of al Yaman. The United States established relations with al Yaman for the first time in 1928 through her consulate in Aden and a good-will visit was arranged. Beginning with 1945 relations became more close, and in 1946 a trade and friendship agreement was signed between the two powers.

The leaders of the Zaydites are called Imāms. The word Imām really means a leader in prayer, the one who stands in front of the congregation. But in connection with the Zaydites, it means the spiritual as well as the political head of the sect, something like *Amīr al Mu'minīn* (prince of the believers, leader of the faithful) with the Sunnīs. The late Imām, therefore, occupied a unique position, a kind of priest-king in this state of the Zaydites. Here church and state are inseparably interlocked. He was accepted by the Sayyids who form the most powerful group in the country, and after being elected and invested with the divine right of kings, he had on the spiritual side all the authority of a pope. The Imām himself never left the country. If he had done so, no laws could have been enacted, no governmental action would have been lawful, and not even a prayer could have been offered by the Sayyids.[6]

The Imām, Yahya called himself the legitimate successor of the Himyāritic line of kings. He kept that idea alive by his use of red powder to dry the ink used in state documents. Red (*ahmar* in Arabic) is present in the word Himyār.[7]

Al Yaman is a closed land to foreigners. Only by invitation of the Imām or the government is a foreigner allowed to enter the country. Further, it is the unchangeable law of the land that no foreigner can own property in al Yaman; and, on the other hand, if a Yamani leaves the country with the intention of taking up his domicile in another country, he ceases to be a Yamani and has no right to his property any longer.[8]

From these statements it can be easily deduced that Christian missions have never had a chance to enter this country, as foreigners in general were not wanted. Al Yaman has never been touched directly by the Christian missionary with the exception, perhaps, of Joseph Wolff, who in his far-flung travels visited San'a', the capital of al Yaman, in 1836, and preached fearlessly to the favoured community, and of the single visits of Dr. Zwemer and of some English missionaries.

In the late nineteen-thirties the Imām requested an English doctor for Ṣan'a'. Dr. and Mrs. Petrie, both of them being doctors, were lent from their mission in Shaykh 'Othmān to work in the Imām's hospital. With them worked different nurses during the years. In his report on al Yaman, Ingrams, an English diplomat, speaks very highly of their work. He states:

'This work has made them greatly loved in Sana and known in distant villages. On my journey I constantly heard Dr.

AL YAMAN, ADEN, AND HADRAMAUT

Petrie's name spoken with respect, and on two occasions owed small courtesies from poor people to being mistaken for him. Although he is by heart a missionary, Dr. Petrie took no steps in active missionizing, which would have prejudiced his success, but he set such a bright and shining example of a Christian life that he had great influence, and it is a pity that on account of the difficulties the medical mission faced it has had to be temporarily withdrawn. . . .

'As regards the cultural level of the Yemen, I think I can best describe it by saying that at its highest level it is completely mediæval. Modern learning is entirely discouraged, and Zeidi theology and history are the only subjects really considered worth writing about.'[9]

Arabia Felix is a forgotten corner in our swift modern time.

ADEN

Aden belongs geographically to al Yaman as the natural outlet to the Indian Ocean. For long centuries it was governed by the Zaydites from San'a', yet during the eighteenth century it fell under the power of the Shaykh of Lahaj, who, of course, had not the strength to repel the British when they occupied the little town of Aden and its surrounding territory in 1839. Aden was placed under the direction of the Bombay Presidency, but in 1932 it was constituted a separate province, and in 1935, by article 288 of the Government of India Act, Aden was separated from India and became a Crown Colony. The administration was transferred to the Colonial Office in 1937.[10]

The area of Aden proper consists of only eighty square miles, and the population is about 48,000, including that of the island of Perim. But the Aden hinterland, or Aden protectorate, embraces 112,000 square miles, including the fertile country of Hadramaut, and a part of the Rub' al Khāli.

Aden greatly gained in importance after the opening of the Suez Canal. It became the British watchtower guarding the traffic on the southern end of the Red Sea. It is a free port and a coaling station, and has attracted a motley population of Arabs, Indians, Parsis, Somalis, Jews, and a limited number of Europeans who have to spend their days in the service of their companies in this oven of the earth. Although very hot, the climate is not unhealthful, and the water supply is sufficient since the erection of the great reservoirs in the Crater. Formerly, mostly sea water was distilled for drinking purposes.

Since Aden came under British control, it has been possible to establish missions there. In 1840, just one year after the British occupation, a Roman Catholic mission was started. It is perfectly independent of all other missions, and is subservient only to the head of the Roman Catholic Church. In 1855 the mission was entrusted to the order of Saint Francis of Assisi (Minor Capuchin Brothers). Their aim is to attend to the spiritual needs of the Europeans, Indians, Abyssinians, Shoas, and Swahilis and of the troops of the garrison. Nuns, Sisters of the 'Good Shepherd,' came to Aden in 1868 with a view to educating girls of all persuasions, and also to offer shelter to any converts or reformed characters.[11] It is now known as the Apostolic Vicariate of Arabia.

A Protestant mission with the definite aim of finding a way to the hearts of the Muslims was established by a young Scot, Ion Keith-Falconer, in 1886. Unfortunately he was stricken with malaria and died the following year in March, 1887. But his work survived. The Free Church of Scotland adopted Aden as a main station. It became primarily a medical mission, and in 1909 the Keith-Falconer Memorial Hospital was completed. It treats nearly a thousand in-patients a year. These are drawn from a wide area.[12]

Besides the Church of Scotland's South Arabia Mission (C.S.M.), the Danish Church Mission (D.C.M.) has been established in the Aden Crater. In 1904 they came to Aden after they were forbidden to work in Makallā by the Sultan. They conduct a kindergarten and an elementary school as well as a night school.[13]

ḤAḌRAMAUT

From Aden we shall direct our steps to another long-forgotten corner of Arabia. This is perhaps the most picturesque and most venerable part of the peninsula—the land of the 'Great Canyon' of Arabia, the land of the Arabian skyscrapers built of

AL YAMAN, ADEN, AND HADRAMAUT

mud. Here are houses of seven or eight stories glittering in the hot Arabian sun and hidden in the deep valleys. This is a country where large palaces in well-shaded gardens surprise the eye, where white-towered mosques pierce the azure sky, and where the most holy shrine of the prophet Hūd is held in reverence. This land is secluded from the rest of the Arabic world, yet it has the most remarkable connections with faraway countries. Its doors are closed hermetically to all foreigners, and here is lived the kind of life that is portrayed in the fairy tales of *The Thousand and One Nights*. Hadramaut is its name. This is derived from the name mentioned in Genesis 10: 26. There we find Hazarmaveth, one of the sons of Joktan of the children of Shem. The Romans knew of this country, and called the inhabitants thereof Chadramotitæ or Chatramotæ.[14]

In Hadramaut we find a well-defined social structure, practically a caste system. There are the Sayyids who are descendants of Ahmad ibn 'Isa from Basra, 'Iraq. The latter settled in the *wādī* (valley) during the tenth century. They are recognized as the spiritual leaders, and being comparatively well educated, they exercise a great influence upon the rest of the population. They belong today to the keenest advocates of modern methods in the country. They do not carry arms.[15] There are the Yafā'is or soldiers, from whose ranks the actual rulers of the country spring. Then there are the tribesmen who stick rigorously to their old tribal customs. Further there are the townsmen, principally derived from families emigrated from 'Iraq, and finally the slaves, mostly under government ownership, but who are exceedingly well treated and can rise to the highest positions. For instance, the governor of the Shibām province (1936) was a slave.[16]

The two seaports of this extraordinary country are Makallā and Shihr, miles away from the inland principalities. The ports have a most oppressive climate, whereas the towns in the *wādī*, like al Qatn, Shibām, Sajjūn, and Tārim, breathe the hot, but dry and invigorating air of the desert. The Hadramīs have always been great travellers. In the tales of *The Thousand and One Nights* we meet Hadramīs in all parts of the East, and so it is until the present day. Practically all the Arabs in Singapore,

Sumatra, and Java are from the upper valley of the Hadramaut. Many on the East African coast are of Hadramī stock, and the bodyguard of the Nizam of Hyderabad (Deccan), India, up to the highest officers of the army are practically all from this part of the Arab world.

Most of these men return to their *wādī* when they have amassed fortunes according to their ambitions in order to spend the rest of their lives in their homeland. But until recently, they spent their means mostly to keep up the perpetual internecine strife between the different tribes and towns. However, beginning with 1936, the British government of the Aden protectorate took a very direct interest in the affairs of this remote yet interesting province. Thanks to the endeavours of her able political officer, W. H. Ingrams, she succeeded in pacifying the country. Ingrams was able to negotiate a three-year truce and when nothing else would help, he enforced it by aerial bombings which did not do much damage. Soon the inhabitants of the *wādī* became aware of the benefits of peace, and this was hailed over the whole of South Arabia as *sulh Ingrams* (Ingram's peace). If peace remains in the valley, an era of great prosperity can be foreseen in this most exclusive spot of the domain of Islām. Tārim in the valley of Hadramaut is a centre of learning, and many interesting documents may be stored away in the mosques and in the homes of the learned Sayyids. Ingrams tried to induce the nobles to send their sons to an English school in Aden; but they do not trust the souls of their sons into the hands of infidels, but prefer to send them to the Muslim institutions in 'Irāq and Egypt.

Besides the official journeys which W. H. Ingrams made through Hadramaut, the Dutch Orientalist D. van der Meulen was one of its first explorers. Later, two courageous travellers passed through that country, and brought back glowing accounts of the life in the *wādī*, revealing to the astonished Western world the existence of a form of life never thought possible in the swift-running twentieth century.[17]

From the point of view of the Christian message, Hadramaut is an unentered territory. As already mentioned, the Danish Church Mission tried to establish a mission station in Makallā

AL YAMAN, ADEN, AND HADRAMAUT

and was unsuccessful. Perhaps it may be possible to influence Hadramīs in the East Indies or in India with the spiritual truth of Christianity, to bring them in contact with Christ, and if God wills, some may return to their valley and become messengers to their own people. They certainly would be much better representatives of God's power than any foreigner could be in that hidden-away land, the Great Canyon of Arabia.

---

[1] A. Rihani, *Arabian Peak and Desert, Travels in Al Yaman*, pp. 35-39.
[2] See *Handbuch der altarabischen Altertumskunde*, ed. D. Nielsen, Vol. I, *Die altarabische Kultur*.
[3] Edward Gibbon, *The History of the Decline and Fall of the Roman Empire*, Vol. I, pp. 216, 217; Th. Mommsen, *Das Weltreich der Cæsaren*, pp. 448, 449.
[4] S. Ochser, 'Yemen,' in *The Jewish Encyclopedia*, Vol. XII, pp. 592-594.
[5] See R. Strothmann, *Das Staatsrecht der Zaiditen* (Studien zur Geschichte und Kultur des islamischen Orients); A. S. Tritton, *The Rise of the Imams of Sanaa*.
[6] W. H. Ingrams, 'A Journey in the Yemen,' in *Royal Central Asian Journal*, Vol. XXXII, 1946, p. 65.
[7] D. van der Meulen, *Aden to the Hadhramaut*, p. 99.
[8] W. H. Ingrams, *op. cit.*, p. 66.
[9] W. H. Ingrams, *ibid.*, pp. 68, 69.
[10] Herbert L. Liebesny, 'International Relations of Arabia,' in *The Middle East Journal*, Vol. I, 1947, No. 2, pp. 148-156.
[11] F. M. Hunter, *An Account of the British Settlement of Aden in Arabia*, pp. 147, 148.
[12] J. T. Addison, *The Christian Approach to the Moslem*, pp. 195, 196.
[13] W. H. Storm, *Whither Arabia*, pp. 109, 110.
[14] W. H. Ingrams, *A Report on the Social, Economic, and Political Condition of the Hadhramaut*, p. 15.
[15] *Ibid.*, p. 40.
[16] *Ibid.*, p. 44.
[17] See D. van der Meulen, and H. von Wissmann, *Hadramaut, Some of Its Mysteries Unveiled* (1932); Freya Stark, *The Southern Gates of Arabia* (1936); Hans Helfritz, *Land Without Shade* (1936).

CHAPTER ELEVEN

'OMĀN AND THE PERSIAN GULF STATES

TRAVELLING east from Hadramaut around the coasts of Arabia, we pass by the interesting little country of Dufar, which is under the suzerainty of the Sultan of Musqat (Muscat). Dr. Storm describes it as unique among Arabian provinces in its combination of forest-clad mountains, groves of frankincense, and coconut palms, cave dwellers and hyenas.[1] From there we reach another secluded yet highly interesting spot of this peninsula. Where the waters of the Indian Ocean and the Persian Gulf mingle and high mountains form a rugged skyline stretches the coast of 'Omān. The Sultanate of 'Omān is one of the most isolated parts of Arabia. It is surrounded on all sides by sea, on the north and east by the waters of the Persian Gulf and the Indian Ocean, and on the south and west by the sea of sand, the fearful Rub' al Khālī. Therefore, it is quite natural that the people of 'Omān have developed certain peculiarities not to be found elsewhere in Arabia.

The estimated area of this district is 82,000 square miles, and the estimated population 795,000. They are mostly Arabs with a strong Negro element and a good sprinkling of Baluchis coming from the not too-distant coast of Baluchistan. The best harbour on this rocky coast is Musqaṭ, where mail boats stop. It is one of the hottest towns in the world. Its high humidity makes it a very trying place in which to live. The heat is so oppressive in summer that even the Arabs try to leave for the mountains. As there was no proper approach from the inland over these mountains to Musqaṭ, Matrah, only a few miles away, became the main marketing centre for the inland trade.

'Omān like al Yaman, is mostly a mountainous country, although its mountains reach not quite so high as those of al Yaman. The Jabal Akhdar is about 10,000 feet high. There are many larger and smaller valleys in these mountains which

'OMĀN AND THE PERSIAN GULF STATES

are often densely populated. Water is abundant, and crops grow in profusion. 'Omān is famous for the quality of its dates. Pomegranates, lemons, quinces, olives, and almonds grow in abundance, and wheat, barley, millet, corn, cotton, and sugar cane are cultivated. 'Omān raises one of the best breeds of camels in Arabia. In the coastal district camels and other livestock feed largely on fish heads boiled with date stones.[2]

The majority of the inhabitants are settled and belong religiously to the Ibāḍīs; the others are Sunnī Muslims. The Ibāḍīs are not a group of the Shī'a as are the Zaydites we encountered in al Yaman, but they are a branch and a last remnant of the Khawārij. The Khawārij were a political group who separated early in Islāmic history, and are first heard of in connection with the murder of Caliph 'Uthmān, because they resented the fact that the caliph ordered all copies of the Qur'ān destroyed in order that his recension should be unchallenged. The Khawārij are really the first Islāmic sect with a politico-religious motive. In later times, especially under Umayyad rule, they rebelled again and again when they believed that the government was not acting correctly. They were scrupulous in their dealings with non-Muslims, but inordinately savage with Muslims who disagreed with their views. The Ibāḍīs, a sub-group of the Khawārij which sprang into existence in the time of Marwān II, around A.D. 748, are the only group which has survived the storms of the centuries. From an early time they appear to have been dominant in 'Omān, where their belief is still the officially recognized form of Islām. Another small group is found in Algeria where they are known as Abādītes.[3]

Ibn Batūta, the famous Muslim traveller of the fourteenth century, came to 'Omān, where he found that the Ibāḍīs repeat the Friday prayer four times at Friday noon and ask God's favour for the first two caliphs but say nothing of the third and fourth. The latter, 'Alī, they call just 'the man.'[4]

In the mountains of 'Omān exist tribes which represent an older civilization than Islām. They speak among themselves different vernaculars and use Arabic only in their connection with the outside world. Towards the desert regions also is tribal territory over which the Sultan of Musqaṭ has hardly any power.

Beginning with 1506 Musqat was occupied by the Portuguese; then it came under Persian domination for a hundred years until the Ghafārī dynasty won the upper hand, and became during the early part of the nineteenth century the most powerful house in Arabia. They even gained control of the island of Zanzibar near the East African coast, and their descendants are the ruling house in the island today. The rulers of 'Omān always leaned toward Britain, and in 1939 the long-standing treaty of friendship with Britain was reaffirmed.[5]

Some very interesting facts about the habits of the people of 'Omān are recorded in Dr. P. W. Harrison's book, *The Arab at Home*. He writes that the people are of an easy-going nature.

'No one seems anxious to accumulate great wealth or fiercely desirous of exterminating infidels.... There is a greater amount of comfort among the rank and file of the people and a more peaceful attitude toward life in general than prevails elsewhere in Arabia.'[6]

Further he remarks:

'Religiously the inhabitants of 'Omān are earnest and faithful in all observances of their own faith; none indeed are more so, but they are tolerant and open-minded to a degree unknown elsewhere in Arabia. Religious discussions are not taboo in that country, and I have even had men ask for a Christian service so that they might come and see what it was like.

'The women have mosques of their own to worship in, a thing that I have never seen elsewhere.... A large percentage of the women can read.... Women do not veil strictly as they do in the towns farther north, and there is a surprising degree of comradeship in married life compared with other parts of Arabia.'[7]

These are certainly remarkable features in a purely Muslim country. Mission work in Musqat was first begun by Bishop Valpy French who, already advanced in age, came from India to 'Omān to bring the gospel of Christ to the Arabs. He arrived in 1890 but in 1891 was laid to rest. On his voyage to Musqat he met a young American, Samuel Zwemer, *en route* to 'somewhere' in Arabia. It was a providential meeting, for the veteran passed on the standard to the young enthusiast.[8] It did not take too long until educational and medical facilities were provided. The Nestor of Protestant missions, Dr. Samuel

'OMĀN AND THE PERSIAN GULF STATES

M. Zwemer, worked here for a long period, and the hospital was operated by the famous desert doctor, P. W. Harrison, from the Arabian Mission of the Reformed Church in America (R.C.A.). And from this centre the influence of Christian teaching and Christian charity has been radiating over the south-east corner of Arabia. As Dr. Storm writes: 'The most hospitable, friendly, and responsive type of Arab in Arabia is to be found in the 'Omān field,'[9] Dr. Harrison states: 'There seems more hope for future progress in 'Omān than in any other province of Arabia.'[10]

PERSIAN GULF STATES

Sailing along the east coast of Arabia in the waters of the Persian Gulf, we find ourselves on one of the oldest traffic lanes of the world. Not only during the time of the Babylonians were these waters crossed, but inscriptions report that at a much earlier date the gulf was traversed by Sumerian vessels. Of Sargon I (before 2200 B.C.) it is said that he subdued Niduk ki, or as it was called in Assyrian, Dilmun, which are probably the islands of Bahrayn. The Sumerian tablets tell of connections with these islands and probably also with India. On the northern part of the main island of Bahrayn a large number of tumuli, or burial mounds, have been found, which for a long time were attributed to the Phœnicians. This view, however, has been discarded. Today these are considered as belonging to an earlier period, and were erected by unnamed conquerors.[11]

When the Seleucids had established themselves in the eastern part of Alexander's empire, the Persian Gulf reached new importance as a trade route. Gerra, a town on the Arabian mainland, became the trade centre and a staple place. The merchants of this town were considered among the wealthiest people on earth.[12] The rich pearl beds near Bahrayn were known, and since the earliest times pearl diving was practised. Persia was for a long time the dominating power in these regions. As soon as the Portuguese had discovered the sea route to India around the Cape of Good Hope, they also sailed towards the north to establish themselves in the Gulf. They left a trail of ruin wherever they went; they burned Musqaṭ and stormed Hormuz in 1507.[13] Therewith the Gulf was brought into the sphere of interest of

European seafaring powers, and their rivalries had their reflections in these waters until the British gained absolute mastery.

North of 'Omān along the Pirate Coast or the Trucial Coast are a number of independent shaykhdoms which are ruled in medieval fashion. Modern influences have not been able to penetrate in any measure, except that some air stations have been erected, and the Arab has become accustomed to seeing these 'magic carpets' descending and ascending. But by the development of longer-range aircraft most of these stations will be abandoned. O'Shea gives a lively description of life on such a lonely outpost.[14] Pearl diving is still the main occupation of the Arabs living on those coasts, where a few shaykhs and merchants amass enormous fortunes but keep the divers in perpetual indebtedness.[15]

Qatar is one of these shaykhdoms, whose shaykh attempts to deal more justly with his people, and the situation has greatly inproved in his domain. He has built a small hospital, and has invited the Arabian Mission to operate it.[16]

Our next step is to the islands of Bahrayn. These islands cover only 250 square miles, but have a population of about 120,000. According to recent history, they were occupied by the Portuguese in 1507, but in 1602 the invaders were dislodged by the Shah of Persia. The Persians were again ejected by Arabs from the mainland belonging to the 'Utayba tribe in 1783, from which the ruling family of Bahrayn stems till the present day. As early as 1820 the East India Company gained a foothold in the islands, and in 1861 they became a British protected area.[17] A treaty was signed with the shaykh in which he agreed to grant concessions of pearl fishing only with British consent. Bahrayn has become the centre of British influence in the Gulf, all the more accentuated after the discovery of large quantities of oil in Bahrayn (1932) and even richer deposits on the opposite shore of the Arabian mainland in the Hasa district, which belongs to Su'ūdī Arabia. Bahrayn has an abundant supply of submarine fresh water, but unfortunately the islands are full of malaria. The Arabs in Bahrayn are mostly Shī'īs. A good number of Iranians and Indians reside there.

These islands being under British administration, it was pos-

'OMĀN AND THE PERSIAN GULF STATES

sible to establish a mission work there. In 1892 a station of the Arabian Mission, later adopted by the Reformed Church of America, was erected. Medical work was started before the end of the century, which won the favour of the ruling shaykh so that he was willing to aid substantially in building a new hospital for women.[18] The medical work has continued ever since, and has proved to be a major factor in dispelling prejudice and breaking down opposition, fear, and superstitution, and in melting the hearts of Muslims, making them gradually inclined to grant a listening ear to the Christian message.

Before leaving the sun-baked shores of the Persian Gulf, we come in its north-west corner to another small independent shaykhdom under British protection. It is the little state of Kuwayt (1,950 square miles) with a settled population of approximately 50,000, and the same number of Beduins. They are mostly Sunnī Muslims and depend on the sea trade. They are sailors and boatbuilders of high reputation. Here, too, it was possible for the Arabian Mission to gain a foothold in 1903, and to start medical work. In 1914 a hospital for women was added.[19]

---

[1] W. H. Storm, *Whither Arabia? A Survey of Missionary Opportunity*, pp. 4, 5.
[2] *A Handbook of Arabia*, compiled by the Geographical Section of the Naval Intelligence Division, London, p. 241.
[3] I. Goldziher, *Vorlesungen uber den Islam*, pp. 195, 196.
[4] Ibn Batūta, *Voyages d' Ibn Batoutah*, Texte Arabe, accompagné d'une traduction par Defrémery et Sanguinetti, Vol. II, pp. 227, 228.
[5] For detailed description of 'Omān, see *A Handbook of Arabia*, Geographical Section of the Naval Intelligence Division, London, pp. 237-283.
[6] P. W. Harrison, *The Arab at Home*, p. 100.
[7] *Ibid*, p. 103.
[8] Storm, *op. cit.*, p. 63.
[9] *Ibid.*, p. 69.
[10] Harrison, *op. cit.*, p. 104.
[11] A. T. Wilson, *The Persian Gulf*, pp. 25-32.
[12] *Ibid.*, p. 34.
[13] *Ibid.*, pp. 113-115.
[14] See R. O'Shea, *The Sand Kings of Oman*.
[15] See P. W. Harrison, *op. cit.*, pp. 71-94.
[16] *The Muslim World*, Vol. XXXVIII, No. 2, April, 1948, p. 146.
[17] Wilson, *op. cit.*, p. 218.
[18] J. T. Addison, *The Christian Approach to the Moslem*, pp. 197, 198.
[19] *Ibid.*, pp. 197, 198; Storm, *op. cit.*, p. 110.

CHAPTER TWELVE

'IRĀQ

IN LEAVING Kuwayt our journey around the coasts of Arabia, or Arabia proper, has come to an end. 'Irāq, which we now reach, is of course an Arabic-speaking country, and is filled with a vigorous, rejuvenated Arabic national spirit, but it has a totally different background from the desert-bred Arabian states. In entering 'Irāq, we have come to the so-called fertile crescent around Arabia, which comprises 'Irāq, Syria, Lebanon, Transjordan, and Palestine, 'Irāq, like Egypt, is the gift of the river, or more correctly, the gift of the twin rivers the Euphrates and the Tigris. Around the banks of these rivers civilizations were born, have flourished, and have died away. History and historical antiquities in 'Irāq do not date back 200 or 300 years as in America, or 1,000 and 2,000 years as in Europe, but 3,000, 4,000, and even 5,000 years.

Here on these river-beds we encounter one of the oldest known civilizations of the world, the civilization of the Sumerians. None of the archæologists is certain of their origin, but after having settled near these great streams, they built towns and cities, organized a government with laws and regulations which were so basically sound that they were to a large measure taken over by the Babylonians. And as discoveries have proved, we are, to a much wider extent than we formerly realized indebted to the Babylonians in many fields of knowledge. Even from a Biblical point of view, Abraham the father of Ishmael and Isaac —Ishmael from whom the Arabs sprang and Isaac from whom the Jews descended—was a Babylonian from Ur in Chaldea. In the northern part of these plains the mighty power of Assyria arose, which for centuries vied with Babylonia for supremacy. Nineveh, Assur, and Babylon were the most marvellous cities of the world in their day. No wonder that Nebuchadnezzar, who had helped to destroy Nineveh and who later embellished

'IRĀQ

Babylon with mighty edifices and beautiful gardens, exclaimed in high exultation, 'Is not this great Babylon, that I have built ... by the might of my power, and for the honour of my majesty?'

The rich soil of this river land and the industry of its inhabitants, who by digging and maintaining thousands of irrigation canals made the river work for them, turned the country into a garden. This abundance has from time immemorial aroused the greed of its neighbours and invited invaders. History, therefore, tells us of wave after wave of invaders flooding the country, either coming from the sandy regions of the south and west, or descending from the mountain passes from the east. Since Nebuchadnezzar's dynasty no indigenous dynasty ruled the country, but foreigners wielded power—Persians and Greeks, Parthians and Romans, Sassanids and Arabs, the Turks, and the English. Only in very recent times has 'Irāq emerged again as an independent nation. In 1932 she was admitted to the League of Nations as an independent, sovereign state.

A BORDERLAND

'Irāq has been a borderland since her remotest past. When the wave of Arabs came, which broke the Persian power then ruling in 'Irāq, it rolled deep into distant Khorasān. Then receding, it mingled and altered; a new borderline began to appear somewhere through 'Irāq. It was the border between the Arabian and Iranian elements. Exactly where this line runs it is impossible to define, but it runs through 'Irāq.

Hence modern 'Irāq is by no means a homogeneous unit either geographically, or ethnologically, or religiously. It was carved out of three Turkish provinces after World War I, and her present population of 4,800,000 includes about 1,200,000 in minority groups as follows:

Kurds ..	800,000
Turcomans	75,000
Persians	80,000
Assyrians	30,000
Other Christians	60,000

Jews	100,000
Yazīdīs	30,000
Mandæans	3,000
Shabak	12,000[1]

Another authority in a reference book on the Middle East gives figures that vary considerably. For instance:

Christians	147,000
Jews	120,000
Yazīdīs	17,000
Mandæans (Sabeans)	40,000[2]

SUNNĪS AND SHĪ'ĪS

Religiously the 4,500,000 Muslims are divided into Sunnīs and Shī'īs, but although the Sunnīs are numerically stronger, they are racially divided into Arabs and Kurds, so the Shī'īs are the largest single community. Moreover, it must be remembered that the most holy shrines of the Shī'a are in 'Irāq, in Najaf, where 'Alī is buried, and in Karbalā where the sons of 'Alī, Hasan and Husayn, are buried. Every Shī'ī yearns in his heart to perform once in his life a pilgrimage to these holy places, just as the Sunnī longs to drink from the well of Zamzam in Makka and to touch the holy black stone in the Ka'ba. When the pious Shī'ī by adverse circumstances during his lifetime is prevented from visiting Najaf and Karbalā, he at least wants to be buried in the sacred soil. Therefore, long camel caravans bringing thousands of dead from all over the Shī'a world could be observed in former times marching towards the golden domes of Najaf. Recently, however, modern quarantine regulations have stopped this endless pilgrimage of the dead.

The Shī'īs, at least in 'Irāq, are in some respects more fanatical and more Francophobe [European-fearing] than the Sunnīs. Whereas it is always possible to enter a Sunnī place of worship, it is strictly forbidden for a Christian to enter a Shī'a mosque because, according to strict Shī'a belief, an infidel defiles everything he touches.

The Sunnīs, as we said, are divided into Arabs and Kurds. The Kurds, a vigorous race of mountaineers, live in the lower

'IRĀQ

and higher ranges of the Zagros mountains towards the north and the north-east. They are not Semites, but are of Aryan stock like the Irānians, and claim to be the descendants of the ancient Medes. They speak their own language and cling tenaciously to their tribal laws and customs. A Kurd will always be a member of his clan first before he is an 'Irāqian, just as a Shī'ī will always be a Shī'ī first. They have developed a modern Kurdish press in Baghdad and Sulaymania, and are for Kurdish independence and unity with the Kurds in Irān and Turkey.[3]

The Sunnī Arabs in 'Irāq, of course, draw much of their spiritual strength from their glorious past in this land. The fame of the 'Abbāsids and the glamour of the court of Baghdad under Ḥarūn al Rashīd and Al Mā'mūn with his likewise famous queens Khayzurān and Zubayda linger still in the air.[4] The Gaylāni mosque and other beautiful edifices point back to a time when Baghdad was the seat of learning and culture in the wide domain of Islām. 'Irāq takes up that ancient heritage, and tries to build upon it a modern nationalistic state with a rejuvenated spirit of Islām.

JEWS IN 'IRĀQ

But these divergent elements in Islām, Shī'ī and Sunnī and Arabs and Kurds, are not the only factors to be reckoned with in the modern life of 'Irāq. Another substantial minority are the Jews, through whose hands a large percentage of the 'Irāqian commerce flows. Two thirds of their number are living in Baghdad. These Jews date back to the Babylonian captivity; they are those who preferred to remain sitting comfortably by the rivers of Babylon and weeping over Jerusalem even when the golden opportunity offered itself to return to rebuild their beloved city. Today they have become so much assimilated with the other part of the population that a stranger at first has the greatest difficulty in differentiating between a Jew and a non-Jew. Perhaps it is even safe to say that they constitute the oldest community in 'Irāq. Living uninterruptedly in the same districts, they have outlived the different conquerors of the country—the Greeks, the Parthians, and the Sassanids—sometimes bitterly persecuted, but often enjoying periods of quiet and comfort in times when learning flourished. Babylonian Jewry assumed the leadership in rabbinical exegesis for a long period.[5] The relationship between the Jews and the Muslims was in general satisfactory. Although they were not greatly respected by the Muslims, there was no direct animosity between the two communities. Only in recent years through the agitation of the Zionists and their claim on Palestine has this relationship become strained.[6]

CHRISTIAN REMNANT GROUPS

Besides this large community of Babylonian Jews in 'Irāq, there exists an equally large group of Oriental Christians—Assyrians and Jacobites, Chaldeans and Armenians. The Assyrians are perhaps the most conspicuous group among these. They are the remnant of the ancient Nestorians and speak Syriac, an ancient Semitic dialect different from Arabic. They have also preserved their ancient Syriac characters in their script. The Nestorians were once the most vigorous Christian church in the East. They were branded as heretics by the official church in Rome and Constantinople, because of their refusal to accept Mary as the mother of God and their rejection of the worship of saints, images, and relics, and of the practice of celibacy. Their schools in Edessa, Seleucia, and especially Nisibin became famous centres of Christian learning in the East and excelled in a true missionary spirit. In these schools a system well balanced between theoretical instruction and vocational training was maintained. From these places missionaries went forth all over the East—to Persia and Afghanistan and to faraway India and China. At one period, the whole Persian church followed the teachings of Nestorius. Many Muslim rulers were favourably inclined towards the Nestorians and did not restrict their activities in any way. On the contrary, Nestorian physicians and secretaries were held in high esteem by the caliphs. Their missionary zeal continued till the thirteenth century when they tried to convert the Mongols to Christianity. When Baghdad was stormed in 1258 by Hulagu Khan, there still existed twenty-five metropolitans in the East who accepted the Nestorian patriarch as their spiritual head. When the Mongols

'IRĀQ

accepted Islām, and Tamerlane, the scourge of the East, destroyed cities and towns and whole flourishing provinces in his sweeping campaigns, these Christian communities were doomed. The Nestorians were driven into the mountain fastnesses of Kurdistan and Eastern Turkey, where they survived, but their zeal and missionary spirit were definitely broken, and they sank into a period of spiritual inertia.[7]

The modern history of the Assyrians is likewise tragic. During World War I, lured by promises of the Christian powers, especially Russia, they revolted against the Turks. They had to flee from their homes, and they came to Hamadan in Persia. When the Russian power collapsed in 1917, they again had to flee and came to 'Irāq, where the British housed them in refugee camps near Baqūba and Baghdad. Many of the able-bodied men were recruited by the British and formed Assyrian levies; others were otherwise employed. With the rising nationalistic spirit in 'Irāq and the enmity against Britain, they became obnoxious in the eyes of the young 'Irāqī. When the Assyrians demanded settlement in certain districts, and autonomy, which was difficult or rather impossible to grant, fighting broke out, in which several hundred were killed by the regular army (1933). After these unfortunate events, thousands of Assyrians crossed into Syria to be resettled in the Jazīra district between Nisibin and Dayr al Zōr. This whole Assyrian question caused no small amount of anxiety and ill feeling to the young 'Irāqī state. It has from the very outset disturbed the relationship between the Muslim majority and the Christian minority in 'Irāq.[8]

Besides the Assyrian Christians, a number of other Christian groups exist in 'Irāq. There are the Chaldeans. They were originally Nestorians, but during the sixteenth century they accepted the supremacy of the pope in Rome, whereupon he granted them the continuance of the use of their language and their ancient rites in the church. Of course, they had to abjure Nestorianism. Subject to the acknowledgement of Rome, they elect their own patriarch, who is called the Patriarch of Babylon and resides in Mōsul. These eastern Christian churches who accept the supremacy of Rome are also called Uniate Eastern Churches. We shall meet other branches when dealing with other parts of the Near East.[9] Another group of Christians are the Jacobites, or Syrian Monophysites.[10] They also look back at a glorious past. George, bishop of the Arabs (A.D. 724) and Abdul Faraj or Barhebræus (A.D. 1286) are names well known outside of their own community. Then we have Armenians of various denominations and a small number of Protestants. The majority of the Christians in 'Irāq are living in towns; only in the plains around Mōsul and towards Jabal Sinjār exist rural communities.

MANDÆANS OR SUBBIS

Two other groups are worthy of mentioning. Although small, they are extremely peculiar and are nowhere else to be found except in 'Irāq. One is called the Mandæans, or Subbis, often called the Christians of John the Baptist. When the Jesuit missionaries, who followed the Portuguese, came to Basra early in the seventeenth century, they found about fourteen or fifteen thousand of these Mandæans around there. They immersed themselves or baptized themselves in the river every day. The Jesuits believed that they were dealing with a remnant of the followers of John the Baptist, a belief which the Mandæans did nothing to dispel.

In reality, they are a remnant of a Gnostic sect, as is evident from their literature, the *Sidra Rabba* and the *Ginza*, which are written in an Aramaic dialect, which resembles closely the language of the Babylonian Talmud. Besides many myths about creation, they hold that the knowledge of good and evil, truth and error, was revealed to the first man immediately after he had received a soul from the higher world. The Jordan is the 'living water,' but all rivers come from the distant 'North' and their waters impart fresh energies to the persons who bathe in them. By immersion the pious become partakers of the virtues brought by the river from a higher world. Immersion with the Mandæans has nothing to do with the Christian conception of baptism as a symbol of the redemption from spiritual evil, the power of sin, and the domination of Satan. Such thoughts are quite foreign to the Mandæans.[11] Today practically all the silversmiths in Baghdad and other towns belong to this group. Their centre, however, is 'Amāra on the lower Tigris.

DEVIL WORSHIPPERS

The second very interesting group is the Yazīdīs, or devil worshippers. They form a solid minority of 30,000, mostly in rural communities north-east of Mōsul and in Jabal Sinjār. Their origin is obscure. Some want to trace them in the old Persian dualistic religion; others consider them to be an offspring of a Muḥammadan group during the time of the Umayyads. Anyway they have developed their own particular set of ideas. Their main book is the *Kitāb al Jilwah*, twelfth century, and their holiest man is Shaykh Ādī. The devil is worshipped in the form of a peacock, the symbol of pride, Malik Ta'ūs, as he is called. Malik Ta'ūs is inferior to the great God, but superior to all others. He was created and is under the command of God, but he is made chief of all.

There is no need to worship God, because God is so good that He cannot but forgive; therefore, it is far more logical to show reverence to Satan in order to appease his wrath and to neutralize his wiles. The word Satan (*Shaytān*) is never pronounced by them, and all words with a similar sound are avoided. It has even happened that the Yazīdīs have put to death persons who have intentionally outraged their feelings by using the devil's name. They adhere to many strange customs. They never wear anything blue, and also do not eat fish, out of veneration to Jonah, the prophet. Marriages in April are forbidden, and New Year is on the first Wednesday in April. They baptize their children, and believe in the transmigration of souls.[12]

To all these various minorities the full protection of life and liberty and the free exercise of any creed and religion or belief is guaranteed by the 'Irāq state. Every 'Irāqī enjoys equality before the law and has the same civil and political rights as every other. Every community has freedom in the use of any language, and the right to maintain its own institutions and educational establishments, and also to have questions of personal status settled in accordance with their customs and usages. They also enjoy full protection of the right to administer their own endowments, and an adequate share for minorities in public funds for educational, religious, and charitable purposes.[13] And although every person has the right to register a change of religion, even from Islām to Christianity, inquirers and converts have an uneasy feeling of apprehension and insecurity as they, even if protected by law, become social outcasts in their community, which means much more in a 90 per cent Muslim society than it would mean here in the West.

EDUCATION AND MISSIONS IN 'IRĀQ

Here in 'Irāq we encounter for the first time in our study the presence of a group of indigenous Christians with a long-established relationship between themselves and Islām. Therefore, the missionary from the West who is preaching Christ does not bring a new revelation to the Muslim. At the best, he brings a long-known fact in a new garb. And the indigenous Christian, having established a *modus vivendi* with his Muslim neighbour, is not overenthusiastic about this new and rather aggressive concept of Christianity which might bring him all kinds of trouble. Hence he often becomes not exactly a positive element on the side of missionary approach, and he is hardly to be blamed for this attitude. For that reason, missions have confined themselves frequently to the educational lines by founding schools for boys and girls, for waifs and orphans. This educational branch was a great asset in former times when the educational level in these countries was very low, and schools were few. But now the young 'Irāqī State is wide awake to the necessity of a proper education of its youth, and also has the means of pursuing this policy on a broad basis and to furnish their schools with all the modern equipment needed. Some figures may speak for themselves:

1943-1944

Type of School	Number of Schools	Enrolment
State Elementary School for boys ..	625	61,954
State Elementary School for girls ..	199	19,069
State Intermediate School for boys ..	27	6,640
State Intermediate School for girls ..	17	1,514

'IRĀQ

State Secondary School for boys	19	2,272
State Secondary School for girls	3	702

In addition there are two technical schools for boys, a school of homecrafts for girls, an agricultural school, a school for health officials, and a school for nurses and midwives. 'Irāq has no university, but the following colleges fulfill many of the functions of a university:

Type of School	Enrolment
The College of Engineering	140
The College of Medicine	302
The College of Pharmacy	144
The Institute of Physical Training	41
The Law College	495 [14]

It is evident from these statistics that it will become increasingly difficult for mission establishments to compete with such a government-sponsored programme. Yet there is one reason which justifies their existence and the expenditures and sacrifices made by the sending organizations. That is their higher spiritual level. If mission schools are operated on a truly Christian basis and radiate a real Christian spirit and atmosphere, then and only then will they still have a good reason to exist in these countries. For example there are the boys' and girls' schools of the Arabian Mission, established in 1913, and headed by Dr. J. Van Ess and his wife. It is only this type of institution that will be rightly esteemed by the Muslims. For instance, a number of high government officials asked the writer to accept their children in the Adventist school at Mōsul, because they wanted them to grow up in a clean and healthy atmosphere where the development of an upright character is one of the main objectives.

If Christian schools yield, however, to the temptation to become institutions for the transmission of knowledge only, with a somewhat Western standard of hygiene and cleanliness, then they will miss their goal completely. They will then too easily become representatives of the Western powers—England, America, or any other, and will be recognized as such. Reciprocally, they cease to be representatives of Christ. The

Easterner quite naturally will link these institutions, and therewith Christianity, with the general aspect of Western civilization, an equation which is by no means correct, but which nevertheless creates in his mind a serious obstacle to understanding Christ as He must be understood, not as an exclusive Western product but standing high above these differentiations of nations, race, and colour—the Son of man for all sons of men, or as a Catholic father in Baghdad once expressed it:

'They see Christianity merely as a phase of Europeanism, which they detest. Before they will ever accept Christ, they must be led to understand that His teachings are independent of all nations and races, the completing crown of all cultures.'[15]

Besides the Arabian Mission in Basra, the United Mission of Mesopotamia was organized in 1924 with stations in Baghdad, Mōsul, Hilla, Kirkūk, and Dohūk. But in general, mission work carried on by Protestant bodies in 'Irāq is rather small.

Catholic missionaries entered 'Irāq at the end of the sixteenth century and the beginning of the seventeenth, at first following the Portuguese trade stations. Later they were attached to the work of the Uniate Chaldæan Church. In Baghdad the Carmelites established their houses and charitable institutions. In 1932 American Jesuits from New England opened a college.

'Irāq in her long history has laid her talents on the altar of humanity and has lavished her gifts for the welfare of mankind. Great sons who enriched the thinking of mankind and opened new avenues to human endeavour and enterprise were born in her borders. 'Irāq being a borderland, and lying across the great trade routes from the West to the farther East, experienced periods of progress and prosperity alternating with periods of subjugation and utter decline, during which only faded memories remained of her former glory. Physical and spiritual stagnation prevailed during the latter periods, and a narrow-minded fanaticism raised its ugly head. Only recently has 'Irāq emerged from such a period of unproductiveness, when she was considered to be one of the backward provinces of the Ottoman Empire, just good enough for the exile of undesirable elements from the capital.

Modern 'Irāq was born after World War I, and bears to the

present day all the characteristics of a young, energetic state full of high aspiration and national ambition. The young generation of 'Irāq is full of ideas and plans, longing to solve the problems of life in a new and better way. She is impatient with the old ways which did not lead to a satisfactory solution. Will she find the solution?

All our problems culminate finally in the one great problem of human relations, the relationship between man and man, man and woman, people and peoples. And here the Christian can make the greatest contribution, because Christ, the Son of man, has solved this greatest of all problems. Christ the Man—not Christ the Westerner, or Christ the Theologian—never fails to speak to the heart of man. It is incumbent upon us, His followers, to place Christ the Man in the midst of the whirling stream of life in 'Irāq.

---

[1] A. H. Hourani, *Minorities in the Arab World*, p. 91.

[2] *The Middle East* (1948), p. 148.

[3] See W. R. Hay, *Two Years in Kurdistan, Experiences of a Political Officer, 1918-1920;* A. M. Hamilton, *Road Through Kurdistan*. For further information see the chapter on Irān.

[4] See Nabia Abbott, *Two Queens of Baghdad* (1946); R. Levy, *A Baghdad Chronicle* (1929).

[5] F. Buhl, art. 'Babylonia,' in *Jewish Encyclopedia*, Vol. II, p. 409.

[6] This paragraph was written before the developments in 1950-51.

[7] See John Stewart, *Nestorian Missionary Enterprise* (1928); L. E. Browne, *The Eclipse of Christianity in Asia* (1933); W. A. Wigram, *An Introduction to the History of the Assyrian Church* (1910).

[8] See Y. Malek, *The Assyrian Tragedy* (1934); W. A. Wigram, *The Assyrians and Their Neighbours* (1929); R. S. Stafford, *The Tragedy of the Assyrians* (1935).

[9] See A. Fortescue, *The Uniate Eastern Churches* (1923).

[10] The Monophysite doctrine will be explained when dealing with the Copts in Egypt, p. 175.

[11] See W. Brandt, *Die mandaische Religion; ihre Entwicklung und geschichtliche Bedeutung*.

[12] See R. H. W. Empson, *The Cult of the Peacock Angel*; I. Joseph, *Devil Worship; the Sacred Book and Traditions of the Yezidis*.

[13] A. H. Hourani, *op. cit.*, p. 92.

[14] These statistics are taken from an official publication: *An Introduction to the Past and Present of the Kingdom of Iraq*, by a Committee of Officials, pp. 76, 77.

[15] J. J. Considine, *Across a World*, p. 20.

CHAPTER THIRTEEN

SYRIA AND LEBANON

IN SYRIA we find ourselves in a Muslim country just as in 'Irāq and the other parts of Arabia. Again, however, we have entered an entirely different world. A different atmosphere seems to lie over this country, to permeate the life of her people, and to penetrate into every *sūq*[1] and every hut. There are deserts. There are the mountains, greener somewhat than in other parts. There are the ancient towns and trading centres. There are the smells of the East, but there are also the azure waters of the Mediterranean which lap gently at her coast, the same waters which lave the shores of Greece and Italy, and which seem to bear upon their tide a breath of the spirit of classical antiquity. Should that have had an influence? Should it have made all the difference? It is true that Syria is a country of the East. However, Syria faces West, whereas 'Irāq faces East, or towards Arabia. Certainly, there have been periods in Syria's long history during which she faced East— but those were not her most flourishing and constructive periods. There were times when she herself was the centre of interest. But now modern Syria has definitely turned her face West.

The boundaries of Syria have often been altered by her various conquerors. For this reason it is not altogether simple to define exactly which stretches of land belong to Syria and which do not. Her natural boundaries, however, are the chain of the Taurus Mountains in the north, the Euphrates and the desert in the east, the Mediterranean in the west, and the Sinai peninsula towards the south. This large territory is subdivided practically in its whole length by two parallel mountain ranges. A deep depression separates the one from the other. In the north it is called Buq'a or Coele-Syria which separates the Lebanon from the lower Anti-Lebanon, and in the south it is the Jordan valley which separates the mountain ranges of Palestine from the mountains of Gilead, Moab, and Edom. Toward the sea there is a smaller or wider coastal strip with a subtropical vegetation and climate; and toward the east, the rolling highland quickly passes from farmland into steppe and desert with its dry and hot inland climate. Between the Lebanon and the Anti-Lebanon two prominent rivers flow. Both have their sources near Baalbek. The one, the Leontes or Litāny, turns south until it finds an outlet to the west and cuts through the southern mountains to pour its waters into the Mediterranean. The other is the Orontes or al 'Āsi, which turns north giving life to such ancient towns as Homs (Emesa), Hama, and Antioch, and finally swings round to find its way into the Mediterranean.

MODERN SYRIA

The modern state of Syria, like 'Irāq, is a creation of World War I. After the revolt of the Arabs against their Turkish overlords, and the final downfall of the Ottoman Empire, the Allies were obliged to make certain new arrangements in order to fulfill to some degree their promises given to the Arabs during the war. At the time the major partners among the Allies were greatly interested in creating strong spheres of influence in these territories. However, it was out of the question to establish new colonies, because self-determination of the small nations was one of the battle cries for which that war had been fought. Therefore, the mandate system was devised. Under this plan these so-called backward nations would be nursed to maturity by a benevolent foster parent. Under this new device the Ottoman provinces on the eastern shore of the Mediterranean were parcelled out. The borders of the state of Syria so created followed roughly the ethnographical boundary line between Arabs and Turks in the north, including, however, large areas east of the Euphrates—the so-called Jazīra—then in an arbitrary fashion cut through the desert, including the lava country of Haurān and Jabal al Drūz. From there in a likewise arbitrary manner the frontier turns to the west until it reaches the Mediterranean north of Akko. This northern portion of the former Ottoman province of Syria was given to France as a mandate; the remaining southern part, comprising Palestine and the country east of the Jordan, which is now known as Transjordan, became a British Mandate. Thus the Arabs of Syria and Palestine, who ethnographically belong together, and who always formed a single unit, were divided—the intelligentsia and the younger generation of the one part were exposed to French thought and influence, and the other part to British thought and influence.

France subdivided Syria into smaller units and created finally the independent republic of Lebanon. The northern part near the Mediterranean coast, with Antioch as its main city and Alexandretta as its harbour, became an autonomous administrative unit, the so-called Sandjac of Alexandretta. As the district contained a large percentage of Turkish-speaking subjects, violent agitation started, after which the Sandjac was returned to Turkey in 1939. The Syrian government raised the strongest protests but was unable to hinder the return. It remains a sore spot in the relations between Syria and Turkey to the present day.

After twenty-two years of French mandatory regime, on November 26, 1941, Lebanon was declared an independent republic, and on the following day, the same declaration was given in behalf of Syria. It took, however, another two years before the administration was finally in native hands, and even heavy fighting in 1945 before the last soldier of the mandatory power left the Syrian soil. The 17th of April, 1946, is really the birthday of complete independence of the Arab state of Syria. We can hardly call it the Syrian nation, as the Syrians themselves feel not so much Syrian as Arab.

Here we might well ask, What is a Syrian? That is a very difficult question to answer as it is practically impossible to pick out a Syrian who could represent the Syrian as a type. In this territory we find the Syro-Phœnician merchant and the Beduin shaykh, the Maronite priest and the Druze 'Ajīl, men who live in mud-built beehive houses around Aleppo and men who live in goat-hair tents. Here we have the young ultra-modern intellectuals of Beirut and Damascus, and the sturdy, stocky ultraconservative peasants of the Ḥaurān, the young emancipated American University-bred women and the heavily veiled women of Ḥama and Damascus. Variety is the key word of Syria, a variety of faith, culture, outlook, and aspiration. And variety has always been the dominant characteristic of Syria. Let us take a brief glance at her past.

GLIMPSES OF SYRIA'S PAST

On the narrow coastal strip between the mountains and the sea, small city states grew up in the dim past. From where their inhabitants came is difficult to ascertain, but records which have been preserved show that these people ventured upon the sea and established connections with Egypt and the isles. A lively trade began, and brought the riches of the world to Tyre and Sidon, Jubayl (Byblos), and Arpad. The Phœnicians became the great seafaring nation of the ancient world until their power waned and finally was broken by the Assyrians and Babylonians. Nothing gives witness today of their immense fortunes. Neither temples nor castles remain, and yet the whole western world is indebted to them. It is true that the origin of the alphabet is today disputed after alphabetic inscriptions have been found in the old copper and turquoise mines on Sinai, but this much is certain: the Phœnicians were the first who grasped the full significance of this phonetic way of writing; they took it and shaped it and used it and passed it on to the Greeks. Thanks to them the alphabet has replaced the ideographic and cuneiform modes of script.[2]

Syria was conquered by the Hittites and the northeastern part was ruled by the Mitannis of whom the Tell el Amarna tablets give ample evidence. Around Damascus and Hamath small Aramæan states rose to power with whom the kings of Israel battled. The story of Naaman, the Syrian commander of the army, is well known. These conflicts continued until the Assyrians crushed friend and foe, and reduced to vassal states Aram and Israel alike.

But the most prosperous period for the fair land of Syria was still in the future. It was to arrive with the coming of the Greeks and the building of Antioch on the banks of the Orontes. Here palaces and temples were erected; and the luxuries of the East filled the markets. Under the Seleucids Syria became the centre of their empire, and Hellenistic thought and initiative coupled with its liberal spirit ushered in a new era.

When the Seleucid administration broke down after a long rule, and Pompey, the Roman, took over in 64 B.C., Syria became one of the most cherished possessions of the Roman Empire, and Antioch, the metropolis of the East, was the third largest city in the Roman world. Soon the influence of Antioch made itself felt in empire affairs to such a degree that poets in Rome mockingly sang that the Orontes would soon flow into the Tiber. In the third century after Christ, Syrians reached for the purple, and Elagabalus (217-222), a native of Emesa, and Philip the Arabian (244-249), a native of Ḥauran, sat on Augustus' throne.[3]

Farther south on the banks of the Orontes, the Syrian West Point or Aldershot was established, the military town of Apamea which housed the 600 imperial war elephants. A population of 120,000 made their livelihood there.[4] The extent of Roman influence in Syria can easily be gauged when wandering leisurely and contemplatively through the temples and ruins of Baalbek.

It was not only that the Syrians reached high positions in the empire or even sat upon the throne of the Cæsars, but in other respects, too, they made their contribution to the world. In Berytus (Beirut) a law school was founded, the fame of which was unsurpassed for centuries, and two of its outstanding doctors helped in the redaction of the likewise famous code of Justinian.[5]

Of even greater interest and importance, however, for the world at large is the fact that Syria is the homeland of Gentile Christianity. Here in Antioch the Christian message established its first foothold among the non-Jewish population, and from here the Christian church started on its victorious march among the Gentiles. Soon Christianity found a foothold in the towns of northern Syria, and many Christian churches, small and large, were erected there. Many were led by venerable Christian bishops. Antioch became the centre of the Greek section of the church, while Edessa, farther east, became the centre of the Aramaic-speaking section. Syrians, as mentioned before, had considerable influence in political Rome. Likewise the Christian Syrians exercised a strong influence in church matters, and many a Syrian rose to a high station in the church. When the church entered into the period of the formation of dogma, some of the most bitter controversies were fought on Syrian soil. Syrian Christianity has without question played an important role in the history of the church, and has certainly deeply influenced the life and outlook of the Near East.

But while Christianity was absorbed in fighting its theological and dogmatical battles, the Arabian storm gathered, and Islām, breaking all floodgates, soon established itself in Syria. Islām changed Syria, but likewise Syria changed Islām. The Syrian spirit nourished by the philosophies of the Greeks, polished and refined, combined with the alert, freedom-loving spirit of the sons of the desert, developed, under the guidance of the famous dynasty of the Umayyads in Damascus, a centre of learning, freedom of thought, art and literature, and laid one of the cornerstones of Islāmic culture. If the Umayyads had continued for a longer period, perhaps even a symbiosis of Christianity and Islām would have been accomplished. It is interesting to note that Aramaic or Syriac, the language of Syrian Christianity, was superseded by Arabic only many centuries later. The House of Umayya in Damascus, however, was not orthodox enough for many of the stern believers. It often did not take the stand for the narrower application of the principles laid down by the Islāmic doctors of law; it was too tolerant, too worldly.

Sinister forces were at work, gained momentum, and finally were able to overthrow the Umayyads. With the downfall of this dynasty, the centre of gravity shifted from Damascus to Baghdad, and Syria, the heart of the empire, was reduced to a mere province. In Baghdad, the new line of caliphs surrounded themselves with Oriental pomp, and soon became Eastern monarchs forsaking the democratic spirit of the desert. Islām again changed to a remarkable degree; its ideas and doctrines crystallized, and found their expression in stereotyped formulæ. Syria, however, welcomed those who were dissatisfied, and her mountains became a place of refuge for many who were persecuted for their opinions, or their faith's sake. It provided a sheltered anchorage in the turbulent whirl of opinion and political strife.

RELIGIOUS DIVERSITIES

The large variety of minorities and sects in Syria is a significant mirror of the role Syria played during the centuries. Although the Lebanon is now a separate political unit, yet the distribution of her minorities bears great resemblance to that of Syria; the latest statistics of both countries will therefore be given at this point:

	SYRIA[6]	LEBANON[7]
	Muslims or related	*Muslims or related*
Sunnīs	1,971,053	235,595
Shī'īs	12,742	209,338
Nusayrīs (or 'Alāwīs)	325,311	(Mutawalīs and Nusayrīs)
Ismā'īlīs	28,527	
Druzes	87,184	74,311
Yazīdīs	2,788	
	Christians	*Christians*
Greek Orthodox	136,957	109,883
Greek Catholic	46,733	64,280
Syrian Orthodox	40,135	3,753
Syrian Catholic	16,247	4,984
Armenian Orthodox	101,747	59,749
Armenian Catholic	16,790	10,048
Maronites	13,349	327,846
Protestants[8]	11,187	10,440
Latins	5,998	3,117
Nestorians	9,178	
Chaldæans	4,719	1,330
Various	—	6,261
Jews	29,770	5,666

These statistics are very revealing. Whereas in Syria there are 393,036 Christians of all persuasions among a total population of 2,870,311, in Lebanon there are 660,691 Christians out of 1,126,601 as total population. Lebanon is therefore the only country in the Near East with a slight Christian majority.

SYRIA AND LEBANON

Furthermore, it is quite significant that in Syria nearly 25 per cent of the Muslims do not belong to the Orthodox Sunna but to the Shī'a and other groups, whereas in Lebanon the Shī'a and Druzes are in the majority, 283,649 against 235,595 Sunnīs. That is all the more remarkable as in these countries the Shī'a has developed a number of offshoots which are worthy of consideration. The figures on the Christian side tell the sad tale of remnant groups of once-strong churches and also of their national affinities and their disunity.

The Shī'īs in the southern Lebanon are called Mutawala.[9] They belong to the ordinary Shī'a, the same as we find in 'Irāq and Irān, who believe in the sanctity of the twelve Imāms.[10]

NUSAYRĪS

In the mountain range east of Tartūs stretching to al-Lādhaqiyya (Latakiya), we find the Nusayrīs or 'Alāwiyyīn. They are an extreme group of the Shī'a. Their origin is shrouded in mystery, and no theory has yet been advanced to command general acceptance. They hold that beneath the inexplicable deity four worlds expand: a spiritual world of heavenly beings, the great world of light, beneath which is the lesser world of light in which half-materialistic beings have their abode, fettered to bodies as to graves, but who gradually will be led back to the great world of light; furthermore there is the lesser dark world, lights which have been extinguished, souls which have lost their spiritual qualities and have been changed into matter—as women and animals, for instance; and last, there is the utter darkness where the demons roam. The existence of the universe is divided into seven periods, and the God of the last period is 'Alī. The Nusayrīs have deified 'Alī and have practically become 'Alī-worshippers. They call him *al ma'na*, i.e., 'meaning,' in contrast to Jesus, whom they call *al kalima*, i.e., 'word.'

It requires a long period of initiation to be accepted as a Nusayrī. The initiation rites are coupled with solemn vows never to divulge the secrets of this spiritual marriage. Only sons of Nusayrīs can be initiated. Besides the Shī'itic feasts, they celebrate the sun festivals of Nawrūz and Mihrgān as well as Christmas, Epiphany, and the day of Saint Barbara. They abstain from camel's meat and rabbit, eel, and catfish, and also from *bāmiya* (okra) and tomatoes.[11]

ISMAʿĪLĪS

Another group we encounter around Banjās and al-Lādhaqiyya are the Ismaʿīlīs, bitter enemies to the Nusayrīs. They, too, belong to the Shīʿa, but they recognize only seven Imāms. The sixth Imām Jaʿfar al Sadīq had nominated his son Ismaʿīl to become Imām, but hearing of his intemperance, he denounced him and transferred the Imamate upon his second son. The Ismaʿīlīs refused to accept this change, claiming that it was not permissible to God to change His opinion, because it is God who speaks through the Imām.

The followers of that doctrine had to flee, and concealed themselves in different parts of the Muslim world. A part came to the mountain fastnesses of Syria. From here they sent out missionaries to preach the doctrine of the esoterics (Bātinīya) and the allegorical explanation of the Qurʾān. Their doctrine is: God is without attributes, incomprehensible, and unperceivable. He did not create the universe directly by an act of will, but He made manifest Universal Reason, in which all the divine attributes rest. Reason thus becomes the real divinity of the Ismaʿīliya. Reason creates the universal soul, whose essential attribute is life. The soul produced primal matter which formed the earth and stars. To gain salvation knowledge must be acquired which can come only from the earthly incarnation of Reason, that is, the Prophet, and his successors, the Imāms.

Paradise allegorically signifies the state of the soul which has reached perfect knowledge. Hell is ignorance, No soul is condemned to hell eternally, but is returned to earth in new incarnations until it has recognized the Imām of the epoch and has learned knowledge from him.[12]

The Ismaʿīlīs at times commanded a large following. At the end of the third century of the Hijra, ʿUbayd Allah ibn Muhammad al Mahdī was recognized as Imām and founded in Tunisia the empire of the Fātimids, which ruled Egypt for a considerable period and which left their deep imprint upon Egyptian life.[13]

SYRIA AND LEBANON

Another offshoot of the Ismaʻīlīs was the Assassins, the notorious secret society which struck terror into the hearts of the Crusaders and all ruling houses of Islām. None of the latter was for a moment sure of his life; suddenly a dagger could be thrown at him by one of these fanatics to bring it to an abrupt end. The founder of this group was Hasan ibn Sabbāh, who from his impenetrable mountain fortress in Persia directed the whole movement. The main seat was Alamut in Persia, but the order possessed many castles outside of Persia in Syria. The Crusaders called the mysterious leader the 'Ancient of the Mountain.' It is said that the members of the secret society were given a drug, Hashīsh, in order to fulfill their often difficult tasks in blind obedience. The addicts of this drug were called hashshāshīn, from which the word 'assassin' is derived. For more than 200 years the Assassins were the terror of the East until the Mongols broke their power in Persia in 1260, and the Sultan Baybars of Egypt in Syria in 1272.[14] Today they are a peaceful community not showing any of their ancient characteristics. The Indian branch of the Ismaʻīlīs is headed by the well-known Agha Khān, who not long ago was weighed in diamonds, the equivalent value of which was distributed for charitable purposes.

DRUZES

Yet another group that should be considered in this connection are the Druzes. They are about 150,000 strong in the Lebanon and Jabal al Drūz. Their origin is also obscure, although they believe themselves to be pure Arabs of South Arabian stock. Professor Hitti, himself a Lebanese, advances a number of rather convincing arguments that point to their affinity with Kurdistan and Persia.[15] But whatever the truth may be, the interesting point is their religious belief. To them the Fātimid caliph Al Hākim bi amr illah (996-1021) is the last incarnation of God. He is venerated, if not worshipped, and is called 'our lord.' He was the most eccentric of all Fātimid caliphs, but his bizarre whims and excesses are interpreted symbolically. He is believed to be alive, living hidden in some kind of spiritual transcendence, but will return to earth some day. The Druzes are strict Unitarians. The door of the Druze religion was closed after the death of Baha' al Dīn in A.D. 1031.

No one can be permitted to enter the Druze fold, but likewise no one can leave it. It is a sacred privilege and a priceless treasure to belong to the Druze people. They have their secret catchwords and the people are divided into initiates and uninitiates. Only the initiates attend their meetings on Thursday nights in secluded spots, the so-called Khalwa. They hold many ideas in common with the Isma'ilīs about the universe. From the universal mind emanates the universal soul, and from the latter again the word, or intelligent expression of mind and soul. All religions are forerunners to Druzism. Adam and Jesus seem to stand above other prophets and share in the divine essence. Jesus is featured according to the Docetistic type, not like the Jesus in the Gospels. They believe in the transmigration of souls, and hold that a pious Druze will be reborn in China or Tibet. They are mostly farmers and winegrowers, and have no inclination for commerce. They are very clean, straightforward, and courageous in battle. In the religious field, however, their straightforwardness is completely reversed, because they consider the doctrine of dissimulation as justified; according to this a member of the Druze religion is free to profess publicly any other dogma or creed, if therein should lie his path of safety. Orthodox Islām never considered the Druzes as a branch of Islām, and Ibn Taymiyya went so far as to proclaim that warring against the Druzes is more meritorious than warring against the Armenians. Modern educated Druzes are fervently pro-Arab and cannot be distinguished from any westernized Easterner.[16]

Most of these aforementioned communities are unknown even to the well-informed Westerner. The West seldom hears about them, and if so, then some queer notion or absurd practices are played up by a casual traveller, which create an altogether wrong impression and leave a distorted picture in the minds of many. The Westerner begins to think that these people are dreadfully backward or that they are simpletons, who have never thought about life, and have no idea of the wherefrom and the whereto; hence they should be treated like children, whereas, the contrary is the case. These people have developed highly elaborate systems of thought, which bear witness to their intense interest in all things supernatural, and in life—its origin and its future. Therefore, if the spiritual forces of the West—that is, Christianity—want to gain a foothold among those people, they must send their best-trained and most tactful ambassadors, who do not consider it a loss to follow the Oriental mind in its highways and byways of subtle reasoning, and who are able to cope with it in presenting the message of Christ in such a way that it will find an echo in the Oriental soul.

ORIENTAL CHRISTIANS

In looking once more at the statistics given before, the reader will see a large variety of Christian bodies, and perhaps here is the proper place to make some remarks in passing. In any survey of the divisions of the church universal, three crucial centuries stand out distinctly: the fifth, when after the Council of Chalcedon (451) the Syrian Nestorian body organized the Church of the East, followed in the next century by the schism of the Syrian Jacobites, Copts, and Armenians who adhered to the Monophysitic view of the nature of Christ; the eleventh century which saw the definite break between the Eastern and the Western Church, that is, the Greek Orthodox Church and the Roman Catholic Church; and the sixteenth century, when the various Protestant churches came into being.

The Orthodox Church has no vicar on earth, but has one common doctrine and practice which binds her followers together. She is subdivided into national churches—the Serbian, Bulgarian, and Russian Orthodox Churches, for example. The original four patriarchs of Constantinople, Antioch, Jerusalem, and Alexandria were equal and independent in administration. The patriarch of Constantinople, being near the seat of the imperial government and later of the Ottoman government, had greater influence, but no greater power. He was *primus inter pares*. There is no celibacy for the lower clergy, but the higher clergy are taken in general from monastic orders.

The difference in points of belief from the Roman Catholic Church could be summed up in the following:
1. Procession of the Holy Ghost from the Father alone.
2. Triple immersion in baptism.
3. The use of leavened bread in the mass.
4. Communion in both kinds.
5. Denial of indulgence and purgatory.[17]

The Syrian Orthodox and Armenian Orthodox are Monophysites. That means that they believe in the unity of Christ's nature, the one nature of the incarnate Word of God. They acknowledge that the *Logos* was made flesh, but did not assume a human soul. He became flesh in order to manifest Himself to us as God through the flesh as through a curtain. They claim that the body of Christ could not be corruptible else we worship the corruptible. However in the Council of Chalcedon it was laid down (and that is what the Greek Orthodox and all the western churches believe) that Jesus Christ is perfect God and perfect man consubstantial with the Father according to His deity, consubstantial with man according to His humanity, in two natures without confusion or change, without division or separation. Those who follow this rule are called Dyophysites.

The Greek Catholics, Syrian Catholics, and Armenian Catholics belong to the Uniates, whom we have already met in the Chaldæans in 'Irāq. These groups have returned to the fold of the Roman Catholic Church, recognize the pope as their head, and adhere to the dogma of Rome but are permitted to continue certain ancient rites and customs of their own, and to read mass not in Latin but in their respective languages. Whereas those who read mass in Latin are called Latins in the Near East, the others are Rūm-Catholics. Rūm is the word the Turks used to signify the Greeks.

Another very important and prominent group in the Lebanon are the Maronites. The real Lebanese, meaning the people of the 'mountain,' are in fact Maronites. So the term Maronite really expresses more than religious adherence; it expresses a national relationship. This was true especially in former times when the 'mountain' formed an administrative unit by itself under the Turks.

SYRIA AND LEBANON

During the sixth and seventh centuries when the Monophysitic controversy was at its height, the emperor Heraclius (610-641) tried to reconcile the warring parties. Finally a new formula was found which stated that in Christ, although being of two natures, the unity of will and purpose (God's and human will) was revealed. But this new formula did not achieve the expected peace between the Monophysites and the Dyophysites. It only helped to create a new faction, the followers of which were called Monothelites. They were living mainly around Antioch and in the plains stretching towards Hama and Homs. When Justinian II, in 685, invaded Muslim Syria and did all he could to persecute the Monothelites and to cripple their influence, they left the plains and retreated into the mountain fastnesses of the northern Lebanon. From there they penetrated farther to the south, and have lived ever since a semi-independent life under their feudal lords. During the time of the Crusades they threw in their lot with the Franks and returned to the fold of the Roman Church in 1182. In 1584, Gregory XIII founded the Maronite College in Rome, which played a decisive part in the organization of the Lebanon Church. The Maronites recognize the pope and have adopted various Roman usages and symbols. They have, of course, abandoned Monothelitism, but they continue to permit the marriage of priests, retain their own fasts and saints and the Syriac liturgy. But for all practical purposes they are Roman Catholics.[18]

The return of the Maronites as a unit to the fold of the Roman Church provided an opening wedge for the entry of many Catholic orders into Lebanon and Syria. The Jesuits entered first in 1595, but closed their work, only to return later a second time. In 1846 they founded the Oriental Seminary at Ghazīr which was transferred to Beirut in 1875, and which developed into the well-known St. Joseph University. Today it is the spiritual and intellectual focus of catholicism in which an elite is prepared in its theological as well as medical colleges. They have a weekly paper *Bashīr* and a bimonthly review *Al Mashriq*. The Jesuits alone have under their care 155 elementary schools scattered all over Syria. The Capuchins have been stationed in Syria since 1627, the Carmelites since 1650, the

BRIDGE TO ISLĀM

Lazarites since 1784. They have 110 schools under their care. Besides these institutions there are numerous institutions operated by nuns, as for example, the Sisters of St. Vincent de Paul, the Sisters of the Holy Family, and so forth.[19] Besides these orders of foreign origin, the Maronites have their monasteries and convents, so that the 'mountain' is just honeycombed with Catholic religious institutions. Lebanon is certainly the bulwark of Catholic Christianity in the Near East.

PROTESTANT MISSIONS

The first two Protestant missionaries arrived at Beirut in 1823. Their force was strengthened by another arrival in 1827. In 1834 the Arabic section of the mission press was transferred from Malta to Beirut,[20] and many books and pamphlets were distributed by colporteurs every year. But these early missionaries felt that the greatest need was the Bible in Arabic. Therefore, the heavy task of translating the Bible was begun in 1847 by Eli Smith and completed by Dr. C. V. A. van Dyck in 1865. It has become the Bible for most Arabic-speaking people in the world, and in 1934 the press could report that it had printed 2,200,000 volumes of Scripture—whole Bibles, Testaments, and portions. The influence and blessing of it, however, cannot be measured in figures. It is one of the best translations of the Bible ever made, and although people at times complain that its Arabic compares unfavourably with that of the Qur'ān, it should never be forgotten that Qur'ānic Arabic has a standard of its own, and cannot be duplicated.

In 1834, the first school exclusively for girls was started. This was certainly a new venture in the Arabic world. In 1870, a large number of small schools could show an enrolment of over 1,200 pupils, including 250 girls. In 1864, the Syrian Protestant College was founded, independent of mission control. It began to operate in 1866 and developed into the famous American University of Beirut to which students flock from all over the Near East. Its graduates return to their respective lands, often to fill posts of high importance, The main interest of the university is to promote knowledge, to raise the moral and ethical standard of all its alumni, and to disregard religious differences.

It could not be said that it exercises a definite Christian influence. Professor Addison sums it up in the following statement:

'The present ideal of the institution, which grows more secular every year, is that each student should remain in whatever religious status he may happen to be. The conversion of a Moslem to Christianity would be as unexpected as it would be inconvenient.'[21]

The first indigenous Protestant church of twenty-seven members, among them three Druzes, was organized in 1848 at Beirut after twenty-five years of labour. Protestant forces, including, of course, the Armenians, have now grown to 10,000, most of them second- and third-generation Protestants, as very few changes of allegiance from one Christian body to another occur. In the early times every small band of Protestants had to undergo strong opposition and often persecution, but today this has practically ceased.

Besides the American Board of the Presbyterian Church, other mission societies entered. The British Syrian Mission, mostly women workers who have made it their primary aim to work among Muslim women; the Edinburgh Medical Mission which operates the Victoria Hospital at Damascus; the Danish Mission which works farther in the interior; and a number of other societies came to Syria. Dr. Bliss mentions thirty-eight Protestant agencies active in Syria in 1912.[22] To unify and to co-ordinate this diversity of Christian endeavour not only in Syria, but also in the other lands of the Muslim East, the Near-East Christian Council was established in 1927 with its executive centre first at Cairo, but later transferred to Beirut (1934).

Considering the enormous efforts which Christian agencies, both Catholic and Protestant, have made in this relatively small area of the Muslim world, we may well ask the question: 'What has been the impression upon the Muslim? What has been the net result? Has the Muslim problem been solved during these long years?' Those who are eager to read the result in statistics about the number of actual conversions will be sorely disappointed. The number is negligible, and the reasons are many. First of all, the Catholics never attempted a really aggressive missionary programme. They worked among the Christians in the main. And the Protestants saw the need of reviving the ancient Oriental churches with the spirit of the gospel, hoping that by this rejuvenation these might become a potent force in evangelizing their neighbours. Therefore, the main missionary effort in former Turkey during the last century was concentrated upon the Armenians and not upon the Turks. The same was true in Syria. These hopes, unfortunately, have not been fulfilled. The influence upon these ancient churches has been less than anticipated, and the members of the various indigenous Protestant churches in general do not seem more inclined than their Orthodox or Maronite brethren to work for their Muslim neighbours.

The indirect influence, of course, cannot be properly gauged. The example of charity, honesty, devotion, and sacrifice of many a Christian ambassador has helped destroy the barriers of prejudice, hate, ignorance, and fanaticism in many a heart, and may have opened many ears to the Christian message which otherwise would have refused to listen. I remember once being invited to a Muslim party where a good number were present. After many secular subjects were discussed, an old doctor stood up and addressed me, saying, 'Today is Christmas, your feast. Tell us something about Christ and let us have a Christian prayer.' Such a request would have been impossible if the silent seed of some other Christian before me had not stimulated this doctor's heart. How deep this influence of silent example has gone cannot be ascertained, but it can always be felt. When one real converted Christian has lived in an area, he is spoken of and even revered for a long time to come.

Missions have largely adopted schools as a means of approach, and certainly countless blessings have been derived from them. But on the other hand, especially in institutions of higher learning the secular, irreverent, agnostic spirit of the West is a most dangerous ferment. It has created a fervent nationalism, eager to imitate Western methods and modes of life which are often based on a purely materialistic concept. The sobering influence of Christianity which makes Western life bearable in spite of its shortcomings is not transmitted to Muslims. This is true because this influence cannot be learned mentally; it must be experienced inwardly, and the result is apparent in modern Turkey, where the church has exchanged one master for another. Formerly it was orthodox Islām which laid all the restrictions upon her. Today it is the well-regimented nationalism, which has no place for a discordant note, which the church with her spiritual claims would strike.

EDUCATION IN SYRIA AND LEBANON

The same situation may eventually arise in Syria and Lebanon, although probably it will be less accentuated. These states have achieved their full independence. Their main concern now is to create a unified national spirit, which is very understandable as it is a matter of life and death to them. In order to achieve that goal their ministers of education have set up a definite programme to which all schools, governmental and private, have to adhere. That again is easy to understand, as a diversity of schools and school systems as was prevalent, especially in Lebanon, would never bring about that envisaged goal. Such a diversity cannot be tolerated. The situation in Lebanon was impossible from a national point of view. There were the Catholic schools modelled according to the French style, making French the medium of instruction and French culture their ideal. There were the Protestant schools based on the American and English systems with the respective attitudes on life. There were the Muslim schools favouring a strong national spirit based on Islām and the glorious past of the Arabs. There were the old mosque schools with a purely religious medieval outlook. The result was four Syrians or four Lebanese who spoke the same language but did not understand one another; as each one of them had received a totally different mental picture, and different ideals were instilled into him by these different educational institutions. Instead of education serving as an agent to bring them closer together, it often separated them and widened the gulf. That a national government cannot tolerate such a situation is evident, but it certainly will mean many readjustments to institutions conducted by mission societies.

In looking through the different curricula published by

BRIDGE TO ISLĀM

Syrian and Lebanon ministers of education, one point stands out clearly. The supreme emphasis is laid upon the study of Arabic and Arabic history, that the medium of instruction shall be Arabic even in the sciences in the higher grades, and that foreign teachers shall be replaced by qualified nationals as fast as circumstances permit, except in cases of experts in certain fields. Further, they require that all private schools come under government inspection and that their pupils qualify in government examinations if they desire a certificate. These restrictions, while they have no important bearing on a school whose purpose is a general education, yet they have a very definitely restrictive attitude toward schools with a particular mission.

These regulations are certainly most reasonable, but likewise they may cause many difficulties. One interesting result is seen in the drop of foreign elementary schools in Syria.

Year	Foreign Schools	Enrolment	Govt. Schools	Enrolment	Private National Schools	Enrolment
1944-45	128	19,878	658	85,540	287	43,010
1945-46	31	3,207	737	99,703	312	47,224
1946-47	41	4,388	839	114,549	303	44,719[23]

I submit these statistics only to show the general trend of developments in the educational field in Syria.

SYRIANS ABROAD

This short survey would, however, not be complete, if it failed to mention one particular feature of Syrian life. Not only the most diversified Islāmic conceptions are to be found in these territories, not only is the Lebanon the stronghold of Latin Christianity in the Near East, and the field of the oldest and strongest Protestant mission work, but the Syrians and Lebanese are moreover the most widely travelled people among the Arabs. Beginning with the last century, a stream of emigrants went forth from Syria and Lebanon, at first mainly directed to Egypt, but later all over the world. In Egypt, Syrians were the first to start newspapers and periodicals, and gave the impulse of the modern literary awakening of the Arabs. Only two periodicals may be mentioned in this place, *Al Muqtaṭaf* and *Al Hilāl*, both of which had a profound influence in shaping the modern spirit of the Near East.

Like the Phœnicians of old, Syrians went farther afield whenever and wherever opportunity presented itself. At present we find large communities of Lebanese and Syrians in the United States of America and in the various republics of Central and South America, as well as on the West Coast of Africa, and in Australia.[24] Some writers believe that an additional 50 per cent of the population figures for Syria and Lebanon should be added to account for those living abroad. Many of these emigrants are absorbed by the countries of their choice, but a good number return to their homeland bringing with them the modern ideas they have imbibed and the spirit of the foreign countries. It can justly be said that Syria, but more especially Lebanon, is the most westernized of all the countries of the Near East, and that a higher percentage of its population has a fair knowledge of the outside world, not only by hearsay but by personal contact, than in any other Eastern country. The inquisitive and versatile spirit of the Syrian makes him more inclined to start out on new ventures in any line than the more static and conservative spirit of his brethren in the neighbouring countries.

---

[1] Sūq = a market or bazaar.
[2] *Achievements of Civilization*, No. 1, *The Story of Writing*, p. 36.
[3] H. Lammens, *La Syrie*, Vol. I, p. 12.
[4] R. Fedden, *Syria*, p. 92.
[5] Lammens, *op. cit.*, Vol. I, pp. 14, 15.
[6] A. H. Hourani, *Minorities in the Arab World*, p. 76.
[7] *Ibid.*, p. 63.
[8] The Protestants are split into different groups—Syrian and Armenian—racially as well as denominationally.
[9] Singular, *Mutawalī*—those who make friends of (understood by the Shī'a, as friends of 'Alī).
[10] F. J. Bliss, *The Religions of Modern Syria and Palestine*, p. 295.
[11] See R. Dussaud, *Histoire et Réligion des Nosairis* (1900); and G. Samné, *La Syri e*, pp. 337-342.
[12] See I. Goldziher, *Streitschrift des Gazālī gegen die Bāṭinijja-sekte*; V. Ivanov, *A Guide to Ismaili Literature*; B. Lewis, *The Origins of Ismā'īlism*.

[13] See Muir, *The Caliphate, Its Rise, Decline and Fall*, pp. 557-586; De L. O'Leary, *A Short History of the Fatimid Khalifate*.

[14] See de Sacy, *Mémoire sur la dynastie des Assassins*; B. Bouthoul, *Le Grand Maître des Assassins*.

[15] P. Hitti, *The Origins of the Druze People and Religion*, pp. 18-23.

[16] See de Sacy, *Exposé de la Réligion des Druzes*, 2 vols.; P. Hitti, *The Origins of the Druze People and Religion*; B. Springett, *Secret Sects of Syria and the Lebanon*.

[17] See W. F. Adeney, *The Greek and Eastern Churches*; S. H. Scott, *The Eastern Churches and the Papacy*.

[18] A. A. Stamouli, 'Maronites,' *The New Schaff-Herzog Encyclopedia*, Vol. VII, pp. 188-190; J. Labourt, 'Maronites,' in *The Catholic Encyclopedia*, Vol. 9, pp. 683-688.

[19] The statistical data are taken from Gabriel Oussani, 'Syria,' *Catholic Encyclopedia*, vol. 14, pp. 404-406.

[20] This and the following data on Protestant missionary endeavours are taken from J. T. Addison, *The Christian Approach to the Moslem*, pp. 113-138.

[21] *Ibid.*, p. 130.

[22] Bliss, *op. cit.*, p. 328.

[23] The figures of 1944-46 are given in the yearly report of the Ministry of Education of the Republic of Syria, 1946, in Arabic, p. 62. The figures of 1947 based on a government report were given to me through the favour of the Syrian Embassy in Washington, D.C.

[24] See P. Hitti, *The Syrians in America*.

CHAPTER FOURTEEN

PALESTINE AND TRANSJORDAN

PALESTINE, the Holy Land, is dear to more hearts in this world than any other country. It unites and has united more men in their thoughts and has inspired more ideals than any other place; but at the same time it splits men far more deeply into antagonistic camps, and raises far more fury and violent hatred than any other land.

Mention the word 'Zion,' and the suppressed hope of millions who have to live in faraway lands, often in squalor and misery, is kindled anew. They are urged on in their struggle for bare existence; and if they approach the valley of shadows and their dreams have never come true, the hope has at least cast some golden rays upon their dreary pathway, and it lingers that perhaps their sons and daughters will experience the joy of throwing off the shackles of bondage and returning home to Zion.

Mention the word 'Bethlehem,' and children's eyes begin to sparkle; and even if that 'Child' which was born there does not hold their allegiance very long, yet Christmas, with all that it stands for, will remain a sweet remembrance for all their days to come. Mention the words 'Galilee,' 'Gethsemane,' and 'Calvary,' and the hustle and bustle in many souls quiets down, and silence and thoughtfulness enter. This may be for a few fleeting moments only; but those moments count, because not the length of time we live is of importance, but the moments which are fraught with inner experiences in which we hear the still voice of God.

Mention the word 'Al Quds' (Jerusalem), and every Muslim feels elated. At the same time, he feels that the strongest appeal is being made upon his manly qualities to protect such a holy place from all aggression and desecration.

Palestine is the most controversial country to be imagined, and ever has been. It is a cockpit of unending conflict. Even its name, intead of being related to one or the other of the three great religions which have their home there, points to the invaders from the Greek islands, the Philistines, who frightened the earlier inhabitants of the land with their chariots of iron and their metal-clad warriors. Such has been the experience of Palestine through the centuries. Conquerors came and conquerors went. They brought death and desolation, but also periods of wealth and prosperity. And in our day, this bridge between the continents has again become a major trouble spot, which may involve many a nation before its problems are finally solved.

It is not the aim of this study to write a political history of the countries of the Near East, nor to delve into the present political controversies. The struggle, however, between the Arabs and the Zionists has such far-reaching repercussions and has such a definite bearing upon the attitude of the Arabs and Muslims towards the West that it cannot be overlooked. No other question has done more to unite the Arabs and to bring about a feeling of solidarity on the one hand and antagonism against the West on the other than the question of Palestine.

Muslims and Jews lived together peacefully for centuries. The Jews were treated like the Christians, as *dhimmīs*; and as long as they accepted that state no difficulties arose. There were no ghettos in Eastern cities, although the Jews themselves liked to live among their brethren, and Jewish quarters were the result just as there existed Christian quarters. There was friendly intercourse between the two communities; and during the glorious age of Islām, Jewish scholars helped to spread the fame of Islāmic culture. Often the Jews became the intermediaries between the Islāmic East and the Christian West. In Palestine the ancient settlements of the Jews in Hebron, Jerusalem, Tiberias, and Safed continued to flourish. There was no strife between the Jews and the Muslims. On the contrary, the Jews had a more peaceful existence under Muslim rule than in many a Christian kingdom. This situation, however, underwent a radical change when Zionism arrived on the scene.

JEWISH MESSIANISM AND ZIONISM

To understand Jewish history in the past, and to have an

inkling of the Jewish future, one must look back to Jewish Messianism. Messianism can be traced to the very beginning of the Israelites, to the hopes and visions of the prophets, and later to the tribulation of the soul under the Roman Empire. It is the Jewish conception of things to come—a complex body of thought and speculation about the destiny of Israel and the salvation of mankind running through Biblical, Apocalyptic, Talmudic, Cabalistic, Rabbinic, and Zionist literature. It finds a different expression in every age, and is subject to many interpretations. Messianism implies faith in the rise of a new order for mankind to be created by persons who are divinely appointed for the task. No matter how long they had to wait, no matter what disasters they had to endure, the Jews were enjoined to have faith in ultimate salvation.[1] Jews seldom gave expression to their Messianic dreams and speculations outside their homes and colleges. There, day and night, Jewish mystics sought contact with deeper reality and searched for the secrets of the universe and dreamed of the salvation of their people.

Zionism began to translate their dreams and aspirations into the political and economic terms of the modern world. That was extremely revolutionary even to Jewish orthodox thought. It meant that the passive waiting for the restoration was to be replaced by an active endeavour to bring about the restoration. Deliverance cannot be expected by a supernatural intervention, but the Messianic hope will find its fulfilment by working for it. In reality in Zionism the Messiah is replaced by the combined effort of the people for the realization of a national goal.

The first fires of Zionism were kindled by Leo Pinsker, a Russian Jew, in 1882, after the pogroms following the assassination of Tsar Alexander II in 1881. Pinsker wrote a book called *Auto-emancipation*. The fires were brought to flame by Theodor Herzl in his book *Jewish State* in 1896. In 1897 the first Zionist Congress was held in Basel, and Herzl spared neither time nor effort to bring his plans to realization. At first no definite country for settling Jews was envisaged. Argentina, Uganda, and Kenya were prospected, but soon the influence of Eastern Jewry made itself felt, which demanded Palestine, the old homeland, and no other. But up to 1911 the idea of the Zionists was not to establish a separate Jewish State but a Jewish home. At the tenth Congress held at Basel in 1911, the president made the following statement:

'The aim of Zionism is the erection for the Jewish people of a publicly recognized, legally secured home in Palestine. Not a Jewish State, but a home in the ancient land of our forefathers, where we can live a Jewish life without oppression and persecution. What we demand is that the Jewish immigrant to Palestine be given the opportunity of naturalizing as a citizen without limitation and that he can live unhindered in accordance with Jewish customs. . . . That and nothing else is our aim!'[2]

The first step for the actual realization of these hopes was made when Dr. Chaim Weizmann as reward for the valuable service rendered to England in chemical warfare received the promise from the British government that it would consider with favour the settling of Jews in Palestine. That is the famous Balfour Declaration of November 2, 1917, which states:

'His Majesty's Government view with favour the establishment in Palestine of a national home for the Jewish people, and will use their best endeavours to facilitate the achievement of this object, it being clearly understood that nothing shall be done which may prejudice the civil and religious rights of existing non-Jewish communities in Palestine or the rights and political status enjoyed by Jews in any other country.'[3]

This declaration not only laid the cornerstone for the aspirations of the Zionists, but it was also lauded by many influential Christian groups in the Anglo-Saxon world who believed that the return of the Jews to the Holy Land constitutes a fulfilment of prophecy and is one of the sure signs which is to usher in the end of the world and the establishment of the millennial reign of Christ. These groups openly support the Jewish claims. The wide circulation given to these ideas in no way helped to increase the confidence of the Muslims in Christian intentions, but made them more suspicious than ever of the trustworthiness of Christian motives.

From the end of World War I, when the Arabs began to realize that the Allied Powers were not going to fulfill their promises of a United Arab State and that their aspirations would not be realized, a bitter controversy has been waged on the interpretation of the Balfour Declaration. The Arabs claim that the aim of this declaration was the establishment of a national home for the Jews in Palestine. The Jews declare that it meant Palestine as a national home. The situation has deteriorated from year to year until open warfare broke out between the Arab nations including Egypt under the auspices of the Arab League and the Jews in Palestine backed by powerful world Jewry. What the final outcome will be is very difficult to foretell. The Zionists have had initial success, and by the pressure and influence of outside nations will most likely be able to maintain a government, at least for a period. It is a wide-open question, however, as to how long they will be able to hold that speck of land in the midst of an Arab ocean. Once before Western powers got a foothold in the Holy Land, and established the Kingdom of Jerusalem, but after a short period the enthusiasm for continued support of that kingdom died down in Europe, and the valiant knights, overwhelmed by the surrounding forces of the Arabs, had to leave the country. The hot wind of the desert which has blown for centuries over the ruins of their seemingly impregnable castles whispers the story of enthusiasm, devotion, and sacrifice, but also of failure and defeat because their ambitious project was built on unsound premises.

A warning signal to the Jews was given by Dr. Abba Hillel Silver on the occasion of the twenty-fifth anniversary of Herzl's death. He made the following statement:

'Many of the spokesmen of our cause were driven to extol nationalism, *per se*, which is after all a quite recent and, demonstrably, a quite inadequate human concept. It is not mankind's ultimate vision. Certainly it is not the substance of our ancestral tradition, whose motive is not nationalism but prophetism. Nationalism is not enough. It is a minimum requirement, not a maximum programme. Our national rebirth was made possible by a war in which nationalism was thoroughly exposed and discredited.'[4]

This fundamental conflict between the Arabs and the Zionists has pushed all other issues and differences into the background. Minority problems among the original Arab population have become practically extinct at the present, as both the Christian Arabs and their Muslim brethren have laid aside their religious differences, and are considering themselves Arabs first in order to repulse the common danger of Zionism.

MUSLIMS MORE UNIFORM THAN IN SYRIA

In comparing figures, it is interesting to note the remarkable difference between Lebanon and Palestine in their respective number of Muslims and Christians. Whereas in Lebanon the Christians formed the majority, and the Shī'īs combined outnumbered the Sunnīs, the relationship between the two communities is exactly reversed in Palestine. Here, according to the figures of 1944, the

Muslims of the Sunnī persuasion numbered	1,053,521
Muslims of the Shī'ī persuasion	4,100
Christians of all persuasions	134,599
Druzes	9,148
Bahai	350
Samaritans	182[5]

The Muslims are overwhelmingly Sunnī, and Christians belong to all persuasions, but are still predominantly Rūm-orthodox. The Christians, in general, form urban communities and live mostly in Jerusalem, Jaffa, Haifa, Ramallah, Bethlehem, and Nazareth, whereas the rural population is in general Muslim.

WESTERN MISSIONS

The interest of Western as well as Eastern Christianity always centred around the Holy Land, and here Islām came into closest contact with all forms of Christianity. Many different orders established houses and institutions in Jerusalem, and the Western and the Eastern as well as the schismatic churches claimed to have a part in the Church of the Holy Sepulcher. The differences between these various factions often became so violent that the Muhammadan guards of the church had to intervene to avoid bloodshed and to restore order. During the past century various Protestant denominations arrived, some with missionary aims, others just to be represented in Palestine. Today a greater diversity of Christian denominations can hardly be found anywhere else in such a relatively small space. This, of course, is rather bewildering to a Muslim inquirer, as he is at a loss what to choose, because each one of these denominations proclaims itself as the only true guardian of the Christian faith.

Before the time of the British regime, mission work was largely conducted among the oriental Christians. Only after complete religious freedom was guaranteed by the mandatory power was the evangelistic approach stressed. The results, however, are very meagre and converts few. The Church Missionary Society of England is the oldest society established in Palestine and has done pioneer work in educational and medical fields.

A light- and power-house for disseminating the spirit of Christ and an example of practical, living Christianity has been the Syrian Orphanage in Jerusalem. It was founded by the German Pastor L. Schneller, who was moved with compassion when he saw the many orphaned Christian children after the fearful massacres of the Christians by the Druzes in Lebanon and Syria in 1860. The institution has grown marvellously, and has provided a practical education and vocational training for tens of thousands of orphaned boys and girls during the years of its existence. It has become a household word in that part of the world, and is remembered with esteem and affection by all. After World War II it was taken over by an American board.

The Y.M.C.A. has one of its finest buildings in Jerusalem, and had become a centre for the modern educated youth of the country before the outbreak of the Arab-Zionist hostilities. The influx of the large number of Jews has opened a new field, but it has also created a new problem for Christian missions. Thus far nothing definite has been done to meet this problem.

TRANSJORDAN

Transjordan emerged as an amirate after the end of World War I, and has recently become the Hāshimite Kingdom of

BRIDGE TO ISLĀM

Transjordan under its ambitious leader, King 'Abdullah from the noble house of the Sharīfs of Makka. King 'Abdullah is the older brother of the late King Faysal of 'Irāq. Before World War I Transjordan was a backward subdistrict of the province of Syria of the Ottoman Empire. Until the present day it is more truly Arab than Palestine and Lebanon and even parts of Syria, as foreign influence and Western ways have not been able to penetrate deeply. The population is about 300,000; 130,000 of whom are settled in towns and villages. Settled Beduins number 120,000, who, however, still live under tribal law, and 50,000 are nomads. About 10 per cent, or 30,000, are Arabic-speaking Christians, Greek Orthodox, Greek Catholics, Latins, and Protestants. Further, there are about 10,000 Circassians, from the Caucasus, who are Muslims, living in Transjordan. They were settled there by the Sultan of Turkey, after they had had to suffer much persecution by the Tsars of Russia during the early part and the middle of the last century. They still speak their own language and preserve their customs and style of dress.

The Church Missionary Society pioneered also in Transjordan, and established a school and a hospital in al Salt. When the Amīr, now King 'Abdullah, chose 'Ammān as his capital, al Salt declined. 'Ammān developed rapidly to a little Damascus, as trading centre for the Beduins. It has become a prosperous new town. Missions followed. The Catholics built a modern hospital at 'Ammān and another in Kerak, and Protestants have their schools erected on the hills of the new city.

The constitution of Transjordan, ratified July 12, 1946, guaranteed freedom of worship and freedom to maintain schools:

'Art. 16—The State shall protect the freedom to perform religious ceremonies and rites in accordance with the customs observed in the Hāshimite Kingdom of Transjordan[6] unless they are injurious to order or are contrary to morals.

'Art. 17—Freedom of opinion is guaranteed and every one may express his thoughts in speech or in writing within the limits of the law. . . .

'Art. 21—Societies shall have the right to establish and main-

PALESTINE AND TRANSJORDAN

tain schools for the instruction of their members, provided that they may meet the general requirements prescribed by law.'[7]

These paragraphs guarantee religious freedom, but agressive missionary work can easily be stopped, as it can cause disturbance and therefore would be injurious to order. It is the typical concept of religious liberty as considered in a previous chapter.

---

[1] Jeremiah Ben-Jacob, *The Future of Jewish Nationalism*, pp. 8, 9.
[2] Nevill Barbour, *Palestine: Star or Crescent?* p. 52.
[3] *Ibid.*, p. 61.
[4] Abba Hillel Silver, 'Herzl and Jewish Messianism,' as an appendix in Jeremiah Ben-Jacob, *The Future of Jewish Nationalism*, pp. 24, 25.
[5] A. H. Hourani, *Minorities in the Arab World*, p. 52.
[6] The name of the country has been changed to *The Hāshimite Kingdom of Jordan*.
[7] *Middle East Journal*, Vol. 1, No. 3, July, 1947, pp. 323 ff.

CHAPTER FIFTEEN

EGYPT

EGYPT, like 'Irāq, is the gift of the river. But whereas 'Irāq lies along the trade routes between East and West, exposed to invasions from all sides, Egypt's position is much more sheltered. Her great life-giving stream flows between two deserts which are sufficiently broad that alien hordes cannot easily traverse them. Therefore a civilization and culture could grow up in this large, secluded valley of the Nile with characteristics all its own. Moreover, the heart of Africa did not harbour great civilizations such as India and the farther East; hence the river was not required for external transit trade but mainly for internal traffic. Ancient Egypt was placed not in the centre, but on the fringe of conflicting world interests, and her development, therefore, was more homogeneous than that of 'Irāq. Certainly, in her long history, she also experienced the heel of foreign invaders, but in many instances the delta alone was involved. Often these invaders found the easy-going life on the banks of the Nile congenial and pleasant, and after not too long a time they were absorbed and became Egyptian.

Egypt is much more uniform in outlook than any of the other countries of the Near East. The casual traveller who visits Alexandria and Cairo will probably object, because he is deeply impressed by the colourful types and the great variety of people he encounters in these two cities. However, it should always be remembered that parts of Cairo and especially of Alexandria are not typical of Egypt. These are international centres.

WHAT ARE THE EGYPTIANS?

Sometimes Egypt is listed among the countries which form the fertile crescent around Arabia, although strictly speaking, that is not correct. Egypt does not belong to Western Asia but geographically to Africa. In crossing the Suez Canal we have entered Africa and have come to a different cultural sphere.

Should the Egyptians then be called Africans or North Africans? That would hardly be acceptable, as we associate in general different groups with these terms, and Egyptians have only slight relationship and very little in common with either the Negroes or the Berbers.

What then are the Egyptians? Are they Arabs as modern Arabic propaganda likes to point out? That again would not be correct. It is true that there was an influx of Arabs into Egypt during the early period of Islām; it is true that the Egyptians have adopted Arabic as their language. For more than a thousand years they have discarded their own original tongue. Furthermore, it is true that the great majority of Egyptians have accepted the religion of the Arabs, and have become thoroughly Islāmized. Egypt has even been the cultural centre of Islām during certain periods, and at present the al Azhar University at Cairo is the mainspring of orthodox Islām, radiating influence and power near and far in the Muslim world.

Yet in spite of all that, the Egyptians are not Arabs but decidedly and distinctly Egyptians. Neither by race nor character are they Arabs. They are not Beduins, roaming herdsmen, split into clans like the Arabs; but they are tillers of the soil. From the very beginning of their history to the present day the great majority of Egypt's millions are *fallāhīn*, peasants, either owning their own small holdings, or working as farm hands on the estates of big land owners, Beks and Pashas. These occupations—wandering tribesmen following their herds, and cultivators of the soil—produce very distinct characteristics, so that in many respects the Egyptian is the exact opposite in type and character of the Arab.

The majority of the Egyptian villagers eke out a bare existence in spite of unrelenting toil and hard work—an existence, however, which becomes more and more precarious because of the rapidly increasing population and the impossibility of increasing the area of cultivated land. In spite of the proverbial fertility of the Nile valley because of the rich sediment which the stream deposits year after year, it becomes wellnigh impossible to nourish adequately an ever-increasing population. The population in 1917 was about 12,000,000. At present (1948) it stands above 19,000,000. These nineteen millions have to live on an arable area not much larger than the state of Maryland. That means about 1,400 persons per square mile, whereas 172 live on the same area in Maryland, and the latter is one of the more thickly populated states in the eastern part of the United States. This makes Egypt one of the most densely inhabited countries of the world, comparable only to some portions of the Ganges valley in India and the Yangtze valley in China.

Such a density of population naturally results in great poverty of the masses, which is increased by the unequal distribution of the land. There is perhaps no other place where people live so crowded together in their villages as in Egypt, as every available inch of ground is cultivated. The lanes between the mud-brick houses are winding and narrow, and it is practically impossible to keep them clean, as donkeys and camels pass through, and cats, dogs, and chickens use them as playgrounds. Thus they become a breeding ground for flies and fleas. To institute real sanitary conditions would mean that these villages would have to be pulled down and rebuilt in a more sanitary style. In addition to the impossibility of financing such a project, there would not be sufficient space on which to build, unless all the villages should be transferred to the edge of the desert. Even the best intentions and efforts for improvement, therefore, will only partly alleviate the situation. As the population increases, the problem becomes more serious. This question of overpopulation has its repercussions in all spheres of life, also in the Muslim-Christian relationship, and must be considered in the planning and the possibilities of mission work.

Egypt in her long history has changed cultures and dynasties, has passed through the stages of ancient Egyptian sun worship and priestly cults, of Roman paganism, and Christianity, and finally Islām. Names have changed, yet the life of the simple tiller of the soil has not been too deeply affected. His life has remained much the same. In many instances he uses the same tools as his forebears used thousands of years ago. With leather buckets he lifts the water from a lower level to a higher, and the creaking sound of the water wheel under the sycamore tree is the eternal song of Egypt. Its melody, plaintive and never ending, is full of melancholy.

The women live in fear of the evil eye and different evil spirits, jinns and afrits, as in times long ago; and in like manner as their sisters in Pharaoh's day, they try to avert the evil influences by charms and talismans. The saints have changed their names into those of the Muslim *walīs*, who are highly venerated.

It is true that all modern inventions have entered Egypt. White luxury trains flash by, bringing visitors from all over the globe to the famous cities of ancient Egypt, as Luxor, Edfu and Siene (Aswan). The automobile reaches practically every village; telephone and telegraph connect the remotest places, but all this has not changed substantially the life of the average villager. Modern life in the larger centres and life as it was lived 5,000 years ago exist side by side.

EGYPT'S CONTRIBUTION TO CHRISTIANITY

The famous past of Egypt does not concern us in our study, but it is worth while to throw a little light upon the development of Christianity in Egypt. It is widely accepted that St. Mark was the first missionary to this land. He was able to win a strong foothold in Alexandria among the large Jewish community there.[1] During the two following centuries Alexandria's theological school had a deep influence upon the dogmatical and theological development of Christianity. Names like Origen and Athanasius may suffice. However, not only in the large cities did young Christianity find its support. Soon it penetrated into the small towns and villages.

The Egyptians added one special feature to the life of the church. That is monasticism, which in later centuries wielded such supreme influence, especially in the church of the West. Antonius (born A.D. 251), a native of upper Egypt, was the first to withdraw from ordinary life in order to live a life of contemplation in the desert. Soon a group of similar-minded gathered around him, and under Pachomius, also an Egyptian, the monastery was developed. For centuries, however, monasticism was not looked upon with favour in the West; only when Benedict of Nursia founded the monastery of Monte

Cassino (529) did it become thoroughly rooted in the Occident.

The Egyptian Church accepted Monophysitism[2] mainly in opposition to the Greek Church, and has not changed her position since, although this resulted in her being cast off from the main stream of Christianity. When the Muslims entered Egypt under 'Amr ibn al 'Āṣ in A.D. 639, the Copts, that is, the indigenous population, did not offer a last-ditch resistance, but on the contrary felt rather relieved to be freed from the imperial yoke and from Byzantine interference. At the beginning, the Copts were not treated badly by the Muslims, and were not forced at the point of the sword to accept Islām. During successive periods, however, the Muslim yoke made itself felt, and it became apparent that a Christian was rated as a second-class being with limited rights. Especially was this the case under fanatical rulers who enforced the segregation laws strictly, and added other degrading conditions. For instance, the Caliph Al Ḥākim bi amr illah, forced the Christians to wear five-pound wooden crosses around their necks. No wonder that many embraced Islām in order to escape such shameful conditions. Therefore, all those who remained faithful should be all the more commended, and those Oriental churches who kept the faith of Christ alive during centuries of most exacting circumstances should be highly esteemed. Perhaps they represent a rather formal, non-spiritual type of Christianity, and often rebuke is heaped upon their heads by Western writers, but have we in the West any reason to boast of the type of Christianity we have developed?

THE FĀṬIMIDS AND THE AZHAR

During the centuries of Islāmic rule in Egypt, the most outstanding period is that of the Fāṭimids (969-1171). The Fāṭimids were Shī'īs, or more exactly Isma'īlīs, and were able during that period to establish a separate caliphate with its centre in Cairo, in opposition to the 'Abbāsid Caliphate, which had its centre in Baghdad. Egypt, therefore, under the Fāṭimids, became the centre of an empire stretching from Tunisia to the borders of the Euphrates. During that period the foundations of a new city were laid north-east of the gates of al Fustāt.

EGYPT

The new city was called al Qāhira al Mu'izzīya (the conquering city of Al Mu'izz), whence Cairo.

In 971 the mosque and school of al Azhar were founded as a Shī'ite institution, of course. But after the Shī'īs were driven out of Egypt, al Azhar was taken over by the Sunnīs and became during the succeeding ages the one great centre of learning and orthodoxy in Islām. At present, since the caliphate has been abolished by Turkey, al Azhar is the one great rallying point of the orthodox forces of Islām all over the world. Al Azhar is the guardian of the faith and the authoritative exponent of the dogma and the Muslim way of life. The Rector of al Azhar, or Shaykh al Azhar, as he is called, exercises a tremendous influence, far greater than his office might suggest. Students from all over the Islāmic world flock to al Azhar to study Islāmic law and theology, and having completed their education, return to become teachers and *qādīs* (judges according to canon law) in their home towns and villages. They are highly esteemed and are destined to play an important role in their communities. An average of 1,500 students are enrolled annually, about 90 per cent of them from Egypt. That country, therefore, is still the stronghold of orthodox and fanatical Islām. Al Azhar is the oldest continuously operating university in the world, and until the beginning of the twentieth century was the only institute of higher learning in Egypt.

MUHAMMAD 'ALĪ AND WESTERN INFLUENCE

On the other hand, Egypt has been longer under Western influence than any of the other Islāmic countries of the Near East. Egypt's modern history begins with Muhammad 'Alī Pasha. He was an Albanian by birth, was sent as an officer in a Turkish regiment to Egypt in 1801, was able to play the different factions then existing in Egypt one against the other, gained a victory over the British, and finally made himself master of Egypt by murdering the Mamlūk Beys who ruled Egypt and had bled it white. Muhammad 'Alī was progressive and laid the foundations of modern Egypt. He started modern irrigation in Egypt, introduced cotton—today one of the major sources of wealth. He also introduced primary and secondary education and sent specially talented students to European universities, mostly to France. He invited scientists and engineers from abroad to help and to supervise the construction of his intended projects, and was thereby instrumental in tying Egypt closer to Europe, and giving French culture a preponderant influence in Egypt even today. Until recently French was more widely used than English, especially in Lower Egypt.

The grandson of Muḥammad 'Alī, the Khedive (viceroy) Isma'īl, opened more widely the gates of Western influence. During his reign the Suez Canal was built. He built an opera house, and the Italian composer Verdi wrote a special opera (*Aïda*) for the inauguration. European players were invited yearly to give their performances. There was more freedom of thought in Egypt than in any other country under Ottoman rule. Many Syrians and Lebanese came to Egypt, daily newspapers were started, and periodicals made it their aim to give translations of the newest developments in Western thought and science. Cairo and Alexandria became important centres where European thought was clothed in Oriental garb and transmitted to the Arabic world. Egypt became the centre of modern intellectual advancement in the Near East.[3] In 1908 the National Egyptian University was established as a private enterprise, which has grown into the great Fu'ād University. In 1945, this institution had over 10,000 students enrolled in its eleven faculties. Egypt began to play a double role. She holds in her midst the most orthodox school of Islāmic thought and the most advanced schools on Western lines in the Near East. Both groups, the orthodox and the progressive, in the Islāmic world, look to Egypt for intellectual and spiritual guidance. Naturally this must lead to tension.

It may be interesting to give some figures of the progress made in Fu'ād University and in education in general.

FU'ĀD UNIVERSITY

Year	Muslim Students	Christian Students	Jewish Students	Total
1935-36	4,861	1,754	36	6,651
1944-45	7,302	2,638	61	10,001

It is remarkable that the percentage of Christian students in the university is much higher (1 to 3) than the proportion of Christians to Muslims in the population (1 to 13). In 1930 the Fu'ād University opened its doors to women students. To show the progress made in education in general some further statistics may be enlightening.

Year	Type School	Boys	Girls	Total
1928	Elementary Schools	470,449	121,552	
	Other Schools	184,333	65,377	
				841,711
1945	Elementary Schools	590,449	450,170	
	Other Schools	263,072	72,276	
				1,375,766[4]

This last figure represents about one-third of all Egyptian children of school age. And although the law makes education compulsory and free to every Egyptian child of both sexes, there are at present not sufficient buildings or teachers available to enforce the law.

Remarkable is the upward surge in the female attendance in schools. Only one who has laboured among the Muslim *fallāhin* of Egypt is able to evaluate what an amount of prejudice had to be overcome to make that rise possible.

The number of pupils who received their education in foreign schools is rather static. In 1928 there were 68,823 pupils and in 1943, 69,179 pupils.[5] All foreign schools have to follow the rules laid down by the Ministry of Education.

Let us now review briefly the political developments. The lavish expenditures of Isma'īl Pasha had burdened Egypt with a tremendous debt. Soon the foreign creditors laid their hands upon every line of revenue, but Egypt was unable to fulfill her commitments. A revolt started among the army under 'Arābi Pasha; a number of foreigners were massacred in Alexandria in 1882. This provided a good reason for England to interfere in order to restore order and to ensure peace and the security of foreign nationals. In practice she took over the administration of the country. Her high commissioners, as advisers to the Khedive, ruled Egypt in fact, although the country remained legally under Turkish suzerainty. Lord Cromer and Lord Kitchener were the shapers of the destiny of modern Egypt.

British rule in Egypt as everywhere else was just and benevolent to the individual. But quite naturally British interests were served first, and this again quite naturally led to clashes when the spirit of nationalism awoke in the country. During World War I, Britain declared Egypt to be a British Protectorate and finally severed her from Turkey. After the war, and after heavy pressure by nationalistic forces, Britain declared the independence of Egypt in 1922. Prince Fu'ād was crowned as King Fu'ād I. In reality, the British 'advisory' administration continued to function. Only after a prolonged struggle, Egypt reached in 1936 the status of complete independence. In 1937 the last vestige of the rule of the foreigners, the capitulation laws, were abolished. These laws granted the foreigner extraterritorial rights. This meant that he could not be arrested by the Egyptian police or judged by an Egyptian court. Now, however, he is under Egyptian jurisdiction. Egypt is one of the Muḥammadan countries which has freed herself from foreign domination during the last decade.

WESTERN CHRISTIANITY IN EGYPT

What part, if any, did foreign mission work have in the shaping of events in Egypt? The Franciscans have had representatives in Egypt practically ever since the time of the Crusades. They were mostly sent out from Jerusalem, and a good number paid for their witnessing with their lives. Toward the end of the fifteenth century and the beginning of the sixteenth, the Bishop of Tama preached for twenty years to Muslims and Copts.[6] Beginning with 1687 Upper Egypt was organized as a separate mission district. But difficulties abounded from both sides—from Muslims as well as Copts. Only after centuries of hard toil were the Roman Catholics able to win sufficient numbers of the Copts so that a special vicar could be appointed for the Uniate Copts.[7] E. L. Butcher writes: 'By the close of the 17th Century the influx of Roman missionaries and European merchants introduced a new factor into the Egyptian world.'[8] These missionaries were working mostly among the Christian population and the slaves, a number of whom had turned Muslim.

The first Protestant missionaries who entered Egypt were from among the Moravian Brethren. Count von Zinzendorf, their leader, had a world-wide vision for missions. He sent his brethren to Labrador and to India and contemplated the revival of the Christian Church in Ethiopia and in Egypt. Therefore, it was resolved to start the work in Egypt, and finally in 1752 a doctor by the name of Friedrich Wilhelm Hocker arrived in Cairo. He laboured there with interruptions until 1782. He and two brethren, a watchmaker and a carpenter, were on a self-supporting basis. The doctor found entrance into many homes, and established excellent connections with the Coptic patriarch and high government officials. Yet the result of their labours expressed in figures was very meagre; in 1782 the home board decided to recall the brethren.[9]

The next attempt was made by the Church Missionary Society of England (C.M.S.). Five young men, trained in the Basel Seminary, Switzerland, were sent to Egypt, among them Samuel Gobat (later Bishop in Jerusalem). They soon discovered that the Muslims were inaccessible, and that the only hope was among the Copts. They began to sell and distribute Bibles and portions of the Bible, and other Christian tracts up and down the Nile. They started a girls' day school and a boarding school for boys, which they developed into a theological seminary for the Coptic clergy. But when this movement for a rejuvenated Christianity began to take hold in larger circles, the government became suspicious and encouraged the most reactionary element in the Coptic Church to take control. Soon difficulties increased, and the work faded out. The missionary force was never large. It started with five men, and for a long period there were only two in Egypt.[10]

In 1854, the 'American Mission' appeared on the scene.[11] Three missionaries sent by the United Presbyterian Church arrived in Egypt. They started, like all missions, by distributing literature and opening small schools, trying to find an opening among Muhammadans. But the only group who seemed to respond was the Copts. In spite of opposition and a denunciation read in all Coptic Churches, the 'Protestant Church' was organized and Protestant churches erected in many Christian quarters, especially in Upper Egypt, because the majority of Christians are living between Minia and Girga with Assiut as centre. Large boarding schools for girls were established, a theological seminary at Cairo, and a large college for men at Assiut, as well as two hospitals, one at Assiut and the other at Tanta in the delta.

These Protestant undertakings have certainly brought a new element into the field of religion in Egypt. And even if the original hope of reforming the Coptic Church has not been fulfilled, it certainly has stirred her to new activity; and just as the Roman Catholic Church after the Reformation abolished many of her former abuses and laid emphasis on points formerly neglected, in like manner the Coptic Church at present is not the same as she was one hundred years ago. And it can be noted that in places of greatest Protestant activity the Coptic Church is most alive.

In 1882 the C.M.S.[12] re-entered Egypt with the sole purpose of work among Muslims. A number of outstanding men among them gave their service, and have done much to prepare the way for that work. Douglas M. Thornton and Reverend W. H. Temple Gairdner are among the most prominent. The latter's book, *The Reproach of Islam*, is an inspiration to every one interested in these questions. In 1905 the Nile Mission Press was founded with the special purpose of providing literature in Arabic suited for Muslim readers, as well as such of a general Christian character. The Nile Mission Press has become the centre of Christian literature publication for all Muslim lands. During 1938 it distributed 500,000 books and tracts for readers in at least twelve countries.[13]

Medical work was also started, and the Mission Hospital in Old Cairo has become well known all over Egypt. Another hospital operates at Manūf in the delta. Besides these two larger missions, the Egypt General Mission works in the delta. The Y.M.C.A. with its centres in the larger towns has had a profound influence in pulling down the barriers of prejudice and bringing together young people of different faiths in an informal manner. The influence has been so great that Muslim's shaykhs started a similar organization and called it Y.M.M.A., Young Men's Muslim Association. But whereas the greatest asset of the Y.M.C.A. is its true Christian spirit of tolerance and forbearance, the Y.M.M.A. soon developed the opposite tendencies and became a stronghold of fanatical Islām.

Inherent in the Protestant way of life is freedom of thought and tolerance, allowing a diversity of opinions. That might be at times detrimental to its own cause, but the conviction that truth by its own valour will be victorious without the help of enforcing laws and restrictions is such a lofty conception that it never should be abandoned, even if we have to go through dark periods during which the lawless forces take advantage of misunderstood liberty.

Side by side with the Protestant schools, sometimes even furthered by them, entered the modern, irreligious, agnostic, materialistic spirit, a spirit which doubts everything, tears down everything without being able to build up a satisfying structure in its place. This, of course, it is unable to do, as it leaves large sections of life out of consideration—all spiritual and supernatural elements. This modern spirit, whose logical outcome is pure materialism, with its enthronement of self, is somewhat tempered in the West by the Christian heritage and the still-existing Christian faith and sentiments in many members of the community. But this modern spirit causes absolute havoc when taken on its face value without the Christian background. And that is just what is going on in the East. This attitude is like a powerful dissolvent; it cuts people from their moorings, and leaves them drifting. It develops cynics. Thus it has come to pass today that not only the often fanatical spirit of Islām has to be met, but also the irreligious attitude of the West with its impact on the Eastern mind.

INFLUENCE OF THE CINEMA

Another extremely detrimental factor towards a right evaluation of the Christian way of life in the Muslin mind is the movies, especially in the smaller centres where only second- and third-class films are shown. Occidentals look at a film story and know it is a bit of fiction. We know where it is exaggerated, highly coloured, sensational. Not so the average Muslim. No other knowledge of Christian ethics are his to correct what he sees, to suggest to him that he should discount a good deal of what passes before him on the screen. He accepts the full story literally and at face value. The life he sees featured on the screen is for him the Christian way of life, because the films are produced in Christian countries, hence are an expression of Christian culture, because for the Muslim, life is not separated into a divine and a secular sphere. It is still one. Do you wonder that he does not cherish a high admiration for Christianity? How often the author felt an undertone of derision in conversation with Muslims when discussing Christian aspects of life. It often took many hours to dislodge some utterly wrong notions which were conceived, quite naturally, from attending the pictures. The harm films have done for the reputation of the Westerner is seldom realized; we only feel shocked when we do not receive the respect from the Easterner that we foolishly imagine is due us.

To be equal to such a situation requires that as Christians we remember that our only power is spiritual power taken from the divine source by constant communion with God, a power which not only changes our lives but which can become through us the greatest uplifting and constructive force in the world. This power does not create biting cynics but men full of vision, inspiration, and love. That is the only power, and yet the mightiest, we Christians have. Political moves, economical schemes, and financial plans count for nothing beside this power of God. It is the only power a Christian worker must depend upon, and he will have to depend upon it in a much larger measure in the days to come.

REACTION OF EGYPTIANS TO FOREIGN CHRISTIAN INFLUENCE

What are the reactions to mission work in Egypt? The conversions from Islām to Christianity are very few, and in no proportion to the effort expended—in fact, they are even offset by the numbers of Copts who accept Islām every year; yet the attitude of Muslims toward missions has always been hostile. Whenever a convert was registered, a storm of protest was raised in all the papers. It was loudly demanded that the work should be closed, and the missionaries expelled. During the year 1942, among other proposals, the following was laid before the Committee for the Protection of Public Morals:

'Fight against missionary work: "A law is being prepared to oppose missionary work and prevent the influencing of Muslim children in foreign schools by any means of propaganda or missionary work, whether by books or publications or requiring them to attend classes for instruction in any religion other than their own, or by any other means." '

The law did not pass. It shows, however, that strong forces are at work which aim at eliminating all foreign religious endeavours.[14] These forces have in no way decreased since World War II. On the contrary they are rather on the increase. Whereas formerly the National Movement, which found its expression in the Wafd Party, tried to bridge religious differences and to create an Egyptian national feeling regardless of religion and ancestry, in recent years radical groups have gained the upper hand, as, for instance, the Muslim Brotherhood (Ikhwān al Muslimīn) of Shaykh Hasan al Banna, who fight fanatically for the realization of Muslim aspirations and are hostile not only to missions but to Christians in general. That spirit of considering Christians as equals on a national basis is fast disappearing. Missions may easily encounter more difficulties and restrictions in the future. That, of course, does not mean that their influence has come to an end, although they may be shown the door. If, however, they have been able to create stalwart Christian characters among the indigenous population, their existence will have been vindicated. Times of storm and stress are always the most fruitful times in spiritual development.

---

[1] E. L. Butcher, *The Story of the Church of Egypt*, Vol. 1, pp. 20, 21.
[2] See pp. 175, 176.

[3] See A. E. Weigall, *A History of Events in Egypt from 1798-1914*.

[4] The statistical figures are used with permission of Dr. Ruth C. Sloan from a report prepared for the State Department, Washington, D.C., entitled *Recent Educational Advances in Egypt*, April 18, 1946.

[5] Ruth C. Sloan, *op. cit.*

[6] Holzapfel, H., *Handbuch der Geschichte des Franziskanerordens*, pp. 250, 251.

[7] *Ibid.*, p. 531.

[8] Butcher, *op. cit.*, Vol. 2, p. 286.

[9] See Th. Bechler, *Die Herrnhuter in Agypten*; and Charles R. Watson, *Egypt and the Christian Crusade*, pp. 131-142.

[10] J. T. Addison, *The Christian Approach to the Moslem*, p. 141.

[11] *Ibid.*, p. 142.

[12] *Ibid.*, p. 144.

[13] *Ibid.*, p. 148.

[14] C. C. Adams, 'Trends of Thought in Egypt,' in *The Moslem World*, Vol. XXXIV, 1944, p. 271 ff.; see also C. C. Adams, *Islam and Modernism in Egypt* (1933).

CHAPTER SIXTEEN

TURKEY

THE whole Arab world is in a process of change. The impact of Western thought, Western science, and Western industrialism is too strong to be ignored. The old social order based upon a patriarchal form of life, fortified by religious sanction and traditional usage, cannot withstand this onrush. But the Arab countries, each of them in a different stage of this process, hope to perfect that change in a more or less gradual manner. They endeavour to find a synthesis between their Eastern way of life, with its deep-set roots in religion and custom, and the Western way with its relentless drive for further subduing and utilizing the forces of nature for its own materialistic end. The Arab countries looking toward the West are trying at the same time to save what can be saved from their old heritage.

TURKEY TURNED WEST

Turkey, on the contrary, has turned West radically, and has severed all bonds which connected her with her past. She accepted the modern scientific principle—which states, 'Truth is what can be proved'—as her guiding star, and discarded wherewith all religious beliefs which accept certain premises by faith.

After the vivisection of Turkey following World War I, and the dividing of Anatolia, her mainland, into spheres of influence of foreign powers, Mustafā Kamāl, later called Kamāl Ata Turk, rallied the Turks around his banner, promising to free Anatolia from the foreigner, and to make Turkey a living place for the Turks. No longer encumbered by a large number of alien races for which the Turk as guardian of Islām had to spill his blood in endless wars, the Turk could fight for the first time in his long history for his own benefit—for Turkey alone. A new nationalism was born, whose watchword was Turkey for the Turks, and Mustafā Kamāl Pasha became its leading force. It was a nationalism backed by the deep interest of self-preservation in the face of overwhelming odds.

In September, 1922, the final military victory over the Greeks was won. As soon as the peace treaty was signed, Mustafā Kamāl set himself to the task of building a new Turkey out of the ruins. It was not a rebuilding of the old nor a reform of the old, but a complete new beginning involving a radical break with the past. As we have formerly seen, religious and political institutions are completely interlinked in Islām, and cannot well be separated. Therefore, any law directed towards a separation of church and state, so to say, is basically against Islām. The significance and importance of any such law has to be evaluated from this angle.

On March 3, 1924, the caliphate was abolished. That meant that Turkey did not wish any longer to take the responsibility for safeguarding Islām. It is true that the caliphate was a tottering institution which had not functioned efficiently for a long time, but as long as the caliph existed, he was a powerful factor in holding up the spiritual unity of the world of Islām. In 1928, Kamāl Ata Turk forbade the wearing of a distinctive dress for religious teachers, which hit both alike—Muslim shaykhs and Christian priests. The wearing of the fēz or tarbūsh was made illegal, and the European hat was introduced. That might seem trivial to Western minds, but in the East, headgear is the distinctive sign of class and religion—an age-old and age-honoured custom. Furthermore, the wearing of a hat made it difficult to fulfill the prescribed ritual of prayer, because the Muslim has to prostrate himself before God, touching the ground with his forehead. At the same time he has to keep his head covered. This is easily done by one who is wearing a fēz or tarbūsh, but it is well-nigh impossible while wearing a modern hat with a brim. Kamāl Ata Turk forbade all religious orders, considering them to be a hotbed of fanaticism. He forbade polygamy, abolished the veil, and gave women equal rights and equal possibilities in education. Today, twenty years after these revolutionary reforms, women can be found in all walks of life in Turkey.

One of his far-reaching reforms was the abolishing of the Arabic script, and the introducing of the Latin alphabet.

Arabic is a most beautiful script, but it requires a scholarly knowledge of the language to read and write it correctly. The Latin alphabet is for the average man much easier to master. Ata Turk himself went from place to place to introduce and teach the new alphabet, and the whole Turkish nation went to school. Hand in hand with the introduction of the Latin characters, the Turkish language, as far as possible was purged from Arabic words, which constituted about 60 per cent of the language. Old Turanian expressions were revived.

At the same time great efforts were made to make the Turks forget their Islamic past and to glorify their pre-Islamic days. when they had lived in the steppes of Turkmenistan and Western Asia. Everything was aimed to set the Turks on the new road of nationalism, unfettered by religious bonds.

Kamāl Ata Turk, although inaugurating a constitutional regime, ruled with dictatorial powers. It is the only way to achieve such far-reaching changes in so short a period among a people who had never known how to express their will, and who were wholly untrained to share in public life. At the same time, Kamāl Ata Turk wanted to introduce a real parliamentary system, but one trial convinced him that the time was not yet ripe for it. Many thought that his more or less dictatorial regime would collapse with his death, but it has weathered the storm. Today Turkey is stronger than before, although she is menaced from many sides.

In a short span of time Turkey has undergone the most complete change ever made by any country. From a medieval state she has passed into a modern state. Turkey has broken with the old traditional Islām and has severed the bonds with her Islāmic past, but has she really broken with Islām? Has she really accepted the full liberal attitude of the United States, for instance, where the state does not interfere with the religious beliefs of the citizens? What is her attitude toward Christians? Is there a more tolerant attitude?

In old Turkey, under the so-called *millet-system*, Christian communities were recognized, and their patriarchs had full legal authority over their respective communities, with the right to operate schools and other institutions according to their own designs. In the new Turkey the number of Christians has been greatly reduced. All those of Greek origin living in Asia Minor have been transplanted to Greece, and Turks formerly living in Greek territory, like Macedonia and Thrace, have been taken over. Other Christians, Armenians and Syrians, have emigrated, so that today practically no Christians are left outside of Istanbul and vicinity, a bare 2 per cent of Turkey's 19,000,000 inhabitants. Turkey is today more solidly Muslim than ever before because a non-muslim is not considered to be a Turk. She has solved her religious problem by eliminating the minorities.

In 1924, education became entirely secular. That means that it was forbidden to teach any religion in schools. Foreign schools which felt they could not comply with this regulation had to close. That was in no way an unfriendly act against Christian schools, because the law was enforced with equal vigour against the teaching of Islām in schools. Religion from this point of view just has no place in a well-ordered state run on modern scientific lines. In the thought of New Turkey, religion would introduce a foreign, transcendental element, which cannot be correctly measured, and its latent potentialities cannot be safely gauged. The result is that Turkey is still a closed country and that there exist fewer possibilities for Christian work today under the modern Westernized government than under the 'terrible' Sultan 'Abd al Hamīd.

ENTRANCE OF WESTERN CHRISTIANITY

Turkey came into closer contact with Western Protestant Christianity when, in 1820, American missionaries landed on her shores. After having made an extensive survey, the American Mission decided to lay its main emphasis on the work among the Armenians (1831), and for the next eighty or ninety years the Armenian work absorbed practically the whole interest and all the energy of the mission.[1] When the fearful massacres broke out in 1895, the Armenian Protestant Church had a membership of about 12,000 and about 20,000 adherents. During the massacre 10,000 were lost.[2]

In Constantinople a famous educational institution, similar to the American University at Beirut, had been developed.

TURKEY

Its name is Robert College. Like the American University at Beirut, it operated independently from the mission board. But whereas in Beirut a good number of Muslims were among the students, in Constantinople the student body consisted mainly of Greeks, Armenians, and Bulgars. This was so because the Sultan had decreed that Turks should receive their education solely in government schools.[3]

The Church Missionary Society arrived in Constantinople in 1858 with the sole purpose of working among Muslims. They brought Gottlieb Pfander to Constantinople from India, where he had worked successfully. Pfander is the author of the famous controversial book, *Mīzān al Ḥaqq* (Balance of Truth). He together with Dr. Koelle from West Africa, a famous linguist, began to work openly for Muslims by preaching and giving Bible studies. In 1864 on one occasion ten adults were accepted into the church. The High Porte became alarmed and acted quickly. It imprisoned the Turkish Christians, closed the assembly hall of the Mission, confiscated all the books of the Bible Society, and ejected the missionaries from their homes. Pfander retired to London, where one year later he died. In 1877 the Church Missionary Society abandoned the station.[4] This experience proved that the indirect methods by schools and hospitals seemed the only advisable way of approach, even if these institutions were not frequented much by Muslims. Their sole existence would help to disseminate the light, truth, and love of a real Christianity. Did these institutions fulfill their purpose?

At present Turkey is again a closed land. This has been brought about by the adoption of Western nationalism. Whither Turkey is moving is the question in many minds. Certainly Turkey is beset with many outside dangers, which may spell disaster, but that does not concern us at present. Whither Turkey at the spiritual crossroads of the world? Many thoughtful Turks who have enthusiastically supported the swing to the West begin to wonder whether modern scientific and purely materialistic thinking is the answer to all questions after all. These men and women wonder whether nationalism alone, however pure its flame, will have sufficient strength to satisfy the soul of the people.

They are disillusioned, because World War II exposed the utter fallacy of the modern materialistic approach to life. They begin to doubt whether the decision to discard Islām was a move in the right direction. There is a widespread feeling that they should return to Islām—a modernized Islām of course—a nationalized Islām, perhaps a philosophy of Islām after the pattern of the Indian thinker Iqbāl. But a modernized Islām is not Islām any longer, and a modernized Islām cannot satisfy the spiritual longing of a people, especially if the only service expected from it is to become the handmaid of nationalism, to furnish the religious trimmings to an otherwise purely materialistic outlook on life, just as Christianity loses all its power and strength when it is summoned only to support some claims of the state.

Turkey is again at the spiritual crossroads either to continue in her course decided upon twenty-five years ago, or to reintroduce Islām in a modernized form. Or do we Christians have a solution for Turkey? Are we able to bring to them a Christianity stripped of all the ballast of the centuries, of all the squabbles of the ecclesiastics, and of all narrow national concepts? Are we in a position to bring a purely spiritual Christianity?—the spiritual message of Christ, pure and simple, which goes directly to the human heart, which does not recognize Greek or Turk, black or white, but which knows only human beings who, with minds bewildered and hearts in trouble, are looking in vain for life's solution? The message of Christ, which reveals human ambitions in their right perspective, changes the whole attitude of life and brings peace and serenity to the heart.

Are there enough Christians who are prepared to bring this kind of Christianity to the Turk? Are there enough among us who have the vision to see the need of the world and to fill that need? Modern Turkey today is a mighty challenge to the spiritual forces of Christianity.

---

[1] J. T. Addison, *The Christian Approach to the Moslem*, pp. 81-83.
[2] *Ibid.*, p. 88.
[3] *Ibid.*, p. 91.
[4] *Ibid.*, pp. 94, 95.

IRĀN

Going east from Turkey, we reach Irān, although the most accessible approach in our days is via Baghdad. The frontier post at Khanikin is really Irān's gate to the West. Irān belongs to the Islāmic sphere, but Islām in Irān is different just as the people of Irān are different. They are neither Semites as the Arabs, nor Turanians as the Turks, but are predominantly Ayran. Irān means the land of the Aryans. The inhabitants of the country never called their land Persia, as it was and still is more widely known in the West. The name Persia is derived from Fars, one of the south-eastern provinces of Irān.

LAND OF THE ARYANS

The original home of the Aryans is believed to have been around the shores of the Caspian Sea. There two main streams of migration set out; the one climbed to the high tablelands of Irān, settling partly there, partly surging further eastward through Afghanistan to settle finally on the plains of Northern India. They subdued the original inhabitants, became the ruling class, and shaped the destiny of India. They produced the songs of the Vedas, and had a large part in developing the different systems of Indian thought and philosophy. The other great stream of migration went West, settling all over Europe and producing the culture of the West. Both streams together formed the great Indo-European group of peoples, or Aryans.

The Aryan relationship of the Iranians can also easily be demonstrated by their language. Not only are the roots of many words the same as those in European languages or with Sanscrit, but also the structure often varies only a little. For instance, Irān has *padér* for father, *madér* for mother, *dochtár* for daughter; likewise, many verbs show the close relationship:

griftan, to grip; in German, *greifen*; *burdan*, to burden, and so forth. Furthermore the grammar is typically that of an Aryan language, and bears no resemblance to that of a Semitic language.

From a religious point of view, ancient Irān produced a system of thought with a resulting philosophy of life that promoted lofty standards of right and honour. In many respects it resembled the Biblical concept. The main difference, however, was that the Iranian system of thought was built on a dualistic principle and not on a strict monotheistic basis. Two powers were recognized: the power of light and the power of darkness. Ahura Mazda was the Lord of Light, of Purity, of Righteousness, of Great Knowledge, of Goodness. Opposed to him was Angra Mainju or Ahriman, the Lord of Darkness, the Lie, the Principle of Evil. Both Ahura Mazda and Ahriman were believed to possess creative powers, whereas according to Biblical conceptions God alone has creative powers, and Satan is able only to use, pervert, and misuse created matter. Life was viewed as an eternal struggle between these two forces. Man was considered to be a creature of value and dignity endowed with the freedom of choice. He was free to align his powers with either one or the other. The path of his duty, was to fight on the side of Ahura Mazda, the Lord of Righteousness, until Ahriman's forces were overcome.

Children from their earliest childhood were taught to shun the lie as the worst of all evils. Finally, on the day of reckoning, they believed that Ahriman would be conquered, evil would vanish forever, and eternal goodness would prevail. The holiest symbol of this religion was fire; it was the great cleansing power. The heavenly fire endowed man with creative powers. Therefore 'fire' received worshipful attention. Such was the religion of the kings of ancient Persia, of Cyrus and Darius, of Cambyses and Artaxerxes, the lords whom Daniel and Esther served.

Another figure was introduced, the figure of Mithra, the lord of wide pastures, the truth-speaking, the thousand-eared, the myriad-eyed, the exalted, the strong, the sleepless, the vigilant, the invincible, the protector of the needy, the mediator, the helper of man in his fight against Ahriman the Lie.

IRĀN

Mithraism, substantially altered by Babylonian influences but still retaining much of its original form, became the cherished cult of the Roman legions. Sanctuaries of Mithra have been found all over Europe, especially at the frontier stations of the Roman Empire. For a long time Mithraism was the strongest rival of Christianity, as the figure of Mithra with all its praiseworthy qualities resembled in a large measure the figure of Christ. Many of the symbols of this cult found their way into Christianity, and today are accepted as genuinely Christian. Among the symbols and ceremonies practiced in Mithraism, we find the use of bells and candles, the use of holy water, and communion. Sunday was a day of worship, and December 25 was sanctified.[1]

At any rate, the ancient Iranian religion, as it was laid down by Zarathustra (Zoroaster is merely a Latin corruption),[2] developed in man a high moral standing and placed upon him the responsibility of combining his forces with Ahura Mazda, the Lord of Light, in the struggle against the forces of darkness. In this system of thought there was no room for complacency or fatalism, which with the spread of Islām has completely enveloped the East. Only faint traces of that original ideal have remained among the Iranians. Thirteen hundred years of Islām, the fearful Mongol invasions under Genghis Khan, and later Tamerlane and his Tartars, have devastated the fair land of Irān and stamped out the lofty ideals of that ancient time.

When the Arabs came, the Zoroastrian religion was officially tolerated, but it rapidly lost its hold on the people, and at present only small groups can be found in Eastern Irān where they are known as Gabrs. A more numerous group went to India and settled in Gujerat mostly around Bombay. There they form the very wealthy community of the Parsees, practicing their ancient rites.

The spirit of 'Ancient Persia,' however, is not wholly extinct. Just as among the Arabs ancient desert poetry is still alive, so among the Iranians, Firdausi's great epic, the *Shah Namah*, completed A.D. 999, has made the ancient legends and history of Irān immortal. And Firdausi's verses are more widely known and recited in their original language and beauty by the common man than any other work of similar nature among Europeans. Firdausi has stabilized the Iranian language, just as the Qur'ān has fixed the Arabic, or Luther's Bible translation the German. Everyone who is interested in gaining an insight into the mentality of the Iranian should have a knowledge of the *Shah Namah*, just as he must comprehend the spirit of *The Thousand and One Nights* and some desert poetry if he wishes to penetrate deeper into the mind of the Arab, or as he has to know something of baseball and football to strike a responsive chord in a modern American's heart.

The battle of Nehavend in A.D. 642 was the great turning point in Irān's history. In this battle the forces of the Iranian dynasty, the Sassanids, which had revived the ancient Persian religion, were finally overwhelmed, and the victorious Arabs swept even to the outer boundaries of the realm, establishing the religion of the prophet wherever they went. The Arabs were not at all numerous in this newly acquired but vast territory, It is, therefore, all the more remarkable that they were able to establish their hold upon Irān for a long time to come, and to exercise such a profound and enduring influence upon this land and ancient culture. They, however, did not succeed in imposing their language upon the Iranians, as they did in Egypt. Iranian remained a separate language, although the Arabic script was adopted, and thousands of Arabic words filtered in.

IRANIAN INFLUENCE ON ISLĀM

The Iranian pulse of life was too powerful to be subdued for long, and as it has happened so often in history, the conquered avenged themselves by subduing their conquerors culturally, changing thereby to a large extent the concept and outlook of the latter's life. Soon the Iranian influence made itself felt in the Arab empire of Islām. The overthrow of the Umayyads in Damascus (A.D. 750) and the establishment of the 'Abbāsids in Baghdad was due mainly to the Iranian support of the latter. Under the famous caliph Harūn al Rashīd, for instance, Iranians were prime ministers, and occupied many of the highest positions in the empire. With them the pomp and grandeur of an Oriental monarchy entered into Islāmic life.

IRĀN

The caliph surrounded himself with bodyguards of foreign extraction, and became more and more remote and unapproachable to the common people of his realm. This was an idea utterly foreign to the simple tastes of the Arabs, where the poorest Beduin may approach his ruler without fear and hesitation.

Besides that fundamental difference in the conception of the state, its ruler, and his function, which was introduced into Islām by Iranian influence, the cultural influence of Irān soon made itself felt. Many famous scientists and philosophers of this and later periods who contributed much to spread the fame of Arabic and Islāmic culture were of Iranian origin.[3] To name only a few: al Ghazālī (1058-1111), the founder of Sūfism and expositor of Islāmic theology, was Iranian; Ibn Sīna, known as Avicenna in the West (979-1037), the famous physician and greatest philosopher of the age, was Iranian; al Birūnī (973-1048), the mathematician and philosopher, was likewise Iranian; furthermore, Abu Bakr Muḥammad al Rāzī (864-925), perhaps the most famous doctor of the Middle Ages, whose discoveries were considered basic, and were unsurpassed during centuries. The poets, as Omar Khayyām (died 1132), Sa'adi (1193-1292), Jalāl al Dīn al Rūmī (1208-1283), and Ḥāfiz (1320-1384), well known also in Western circles, wrote in their mother tongue. Their verses are still repeated and sung by high and low, by shah and muleteer, in Irān. Even the formerly mentioned collection of *The Thousand and One Nights* is largely Iranian in origin. Iranian influence penetrated into all spheres of life, but as it used Arabic largely as its mode of expression, and as it was eagerly absorbed by the Arabs, it is difficult to establish a distinct demarcation line between the Arabic and the Iranian element in Islāmic culture. Both elements together with further additions from Christian and Oriental sources form the complex body of Islāmic culture.

The Shī'a preachers early lent their power and talent to support Iranian nationalism in opposition to pan-Islāmic imperialism. Hence, when the central power of the 'Abbāsids waned, Iranian nationalism was able to assert itself, and Iranian dynasties followed, adopting officially the Shī'ite form of Islām. Irān has clung to the Shī'a ever since, alienating herself thereby from her neighbours to the west and to the east, so that her relations with Turkey and Afghanistan were often not only strained but openly hostile, as both are staunch supporters of the Sunna.

The Shī'īs are in some respects more fanatical than the Sunnīs, especially in their particular beliefs regarding the imamate. On the other hand, they are more easily accessible to outside and also to Christian ideas than the Sunnīs, as their religious conceptions are not confined to a vigorous formalism. For instance, in their belief in the imamate and the hidden Imām as an everlasting guide, they find a clue to understand the doctrine of the incarnation. As most of their imāms have met with a violent death, to which a vicarious meaning has been attached, the cross on which Jesus expired to redeem the world does not become to them the fatal rock of offence, as it does to the Sunnīs. During the first days of Muharram until recent years thousands marched through the streets lashing themselves with whips and chains, and inflicting wounds upon themselves with swords. The doctrine of atonement is more easily comprehensible to them because of the sufferings of Ḥusayn, which gave him the right to be an intercessor before God in behalf of his followers, and which are remembered yearly throughout the land. Furthermore, their belief in the *paighambar akhira zamān* (the messenger of God or prophet of the last time), who will restore righteousness, helps them to understand the second coming of Christ in which the Christian hope finds its ultimate consummation.

These foregoing remarks might convey the impression that Christian mission work should have found a ready welcome in Irān, and that it should not be too difficult to bring a Shī'ī into contact with Christ. To draw such a conclusion, of course, would be premature. It has been proved, however, that it is easier to win an Iranian than an Arab, and churches exist in Irān whose members are without exception converts from Islām. Before we enlarge on this topic, a few remarks on Irān might be in order.

GEOGRAPHICAL AND ETHNOGRAPHICAL REMARKS

Irān is the connecting link between Western and Central

IRĀN

Asia. Her high tablelands, which have an average altitude of 4,000 feet, are surrounded by mighty mountain ranges, which fan out from the Armenian highlands and the Caucasus mountains, stretching eastward towards the Hindu Kush mountains and the Pamir plateau, and south-eastward parallel to the Persian Gulf, towards the mountain ranges of Baluchistan. Their peaks often reach the height of 10,000 feet, and the Demavend north-west of Teheran towers with his 18,600 feet far above all the others. Large tracts of land are barren wastes due to the lack of rain, but wherever water is found, beautiful oases have sprung up, in which larger and smaller towns thrive. The climate in general is healthful, although the temperature varies from extreme heat in summer to a biting cold in winter. During a considerable time of the year strong, persistent, north-westerly winds blow, so that the Iranians were the first to conceive the idea of harnessing the powers of the wind, and invented the windmill. The narrow strip of lowlands around the Caspian Sea is of an entirely different nature. Its climate is tropical, and a dense subtropical vegetation flourishes. Also the lowlands towards the Persian Gulf and along its coast are extremely trying and unhealthful for foreigners because of the sweltering, oppressive heat.

The territory of modern Irān comprises 628,000 square miles, about the size of Texas, Arkansas, and New Mexico. It contains a population variously estimated to be between thirteen and fifteen millions. The first estimate is probably more correct, as the population of thirty-five larger towns amounts to only three million. Twenty-five per cent of the population are nomads with their own tribal constitution and their ancient tribal customs. Under the late Riza Shah Pahlevi, great efforts were made to break up these tribes, and settle them in their respective districts in order to bring them under the authority of the central government in Teheran. The encouraging results obtained were largely undone by the effects of World War II.

The population of such a vast mountainous territory is, of course, not homogeneous. Besides the true Iranians, who constitute the absolute majority of the population, we find in the north-western province of Irān in Azerbaijan, people mainly of

Turkish origin. They are descendants of hordes from Central Asia who invaded Irān during the Seljūk period (11th and 12th centuries). Their language is Turki, a coarser form of the more polished and refined Osmanli Turkish spoken in Istanbul and Ankara. Only the upper classes among them understand Iranian and a great difference is noticeable in mental and physical characteristics between Turkis and Iranis. Azerbaijan probably is the most fertile province of Irān. The capital is Tabriz which in former centuries was one of the main exchange centres of commerce between Europe and Asia. Soon after World War II, claims for autonomy of Azerbaijan were raised, based on the racial differences from the Iranians. Other powerful influences were behind the scenes. The revolt which followed ended in failure. Azerbaijan is again incorporated in the structure of the Iranian state, but with a grant of considerable powers of local administration.[4]

This same north-western district, especially around Lake Urmia, was the home of large Christian groups, Armenians as well as Nestorians. During World War I the Nestorians cast their lot in on the side of Russia and England, hoping that they would find help and freedom through their Christian brethren. This disastrous decision brought only hardship. They were driven out of their homes by the Kurds and Turks, and had to live the life of unwanted displaced persons, until they were finally permitted to settle in north-eastern Syria, around the river Khabur.

In the mountain ranges to the west of Lake Urmia, towards the 'Irāqi and Turkish borders, is the homeland of the Kurds. They speak their own language, which is related to Iranian, but yet distinct, and which only during this century has been put into written form. In appearance they are distinct from the typical Iranians. They are more stocky, with aquiline features and dark eyes with beetling brows, and are fond of a hazardous life and warfare. They pay only lip service to the central government; in reality they recognize only their own tribal chiefs and their own tribal laws. In former times they often descended from their mountain fastnesses to raid and decimate the Christian towns and villages of the Nestorians and Armenians around

IRĀN

Lake Urmia and Lake Van. Their most famous son was Salah al Dīn al Ajjūbī, the Saladin of the West, who defeated the Crusaders and excelled in chivalry and nobility.

In the north-eastern province of Irān, in Khorasan, are numerous Turkmenes. In the south-eastern parts of Irān the Baluchis have their home. They form a racial unit with their brothers beyond the border in Indian Baluchistan, which forms today a part of Pakistan. They speak their own language. Arabs are found in the lowlands around the northern part of the Persian Gulf. They make a living by cultivating dates and fishing.

Some of the most powerful tribes are the Lurs and the Bakhtiaris. They marry only inside their tribes, and are therefore pure bred. Nominally they are Muslims, yet these free sons of the *dasht*, as the untilled land is called, obey nobody except their chief.

That is the picture of Irān over which the shahs of the different dynasties ruled with more or less success. It was a medieval system: an autocratic emperor with his feudal lords, assisted or hampered by a zealous clergy, the *mujtahidīn* and mullahs of the Shī'a faith. It worked well as long as Europe was ruled by the same system. But with the change in Europe during the eighteenth and nineteenth centuries, Irān was soon outpaced and became the prey of the stronger European powers, until it was parcelled out into spheres of interest between Russia in the north and Britain in the south-east.

RIZA SHAH

This situation, however, underwent a radical change when Riza Khan, later Riza Shah Pahlevi, an officer of the Cossack guard, seized power in 1921. With a strong hand, he began to set the house in order and did everything possible not only to free the country from the foreign political and financial influence, but also from the reactionary influence of the powerful, fanatical, and superstitious clergy. The influence of the Sharī'a law was gradually abolished, and therewith the power taken from the hands of the mullahs. The veil was discarded and women partially emancipated. When the leading *mujtahid* of the mosque of Qūm publicly derided the queen, who had advertently or inadvertently unveiled her face during the sermon, consequently causing a demonstration against the queen, the shah proceeded immediately to Qūm with troops, entered the mosque without removing his boots and administered a severe flogging to the *mujtahid* with his own hands.[5] The religious holidays were drastically reduced, and the Muharram procession with its accompanying religious frenzy was forbidden.

Like Kamāl Ata Turk in Turkey, Riza Shah endeavoured to make the Iranians Irān-conscious, and no effort was spared to link them again to their glorious pre-Islāmic past, and to make them forget if possible, the long predominance of Arab influence. The same process as in Turkey went into operation in Irān. The language has been purged of its Arabic elements, and old Iranian words revived. The ethics of Zoroaster are restudied and praised, and to Iranian poets, old and new, a wide publicity is given. Many reforms were inaugurated which were detrimental to Islām. A secular-minded nationalism was created, in which religion has to play a second fiddle. The result of this trend, of course, is that many, especially among the educated classes, are led away from all religion towards modern scepticism. But beside the evil consequences which such a falling away from all religion brings forth, it has on the other hand given rise to a tolerance in religious matters, a tolerance never experienced in former times, so that a convert from Islām, apart from petty annoyances, is hardly ever threatened with death, as was the case in the past.

On the other hand, in this effort to create an Irān-consciousness, the state has decreed the closing of all foreign and sectarian schools, and has put all education under its direct control. Although it was by no means particularly aimed at them, it was a hard blow to missions, because most mission work was done along educational lines. But it might be a blessing in disguise, as missionary energies and funds will thereby become free to be used for the main objective of missions and the only reason for their existence: namely, the proclamation of truth revealed in Christ Jesus. Missions have done a most difficult spadework in education in Irān, and have nobly executed it, but this phase of their work seems to have come to an end definitely. The government has taken over and has larger means at its disposal than ever could be gathered by private initiative. Let us hope that the high ideals of Christian influence will be taken over at least partially by the new agency.

FOREIGN MISSIONS IN IRĀN

Foreign missions were represented in Irān by the Lazarites who came to Irān in 1625. Their work and that of other Catholic orders is mostly confined to the ancient Christian communities and to the foreigner residing in Irān. Christian charity, of course, is extended to all, and that silent witness is often more forceful than the best sermon.[6]

Protestant missions in an organized form came to Irān in 1833, when the Basel Mission opened a station in Tabriz. They soon found out, however, that there was little opportunity to work among Muslims, and they left after a few years.[7] But before organized work began, one of the greatest modern missionaries, the pioneer of work among Muslims in modern times, spent some time in Irān. He was Henry Martyn, whose heart was aflame to bring the message to his Muslim brethren. He was a chaplain, employed by the East India Company, and spent a number of years in India. In 1811 he went to Irān and lived for ten months in Shirāz, where he completed and revised his translation of the New Testament and the Psalms into Iranian. During his stay in Shirāz he had daily talks and discussions with the leading Muslims. But he came to the conclusion that it is of no avail to convince Muslims by argument, and he cried out in despair: 'I know not what to do but to pray for them.'[8] After the completion of his translation, a copy was presented to the shah, and then Martyn took the overland route to Constantinople. Before he could reach that city, however, his already weakened health failed, and he died.

The American Mission, later taken over by the American Presbyterian Board, started work in 1834 among the Nestorians around Lake Urmia. After a survey of the situation, public preaching to Muslims was not recommended. Later a station in Hamadan was opened, and medical work begun at Tabriz and Teheran.⁹ Shortly before World War I, Meshed, one of the most fanatical towns of Islām, was entered, and medical work established. Today there exists a church in Meshed, the members of which are all converts from Islām.

Besides the American Mission, the Church Missionary Society of England (C.M.S.) is working in Irān. Their stations are in Isfahān, Shirāz, Yezd, and Kerman. The work started in Isfahān (1869 and 1875). In each of these places, hospitals and dispensaries were established, besides the schoolwork for boys and girls. Their main object was to reach the Muslim population. The results were at first very sparse, but later became more abundant. In 1911 the C.M.S. could report that they had 100 converts from Islām.¹⁰ In the beginning these converts were mostly around the mission centres and enjoyed their protection, so that the reproach could be levelled against them that they were rice Christians. In recent times, however, churches have sprung up independently from the mission, as for instance in the village of Qalat near Shirāz, where there exists today a church entirely of Iranian-Muslim descent.¹¹

The work of the Protestant missions was considered advanced enough that in 1933 the first synod of the diocese of Irān as an independent see could be held. There is now Iranian leadership in the councils of the church as well as in the evangelistic work, a factor of utmost importance, as it will become increasingly more difficult for foreigners to live in those countries and have a direct hand in the management of the affairs of the church. The work has to be done by nationals. Christ on the Iranian road must be carried by Iranians clad in Iranian garb.

Irān today, more than any other Muslim land, presents an open door. There is greater tolerance at present towards religion than in any other Muhammadan country, and the tenets of the Shī'a make it easier for the inquirer to understand, to a certain degree, the essential points of Christianity. Moreover, Irān is in a most strategic position from which the light of Christianity can spread further. To the east lies Afghanistan, a country which has never consented to let a Christian messenger enter. To the west lies Turkey, the doors of which likewise seem closed; to the north lies Soviet Russia, with all her Central Asian peoples, who never have had the opportunity of hearing the message of love in Christ. And here in Irān an open door exists, and tolerance such as has seldom been experienced in her history. There is an awakening and longing among the people for something better than what they have had before. Perhaps from Irān will go forth the messengers again as the Nestorians of old to preach the message of salvation to the countries of Central Asia. Let us not pass by this open door.

---

[1] See H. Stuart Jones, 'Mithraism,' in Hastings *Encyclopedia of Religion and Ethics*, Vol. 8, pp. 752-759; also F. Cumont, *The Mysteries of Mithra*; English translation by T. J. McCormack, 1903.

[2] The birth of Zarathustra is variously given from 1000 B.C. to 600 B.C.

[3] Many of them wrote in Arabic, and are therefore counted as belonging to the Arabic sphere.

[4] E. Groseclose, *Introduction to Iran*, p. 240.

[5] *Ibid.*, p. 131.

[6] B. Arens, *Handbuch der Katholischen Missionen*, pp. 36, 37.

[7] J. T. Addison, *The Christian Approach to the Moslem*, p. 180.

[8] *Ibid.*, pp. 178, 179.

[9] *Ibid.*, p. 180 ff.

[10] *Ibid.*, p. 182.

[11] J. N. Hoare, *Something New in Iran*, pp. 40, 41.

CHAPTER EIGHTEEN

THE BRIDGE AND ITS BUILDERS

IN BUILDING a bridge over a deep gorge or a wide, swift-flowing river, the engineers have to do a vast amount of planning before the first digging can be done. They have to survey the terrain with the greatest care in order to be able to select the most suitable spot where the future structure is to be erected. They have to plumb the depth of the river, measure the swiftness and volume of the current, and observe the high and low watermarks, before they decide what kind of bridge they are going to build. They have to make most exact calculations in order to choose the kind of material best suited to the amount of stress and strain which the structure must bear. Only after having laid these plans most carefully and after having estimated the costs closely is work begun on the great enterprise.

In the preceding chapters of this study our work was mostly that of surveying the territory, of measuring the width of the gulf which separates Islām from Christianity, of plumbing the currents and crosscurrents which have to be reckoned with. Everyone who has had the patience to follow these chapters will realize that the shores along this gulf run parallel for long distances, that at some points they approach each other rather closely, but at others they draw far apart. Certainly, he will have recognized that the other shore is not just a barren desert, but a country full of life, with its own forms and patterns—that Islām is a way of life just as Christianity has developed its own distinct culture.

But he will also have discovered on the long march up and down the stream that there is no bridge anywhere between the two banks. On the contrary the relationship between Christianity and Islām during the past was mostly overshadowed by political considerations. This resulted in a state of permanent tension, with frequent outbreaks of bitter hostilities and a deep-seated fear and suspicion toward the sincerity of the motives of each other. He may have noticed with dismay that the best-meant Christian endeavours during the past hundred years have not accomplished much in this respect.

On the other hand, he may point out that Western civilization and the modern application of science with all its material benefits has finally bridged the gulf. However, that latter aspect is rather deceptive; it is only seemingly true, whereas the inner life of the two peoples still runs far apart, each in its own course. Where Christians and Muslims have met is on neutral ground—a few highly educated persons from both camps on a scientific level. It would therefore be more appropriate to point to the mystics of both groups who really do stand on common ground in their adoration of a highest deity.

But why, many will ask, is it necessary to build a bridge to Islām? Is it not just as well that the two religions and systems of thought run parallel without mixing and intermingling, especially as there does not exist on the side of official Islām the least inclination to lay the foundation for such a bridge on their side of the gulf? This question has often been asked, and rightly so. It can only be answered by another question: Why did God send Christ to bridge the gulf between heaven and earth, between divinity and humanity? The people of this world did not ask for it, and when Christ came He was not accepted even by those who should have been prepared for His coming. God's love constrained Him to do so, and the same love constrains Christians to do likewise.

God himself built the bridge to humanity. Should we fail to build the bridge to our fellow men? God knew that when His love would become fully revealed in Christ, this very love would draw men to Him. He had to condescend to make our salvation and partaking of the divine life possible. Or, as Paul has expressed it so eloquently, Christ 'thought it not robbery to be equal with God: but made Himself of no reputation, and took upon Him the form of a servant, and was made in the likeness of men: and being found in fashion as a man, He humbled Himself, and became obedient unto death, even the death of the cross.' Christ spanned the gulf between divinity and humanity in Himself, that we might have access to the Father, no longer to remain aliens and foreigners to the household of God, but to be children and heirs. The spirit that was in Christ should be in us also, is the admonition of Paul.

That is the answer. And thank God there will always be men and women who will attempt to build that bridge to Islām and who will not rest until they have succeeded. And this word of Paul's about Christ gives the directive concerning the conditions under which this work should be undertaken, and what attitudes should inspire the bridge-builders. Just as Christ Himself became the bridge between God and man and the channel through which the divine blessings flow, in like manner we have to become bridges to our fellow men—here to the Muslims—and channels through which the life-giving waters flow. That alone should be our objective and that alone justifies our going to these foreign lands as missionaries.

Are these the reasons why we go to the lands of the Muslims? Why do we do mission work, as we call it nowadays? Are we clear in our objectives? Mission work has taken on so many aspects, partly through our western fondness for organization, that only too easily our objectives become blurred. It is of utmost importance that we ask ourselves this question again, and again that we keep our objective clear. Why do we go? Do we go to the Muslims because we long deep in our hearts that they may share with us the abundant life in God which we have experienced in Christ Jesus? Do we long to make them acquainted with Christ, the Healer of the soul, who alone can free man from the bondage of fear and from the fetters of sin and guilt? Does the love of Christ constrain us to do so?

Where do our objectives lie? Do they lie on a different level? Do they lie more on a cultural level, or a modern scientific level? Do we go to clean up these people somewhat, to give them the benefits of carbolic acid and make them microbe-conscious? And are we highly pleased if they start to use a toothbrush and adopt some of our hygienic requirements? Let us not forget that they have survived the microbes for thousands of years, and were never haunted by the fear of microbic warfare which now lurks in the back of our minds. Or do we go to put them on their feet socially by educational methods? Do we go to give them some uplift in their agricultural or other economic problems? What is our aim? Are we messengers for Christ, or messengers for a Christianity as we understand it—a Christianity clothed in the garb of western civilization?

Perhaps you will say, Do not the preaching of Christ and educational as well as medical work go hand in hand? Are not teaching, healing, and helping essential to the Christian faith? Are not these practical virtues better than any amount of theorizing? Why put the alternatives so crassly?

The answer has been given most effectively by Professor Duncan B. Macdonald in an article which appeared in the *Moslem World* under the title, 'The Essence of Christian Missions.' The author states, after having put the question in similar lines:

'The answer, in all gentleness and charity, must be that this objection rests simply on confused thinking and is, also, a misreading of the facts in the case. It may easily be that our Western world is not theologically minded, that its religion is not theocentric—which is a pity—but the whole Eastern, non-Christian world is theologically minded, and when our missionaries go to them with a non-theological temper of mind, they are simply unintelligible. The East is quite certain that these men know nothing of Religion, that the Divine Spirit has never spoken to them. They may bring in their hands many very useful things for our present life, here and now; they may be teachers, physicians, and helpers in many ways. But if they do not come to proclaim a definite theological teaching which produces a life-transforming faith they are a puzzle to the Oriental. Why do they come? What is their motive? The whole East understands a theological motive; but when that is obscured the East is only too ready to impute other and discreditable motives.'[1]

These words are only too true, as the author can testify from personal experience. Most of our philanthropic work is not understood. Often it is considered to be a bait for catching converts and is resented. Or as many simple souls put it: Why not take advantage of the generosity of the foreigner, which he displays so lavishly, and give him the opportunity to perform some good works? These will surely stand him in good stead in the day of reckoning when hope is against him.

These lines are not written with the intention of depreciating educational or medical work, nor do they mean that we should stop all of this type of work. Not at all. The writer simply wishes to point out that we should never lose sight of the main issue of our calling, namely, to be witnesses for Christ; and that we should never allow ourselves to be sidetracked by the busy routine work which is involved in the upkeep of such institutions.

Furthermore, as has been pointed out in the separate studies on the different countries of the Near East, the educational as well as the medical lines of mission work face increasing difficulties because the respective governments of these countries are taking education and medical welfare work into their own hands, and have much larger means at their disposal than missions ever can hope for. It would be unwise, therefore, to embark into big ventures without very careful counsel. On the other hand, this development brings home the fact that spiritual truth must be proclaimed by spiritual means; not by human strength and human achievements can this be brought about, but by the Spirit of the everlasting God.

Before considering some special points necessary in the work with Muslims, some general remarks about the attitudes and qualifications these bridge builders should possess or at least aim for, will not be out of place. Fishermen must love fish. You must love people. You want to win hearts, but hearts can only be won by heartfelt love and sympathy. Be natural in your dealings. Do not try to impress others regarding your own importance. The Arab, and the Oriental in general, has a sharp mind to detect the genuine from the false. Never consider yourself superior to them because your skin is a shade whiter than theirs. Never allow a feeling of superiority to lead you into a back-slapping attitude. This is not at all appreciated. Remember, you did not choose your mother or the country in which you first saw the light of day. Be honest and frank, as a man to man should be, and soon you will not see the difference in colour or habit, but only the other man whose innermost being longs for honesty and frankness. Never consider your habits superior to theirs and commit the tactless offence of comparing their ways with your accustomed ways in a depreciating manner.

The Easterner likes to invite you to eat with him. It means more than to provide a meal for you; it is a gesture of friendship. Eat heartily of that which is set before you. You will cause great joy and establish a friendship never forgotten. If you have a weak stomach, or if you are over-sensitive about what you eat, then it will be better for you to choose another country for your endeavours. Principles of healthful living are very important, but to avoid offence and win the friendship of those we have come to bring in contact with Christ is more important than some slight digression from our usual habits of eating. Certainly health reform faddists are unsuited for pioneer mission work.

Never consider Western ways essential to a Christian life. Remember that Christ and His apostles were Easterners. Those who would have greater right to object are the Easterners when they observe our Western ways. Be courteous and hospitable, two virtues which are inborn in every Easterner, even if he does not pretend to be religious. If you lack in those, you have little chance to impress them with your message.

Tact includes the ability to speak respectfully of their religion and religious institutions. Speaking of Muḥammad as the false prophet would be just as helpful as if a Muslim coming to this country in order to win Christians would speak of Christ as the son of a harlot. You have conceded nothing when you call Muḥammad the 'Prophet of Islām.' If you call him 'a prophet,' that would lead to misunderstandings.

Do not be hasty! Haste is not a manifestation of energy, but a sign of confusion and nervous tension. 'Haste is from the devil,' says an Arabic proverb. Therefore, do not associate yourself with this bedfellow in the minds of the people you have come to work for. It might ruin your usefulness for quite a long time to come. Do not think when some wheels are turning that you have accomplished a great deal in their hearts. A steadfastness in adversity, a loyal stand at their side in their sorrows, big or small, will give you a place in their hearts. To have a place in their hearts is the greatest achievement towards which you should aim, because, remember, *you are the bridge* over which Christ will walk to them and they to Him. Christianity in its highest sense is never propagated by methods but only by Christian hearts through which pulsates fully the stream of love coming from that greatest of hearts which ever beat for human beings, the heart of Jesus.

In order to be able to enter fully into the lives of your friends, to share their joys and their sorrows, you must know their language. If you do not know their language you will forever remain an outsider, and your working capacity and outlook for a successful life are at least 50 per cent reduced. Imagine a Muslim coming from Cairo or Baghdad trying to convert people to Islām in New York or any other great centre, preaching only in Arabic, understanding only a few sentences of English, relying on translators whose qualities he is unable to check. What measure of success would you grant to such a person? Therefore, language study is absolutely essential, and your aim should be no less than mastery of the language.

Only if you are able to talk to the people on all subjects concerning their lives, only if you are able to read their books and to understand their way of thinking, only if you can join in their jokes and laugh heartily with them, have you become one of them, and one who will be able to exercise a permanent influence upon them. Without knowing their language you have little more than a curiosity value.

Until recent times missionaries in Muslim lands worked under one great handicap. They belonged in most cases to a nation which was dominant politically in the country in which they worked. Their message, therefore, was quite naturally linked with all the acts of aggression and oppression of that hated foreign power, and often was even considered part and parcel of that domination. It is evident that the true spiritual values of Christ's message were thereby blurred or not seen at all. On the other hand, the missionary had that pleasant feeling of security, that in the time of trouble the strong arm of his government would always be available to help and to protect him. Some missionaries even played up that point.

THE BRIDGE AND ITS BUILDERS

Recently, however, most of these countries have become independent. Foreign governments have nothing to say any more in their domestic affairs. The missionary cannot call for protection by his home government at any moment. Such protection is no more available. He stands on his own, more or less, among the people he has come to serve. That might at times be quite uncomfortable, but it has made him and his message a thousand times stronger than before. It dissociates him from all Western political influence. The accusation that he is an agent of a foreign power cannot be levelled against him any longer. He is not there because his government is there, or because his government looks favourably upon his being there. He is not there to protect some vested interests, but he stands at his post because he came to proclaim Christ. For Christ's sake he lives among these people. Christ is his protection, and for Christ's sake he is willing to die if need be.

If missionaries accept this clear attitude, and are willing to work under such conditions, then their message has a chance to be heard on its own merits, and Christ has a chance to be seen in His own beauty and holiness, not dressed up with Western paraphernalia. Therefore, unpleasant as the political development in the East may appear at first sight, in reality it is a blessing in disguise, and offers greater prospects for success than ever before.

It might happen that some countries will close their doors completely to all foreigners. That would be regrettable. Yet it does not matter by whom Christ is proclaimed, whether by foreigners or nationals of the country. The witness of the latter will be more valuable and eventually the work will be done by them. These national workers often become more effective by the withdrawal of the foreign political influence, because the horrible accusation that they are fifth columnists, tools in the hand of a foreign power, traitors to their own country, cannot be hurled against them any more. If they now proclaim the message of Christ, then they witness for Christ and for Him alone.

The foregoing remarks may be applicable to missionaries in general. However, the missionary to Muslim countries should possess some other qualities in addition to the foregoing. Everyone who has followed these chapters will have recognized that the Near East is full of religious ideas and speculative systems, and has ever been. A missionary going to these countries should have the best possible mental equipment, and should be well trained in religious and philosophical thinking. First of all he must do all his work in a difficult language. Then, too, he should be capable of understanding these systems, and be able to reason soundly and logically without bias. However, he should never make reasoning and arguing his business.

The more practical type of man finds himself somewhat out of place. His ability to do all sorts of things, which would be highly appreciated in Central Africa or some other field, is not so much needed in the Near East, where workmen for nearly all purposes can be found. In laying all due stress upon the good intellectual qualities of the missionary candidate, it should never be overlooked that the best intellect is of no avail when the heart is not full of the love of Christ. Both should be found together.

The work for Muslims requires full attention and concentration. It is therefore advisable to let him specialize in this field, and not have him do work for Christians and Muslims at the same time. Not only is an entirely different approach needed to reach Muslims, but even a different vocabulary. For example, in speaking to a Christian audience, the term, Christ the Son of God, is perfectly understood. To Muslim ears it is a blasphemy. The same holds true for many other fundamental terms which we Christians use as a matter of course.

For that same reason it is impracticable to translate Christian literature of the West even of the best quality. It has to be rewritten to make it suitable for the understanding of the Muslim. That does not mean that truth should be watered down or even hidden. It means only that it should presented in such a way that it does not repel the reader from the very outset. Only a man who is well acquainted with Islāmic thought and deeply versed in its literature is able to produce such books.

Furthermore, the two communities, the Muslim and Christian, do not mix much in a social way, except perhaps on the higher social stratum, or among some modernly educated young people. They live in watertight compartments; in most places they live in different quarters of the town. Most Christians have not the faintest inkling of Muslim literature and religious thought. The Muslim is likewise ignorant of Christianity. He knows just a few points by which he can deride and ridicule Christianity, and the Christian retaliates in the same coin. Therefore, a man who finds ready entrance in the one community will have difficulty in finding acceptance at the same time in the other. All these points speak strongly in favour of a separation of the work for Muslims from that for other communities.

In bringing Christ to Muslims we face a difficulty which is to be met nowhere else. That is that Muslims assume that they know Christ and that their knowledge of Him is more accurate than ours. We are, therefore, not introducing a new figure to their thinking in bringing Christ to them, but on the contrary, we are trying to impose our wrong ideas about Christ upon their better understanding of Him.

To us, Christ is the Incarnate Word of God. He is the Redeemer, the only Mediator between God and man. To Muslims, Christ is highly exalted. He is a sign to the worlds, a spirit from God, the messenger of God, illustrious in this world and in the next, but otherwise he is considered to be on the same level as any other prophet.

By no other religion is Christ's position challenged in such a definite manner as it is in Islām. Therefore, everything depends upon our right representation of Christ. If we are able to represent Christ in His full spiritual power, every other problem will be solved. And here lies the crux of the matter. We can only represent Christ in such a manner if we have become partakers of His spiritual power. But often we ourselves have only touched the fringe of His garment, and are not aware of the spiritual resources which are in store for everyone who maintains an uninterrupted communion with Christ. In our own experience we often mistake the belief in a set of doctrines for faith, an adherence to some formulæ for the life-changing power of the Spirit of God. Islām, however, arouses us from our lethargy, because Islām not only challenges the Christian creed, but it challenges the spiritual power revealed in Christ Jesus.

The Muslim is always ready to bring up the subject of the Trinity, the Sonship of Christ, and the death of God. If the Son of God died, then God, they say, died. The Christian church for many centuries has defended her creed against these attacks. In the course of this very noble undertaking, she has tried to find similes, metaphors, and symbols in order to prove convincingly the truth of such doctrines as the Trinity, the two natures of Christ, redemption, and so forth. But in spite of all this endeavour she has failed. No amount of discussion and argument over these points will ever convince anybody, because the truth of these doctrines does not lie on the intellectual level where it can be reached by the power of reasoning. It lies on the spiritual level to which we find entrance by listening quietly to the Spirit of God, who is willing to reveal Himself to everybody, Muslim and Christian alike.

Let us remember that none among ourselves has become a true, living Christian because he suddenly understood and was able to explain the Trinity, but he has become such because of a personal experience with Christ. At the same time he understood inwardly on a higher level that the Trinity must be true, although he will forever be unable to explain it satisfactorily. But how many simpler things become distorted when we try to explain them in words or draw them on paper. For instance, we are unable to project a spherical body on a level surface. Therefore, all global maps give us a somewhat distorted picture of the earth.

The peculiar problem in the work with Muslims arises because Islām has a great similarity with Christianity in its outward form. Muslims believe in one God, and so do Christians. Muslims have a book, the Qur'ān; Christians have a book, the Bible. Muslims have a founder, the messenger of God, Muhammad; Christians also have a founder, Christ, the Son of God. Muslims have a creed; Christians have a creed. Muslims have a number of religious duties to perform; Christians seem to do likewise.

Comparing the two systems according to their *outward* structure and appearance, there does not seem to be much difference between the two, and comparing form with form, Islām would probably take the first prize. Muslims contend that Islām is simpler, easier to comprehend, and more reasonable, that its requirements can be met by everyone, whereas the sayings of Christ, although pointing to high ideals, are difficult to attain and nobody or only a chosen few are able to live up to them. Therefore, they affirm, Islām is more practical for this world.

And yet this conclusion is subject to the reservation that a religion which is fully comprehensible by reason, and its requirements fully adapted to human possibilities is not a religion at all; it is just an ethical system. The purpose of religion is to raise man from his human level to a higher level, to the divine level. It is to awaken in him, besides the faculty of reason which he has so well developed, a greater and higher faculty, the faculty of faith, which has its own laws. Religion must set before man a goal which he is unable to attain by his own strength in order to bring him into contact with the divine power. In doing so, the necessary tension is created to bring about the full development of man's personality, spiritually and mentally. This aspect of true religion is most beautifully expressed by the ageing Apostle Paul in his letter to the Philippians:

'Not as though I had already attained, either were already perfect: but I follow after, if that I may apprehend that for which also I am apprehended of Christ Jesus. Brethren, I count not myself to have apprehended: but this one thing I do, forgetting those things which are behind, and reaching forth unto those things which are before, I press toward the mark for the prize of the high calling of God in Christ Jesus.'[2]

If any religion lacks this fundamental element, its followers will soon settle down to a self-satisfied complacency, adhering to a rigid formalism. Islām by its own admission lacks this element of spiritual tension; it does not even claim to have such aspirations.

It is therefore perfectly logical that Muslims consider the Christian teaching in the same formalistic, mechanical way as they consider their own. The Bible is a mechanized, word-for-word revelation like the Qur'ān. Christ, the Son of God, can only be such in a physical way, a repulsive thought indeed. The same holds true for all the other points. Abstaining from alcohol or certain foods will surely be praised by Muslims, but the motive for so doing would be misunderstood. We do it, of course, they assume, to gain favour or merit with God. To present to Muslims a certain set of forms in order to replace their own set means no gain at all. Even if they should accept this new set, we have achieved nothing so long as they do not understand that Christianity is not a form, but spiritual life.

To understand the fundamental difference in the conception of inspiration of the two books, the Qur'ān and the Bible, is of utmost value. In this connection one other aspect of the Bible deserves special mention here. This is totally absent in the Qur'ān, and that is the 'Word of Prophecy.' Unfortunately Christians in general have failed to heed it and have practically forgotten to use that mighty weapon of their spiritual armour. The Apostle Peter says:

'We have also a more sure word of prophecy; whereunto ye do well that ye take heed, as unto a light that shineth in a dark place, until the day dawn, and the day star arise in your hearts: knowing this first, that no prophecy of the Scripture is of any private interpretation. For the prophecy came not in old time by the will of man: but holy men of God spake as they were moved by the Holy Ghost.'[3]

By the prophetic word, God has thrown rays of light upon earth's dark pathway. He has built lighthouses beforehand that man may recognize the times in which he lives. The great prophecies of Isiah concerning the Messiah, the prophecies of Daniel which span human history and reach unto the time of the end, and the prophetic words of Jesus Himself are the most eloquent witnesses of the manifestation of God's Spirit through all the ages, and one of the most convincing elements even to the sceptic that God does not leave Himself unrevealed.

Muhammad brought laws, often going into great detail; Christ laid down principles upon which true life is based and can grow. He led us from the adherence to law to the realm of faith and its righteousness, from the confession of a creed to the self-sacrificing service of love, from a hope to the privilege of sonship of God.

Islām is proud of its brotherhood and has a right to be proud of it. But this brotherhood is confined to its own members and based upon a hereditary selection. It considers all outsiders to be in the 'House of War,' certain groups of which even should be annihilated. Christ, on the other hand, spoke of the general human brotherhood, and in a special sense of those who are reborn by the Spirit of God. The acceptance into this spiritual brotherhood does not rest on hereditary merits, but on the willing reception of the Spirit of God. Islām requires a strict ritual in worship which only too easily develops into a rigid form bare of all spiritual significance. Christ laid down no special rule or form for worship, but requested that worship should be in spirit and in truth. Islām claims finality; that means that no higher thought about God and our relationship to Him can be possible than what has been revealed in the Qur'ān. Now, however, it is evident that more advanced thoughts on this God-man relationship have been revealed and can be conceived. Thoughts and revelations raise this relationship from the level of man's abject submission to God to that of a spiritual intercourse with God, from that of blind obedience to that of an intelligent acceptance of God's purposes. This opens up the whole realm of the Spirit, a sphere in which orthodox Islām has nothing to offer. Therewith its claim of finality is invalid.

Is there still need for us to go to the Muslim world? Have we something to offer? Should we offer it, even if we are not welcomed? Friends, when we have drunk from the stream of life, when we have come to the fountainhead of life—to Christ Jesus—and He has filled us with His Spirit, then streams of living water flow forth from us. Then in accord with Paul the apostle we exclaim: 'I am a debtor to the Arab and the Turk, to the Iranian and the Afghani, to the Christian in ignorance, and to the Muslim alike.'

As long as we Christians set form against form, our contribution will be very meagre, but the moment we are able to bring the full power of Christ's spiritual message to the Muslims, this power will perform its work upon their hearts. Spiritual power cannot be resisted forever. Spiritual power leaves its influence even if the results are not immediately apparent. Spiritual power is never lost; it is a seed which will blossom and bloom at its time. To pray for this power is our greatest need. Islām is the greatest challenge to the Christian church, but perhaps also her best handmaid in making her realize the one thing she needs most, spiritual power.

---

[1] *The Moslem World*, Vol. XXXIV, p. 7, Jan., 1944.
[2] Philippians 3: 12-14.
[3] 2 Peter 1: 19-21.

APPENDIX

RULING HOUSES IN ISLĀM

1. Orthodox Caliphs

A.H.		A.D.
11-40		632-661
11	Abu Bakr	632
13	'Umar	634
23	'Uthmān	644
35-40	'Alī	656-661

2. Umayyad Caliphs

A.H.		A.D.
41-132	*Damascus*	661-750
41	Mu'āwiya I	661
60	Yazīd I	680
64	Mu'āwiya II	683
64	Marwān I	683
65	'Abd al Malik	684
86	Walīd	705
96	Sulaymān	714
99	'Umar II	717
101	Yazīd II	719
105	Hishām	723
125	Walīd II	742
126	Yazīd III	743
126	Ibrāhīm	743
127-132	Marwān II	744-750

3. 'Abbāsid Caliphs

A.H.		A.D.
132-656	*Baghdad*	750-1258
132	Al Saffāh	750
136	Al Mansūr	754
158	Al Mahdī	775
169	Al Hādī	785
170	Harūn al Rashīd	786
193	Al Amīn	809
198	Al Mā'mūn	813
218	Al Mu'tasim	833
227	Al Wathīq	842
232	Al Mutawakkil	847
247	Al Muntasir (Followed by a long list of mostly unimportant rulers)	861
640-656	Al Musta'sim	1242-1258

APPENDIX

A.H.	4. Umayyads of Spain	A.D.
138-422	Cordova	756-1031
	then followed by minor dynasties, among them the	
448-541	Almoravides (Al Murābiṭs)	1056-1147
	(Morocco, part of Algeria, Spain) and the	
524-667	Almohades (Al Muwahhids)	1130-1269
	(All North Africa and part of Spain)	
629-897	The Nasrids (Granada)	1232-1492
	(1492, expulsion of the Arabs from Spain by Ferdinand and Isabella of Castile)	

	5. Fātimid Caliphs in Egypt	
297-567	Cairo	909-1171
297	'Ubayd Allah al Mahdī	909
322	Muhāmmad al Qā'im	934
334	Al Mansūr, Isma'īl	945
341	Al Mu'izz	952
365	Al 'Azīz	975
386	Al Hākim bi amr illah	996
411	Al Zāhīr	1020
427	Al Mustanir	1035
487	Al Musta'li	1094
495	Al Amīr Abu 'Ālī	1101
524	Al Hāfiẓ	1130
544	Al Zāfir	1149
549	Al Fa'iz	1154
555-567	'Abd-Allah al 'Adīd	1160-1171

	6. The Ayyubids	
564-650	The most important was:	1169-1252
564-589	Salah al Dīn (Saladin)	1169-1193

	7. Mamlūk Sultans in Egypt	
650-922		1252-1517
648-792	a. Bahrī Mamlūks	1250-1390
784-922	b. Burjī Mamlūks	1382-1517

	8. The Seljūks	
429-700		1037-1300

(They are Turkomans from the steppes of Central Asia, and appeared at a time when the Empire of the Caliphate was dying. They accepted Islām and reunited Muhammadan Asia, until they split among themselves. Their greatest names are:

APPENDIX

A.H.		A.D.
429	Tughril Bek	1037
455	Alp Arslān	1063
465-485	Malik Shah	1072-1092

Later, we have separate dynasties of Seljūks, of Kirman of Syria, 'Irāq, and Asia Minor. Among the latter the tribe of the 'Othmanlis gained the upper hand.)

9. *'Othmanli Sultans of Turkey*

A.H.		A.D.
699	'Othmān I	1299
726	Orkhan	1326
761	Murād I	1360
792	Bāyazīd I	1389
805	Muhammad I	1402
824	Murād II	1421
855	Muhammad II	1451
886	Bāyazīd II	1481
918	Selīm I	1512
926	Sulaymān the Magnificent	1520
974	Selīm II	1566
982	Murād III	1574
1003	Muhammad III	1595
1012	Ahmad I	1603
1026	Mustafa I	1617
1027	'Othmān II	1618
1031	Mustafa I (restored)	1622
1032	Murād IV	1623
1049	Ibrāhīm I	1640
1058	Muhammad IV	1648
1099	Sulaymān II	1687
1102	Ahmad II	1691
1106	Mustafa II	1695
1115	Ahmad III	1703
1143	Muhmūd I	1730
1168	'Othmān III	1754
1171	Mustafa III	1757
1187	'Abd al Hamīd I	1773
1203	Selīm III	1789
1222	Mustafa IV	1807
1223	Mahmūd II	1808
1255	'Abd al Majīd	1839
1277	'Abd al 'Azīz	1861
1293	Murād V	1876

APPENDIX

A.H.		A.D.
1293	'Abd al Hamīd II	1876
1327	Muhammad V	1909
1336-1341	Muhammad VI (Wahid al Dīn)	1917-1922
1341-1342	Prince 'Abd al Majīd—elected—deposed	1922-1923

(Turkey became republic under Mustafa Kamāl Ata Turk.)

10. The Khedives of Egypt

A.H.	(Under nominal subordination to the Porte)	A.D.
1220	Muhammad 'Alī	1805
1264	Ibrāhīm	1848
1264	'Abbās I	1848
1270	Sa'īd	1854
1280	Isma'īl (adopted the title Khedive)	1863
1300	Tawtfīq	1882
1309	'Abbās Hilmi	1892
1332	deposed by the British	1914
1333	Husayn Kamil declared Sultan of Egypt	1914
1336	Prince Fu'ād becomes Sultan of Egypt	1917
1341	King of Egypt	1922
1355	Farūq	1936

11. Dynasties in Irān

250-316	'Alids (Tabaristān)	864-928
205-259	Tahirids (Khorasān)	820-872
254-290	Sāfārids (Persia)	867-903
261-389	Sāmānids (Transoxania and Persia)	874-999
320-447	Buwayhids (Southern Persia and 'Irāq)	932-1055
470-628	Shahs of Khwarizm	1077-1231
654-750	Il-Khāns (Mongols, descendants of Jenghiz Khan)	1256-1349
907-1148	*Safarids*	1502-1736
985-1038	Abbās I	1577-1629
1052-1077	Abbās II	1642-1667
1135-1142	*Afghans*	1722-1729
1148-1210	*Afshārids*	1736-1796
1148-1160	Nādir Shah	1736-1747
1163-1209	*Zands*	1750-1794
1193-1342	*Qājars*	1779-1923
1344-1362	Riza Shah Pahlevi	1925-1943

BIBLIOGRAPHY

Abbott, Nabia. *Two Queens of Baghdad.* Chicago: The University of Chicago Press, 1946.
Adams, Charles Clarence. *Islam and Modernism in Egypt.* London: Oxford University Press, 1933.
Addison, James Thayer. *The Christian Approach to the Moslem.* New York: Columbia University Press, 1942.
Adeney, Walter F. *The Greek and Eastern Churches.* New York: Charles Scribner and Sons, 1908.
Ameer Ali, Syed. *The Spirit of Islām, A History of the Evaluation and Ideals of Islām.* London: Christophers, 1946.
Andræ, Tor. *Mohammed, the Man and His Faith.* London: George Allen and Unwin Ltd, 1936.
―――. *Die Person Muhammeds in Lehre und Glauben seiner Gemeinde.* Stockholm: P. A. Norsted, 1917.
Arens, Bernard. *Handbuch der Katholischen Missionen.* Freiburg/Breisgau, Herder & Co., St. Louis, Mo., 1920.
Armstrong, Harold Courtenay. *Lord of Arabia, Ibn Saud.* London: A. Barker, 1934.
Arnold, Sir Thomas, and Alfred Guillaume. *The Legacy of Islam.* Oxford: Clarendon Press, 1931.
Arnold, T. W. *The Preaching of Islam.* Westminster: Archibald Constable and Co., 1896.
Barbour, Nevill. *Palestine: Star or Crescent?* New York: The Odyssey Press, 1947.
Batūta, Ibn. *Voyages d'Ibn Batoutah.* Texte Arabe, accompagné d'une traduction par C. Defrémery et Dr. B. R. Sanguinetti. 4 vols. Imprimerie Impériale. Paris: 1853-1859.
Bayḍāwī, Al. *Tafsīr* (Commentary).
Bechler, Theodor. *Die Herrnhuter in Agypten. Hefte für Missionskunde* (Herrnhuter Missionsstudien, No. 32). Missionsbuchhandlung Herrnhut.
Ben-Jacob, Jeremiah. *The Future of Jewish Nationalism* (with appendices). London: Carmel Publications, Midget Books, Ltd., 1947.
Björkman, W., 'Kāfir,' in *The Encyclopædia of Islam,* Vol. II.
Bliss, Frederick Jones. *The Religions of Modern Syria and Palestine.* New York: Charles Scribner and Sons, 1912.
Bokhāri, El. *Les Traditions Islamiques,* traduites de l'Arabs avec notes and index par O. Houdes et W. Marçais. Paris: Imprimerie Nationale, 1903.
Bouthoul, B. *Le Grand Maître des Assassins.* Paris: Libraire Armand Colin, 1936.

BIBLIOGRAPHY

Brandt, Wilhelm. *Die mandäische Religion; ihre Entwicklung und geschichtliche Bedeutung*, Leipzig: J. C. Hinrichs, 1889.

Browne, Lawrence Edward. *The Eclipse of Christianity in Asia.* Cambridge: Cambridge University Press, 1933.

Buhl, Frantz. 'Babylonia.' *The Jewish Encyclopedia*, Vol. II.

Bukhāri, Al. *Kitāb al Jāmi' al Sahih.* Leiden: Brill [n.d.].

Burton, Richard F. *Personal Narrative of a Pilgrimage to El-Medinah and Meccah.* London: Longman, Brown, Green, and Longmans, 1855. 3 vols.

Būṣīrī, Al. *Al Burda.*

Butcher, E. L. *The Story of the Church of Egypt.* London: Smith/Elder and Co., 1897. 2 vols.

Cash, W. Wilson. *Christendom and Islam.* New York: Harper and Brothers, 1937.

Catholic Encyclopedia, The, 15 vols. New York: Robert Appleton Company, 1907.

Columbus, Christopher. *First Letter of Christopher Columbus to the Noble Lord Raphael Sanchez*, dated Lisbon, March 14, 1493. Boston: Public Library, 1891.

Committee on Materials of Instruction of the American Council on Education. *The Story of Writing.* (Achievements of Civilization, Number 1.) Washington, D.C.: The American Council on Education, 1932.

Considine, John Joseph. *Across a World.* Toronto and New York: Longmans, Green and Co., 1942.

Corpus Reformatorum. 13 vols.

Cumont, Franz Valery Marie. *The Mysteries of Mithra*, trans. from the second revised French edition by Thomas J. McCormack. Chicago: The Open Court Publishing Co., 1903.

Dante Alighieri. *Divine Comedy.* Trans. by Melville B. Anderson. London: Oxford University Press, 1933.

Doughty, Charles M. *Travels in Arabia Deserta.* New York: Random House, 1937.

Dussaud, René. *Histoire et Religion des Noṣairîs.* Paris: Libraire Emile Bouillion, 1900.

Empson, Ralph Horatio Woolnough. *The Cult of the Peacock Angel.* London: H. F. and G. Witherby, 1928.

Enan, Muḥammed Abdullah. *Decisive Moments in the History of Islam.* Lahore, India: Sheikh Muh. Ashraf, 1940.

Encyclopædia of Islam, The. A Dictionary of the Geography, Ethnography, and Biography of the Muhammedan Peoples. Leiden: E. J. Brill, and London: Luzac and Co., 1913-1934, 4 vols.

Fedden, Robin. *Syria, An Historical Appreciation.* London: Robert Hale, Ltd., 1946.

Fortescue, Adrian. *The Orthodox Eastern Church.* London: Catholic Truth Society, 1907.

BIBLIOGRAPHY

———. *The Uniate Eastern Churches*. Ed. by George D. Smith. London: Burns, Oates, and Washbourne Ltd., 1923.

Gibb, H. A. R. *Modern Trends in Islam*. Chicago: University of Chicago Press, 1945.

Gibbon, Edward. *The History of the Decline and Fall of the Roman Empire*. London: Methuen and Co., and New York: Macmillan and Co., 1896-1906. 7 vols.

Goldziher, Ignaz. *Mohammed and Islam*. New Haven: Yale University Press, 1917.

———. *Streitschrift des Gazālī gegen die Bāṭinija-sekte*. Leiden: Brill, 1916.

———. *Vorlesungen über den Islam*. Heidelberg: Winter, Universitatsbuchhandlung, 1925.

Görlitz, Walter. *Wächter der Gläubigen. Der Arabische Lebenskreis und seine Arzte*. Hamburg: Sieben Stäbe Verlag, 1936.

Gottron, Adam. *Ramon Lulls Kreuzzugsideen*. (In Abhandlungen zur mittleren und neueren Geschichte Heft 39.) Berlin-Leipzig: Dr. W. Rothschild, 1912.

Groseclose, Eligin. *Introduction to Iran*. New York: Oxford University Press, 1947.

Hamilton, Archibald M. *Road Through Kurdistan*. London: Faber and Faber Ltd., 1937.

Handbook of Arabia, A. Compiled by the geographical section of the Naval Intelligence Division, British Admiralty, London: H.M. Stationery Office, 1920.

Harrison, Paul W. *The Arab at Home*. New York: Thomas Y. Crowell Co., 1924.

Hay, William Rupert. *Two Years in Kurdistan. Experiences of a Political Officer, 1918-1920*. London: Sidgwick and Jackson, 1921.

Helfritz, Hans. *Land Without Shade*. Trans. from the German. New York: National Travel Club, 1936.

Historians' History of the World, The, Vol. VIII. New York: The Outlook Co., London: The History Association, 1904.

Hitti, Philip Khuri. *The Origins of the Druze People and Religion*. (Columbia University Oriental Studies, Vol. XXVIII.) New York: Columbia University Press, 1928.

———. *The Syrians in America*. New York: G. H. Doran and Co., 1924.

Hoare, J. N. *Something New in Iran*. London: Church Missionary Society, 1937.

Holzapfel, Heribert. *Handbuch der Geschichte des Franziskanerordens*. Freiburg in Br.: Herder, 1909.

Hourani, A. H. *Minorities in the Arab World*. London: Oxford University Press, 1947.

Hunter, Frederick Mercer. *An Account of the British Settlement of Aden in Arabia*. London: Trübner and Co., 1877.

BIBLIOGRAPHY

Ingrams, William Harold. *A Report on the Social, Economic, and Political Condition of the Hadramaut.* London: H.M. Stationery Office, 1936.

Iraq, An Introduction to the Past and Present of the Kingdom of Iraq. By a committee of officials. Baltimore: Lord Baltimore Press, 1946.

Ivanov, Vladīmir Aleksīeevīch. *A Guide to Ismaili Literature.* London: The Royal Asiatic Society, 1933.

Jeffery, Arthur. *Materials for the History of the Text of the Qur'ān.* Leiden: E. J. Brill, 1937.

Jewish Encyclopedia, The. 12 vols. New York and London: Funk & Wagnalls Company, 1907.

Jones, H. Stuart. 'Mithraism,' in James Hastings, *Encyclopædia of Religion and Ethics,* Vol. 8, pp. 752-759.

Joseph, Isya. *Devil Worship; The Sacred Books and Traditions of the Yezidis.* Boston: R. G. Badger, 1919.

Juynboll, Theodor Willem. *Handbuch des islamischen Gesetzes nach der Lehre der schafi'itischen Schule.* Leiden: E. J. Brill, 1910.

Kheirallah, G. D. *Islam and the Arabian Prophet.* New York: Islamic Publishing Co., 1938.

Kiernan, Reginald Hugh. *The Unveiling of Arabia, the Story of Arabian Travel and Discovery.* London: G. G. Harrap and Co., 1937.

Koehler, Manfred. *Melanchthon und der Islam.* Leipzig: L. Klotz, 1938.

Koran, The. Translated from the Arabic by J. M. Rodwell, 1945. (Everyman's Library.)

Labourt, J. 'Maronites.' *The Catholic Encyclopedia,* Vol. IX, pp. 683-688.

Lactantius, *The Epitome of the Divine Institutes,* in The Ante-Nicene Fathers, Vol. VII., pp. 224-255. New York: Charles Scribner's Sons, 1913.

Lammens, Henri. *La Syrie, Précis Historique.* Beyrouth: Imprimerie Catholique, 1921. 2 vols. in one.

Levy, Reuben. *A Baghdad Chronicle.* Cambridge: Cambridge University Press, 1929.

Lewis, Bernard. *The Origins of Ismā'īlism.* Cambridge: W. Heffer and Sons Ltd., 1940.

Luther, Martin. *Sämmtliche Schriften.* Walch ed. St. Louis: Vol. 20.

Malek, Yusuf. *The Assyrian Tragedy.* Annemasse: Imp. Granchamps, 1934.

Margoliouth, D. S. *Mohammed and the Rise of Islam.* New York: G. P. Putnam's Sons, 1905.

Maulana Muhammad 'Ali. *The Religion of Islām.* Lahore: The Ahmadiyya Anjuman Ishā'at Islām, 1936.

Meulen, Daniel van der. *Aden to the Hadhramaut, a Journey in South Arabia.* London: J. Murray, 1947.

———, and H. von Wissmann. *Hadramaut; Some of Its Mysteries Unveiled.* Leiden: E. J. Brill, 1932.

Mez, Adam. *Die Renaissance des Islams.* Heidelberg: Carl Winter, 1922.

Middle East, The. 1948. London: Europa Publications Ltd., 1948.

Migne, J. P. *Patrologiæ, Cursus Completus,* S. G. Vol. 94.

BIBLIOGRAPHY

Moberg, Axel. *The Book of the Himyarites.* Lünd: C. W. K. Gleerup, 1924.
Mommsen, Theodor. *Das Weltreich der Caesaren.* Wien and Leipzig: Phaidon Verlag, 1933.
Muir, Sir William. *The Caliphate, Its Rise, Decline, and Fall.* A new and revised ed. by T. H. Weir, Edinburgh: John Grant, 1924.
———. *The Life of Mohammed.* Edinburgh: J. Grant, 1912.
Newman, A. H. 'Ignatius of Loyola,' *The New Schaff-Herzog Encyclopedia of Religious Knowledge,* Vol. V.
Nielsen, Ditlef, Fr. Hommel and N. Rhodokanakis eds. *Handbuch der altarabischen Altertumskunde.* Vol. I: Die altarabische Kultur, Kopenhagen: Arnold Busck, 1927.
Nöldeke, Theo. *Geschichte des Qurāns.* 2nd ed. Edited by Friedrich Schwally, G. Bergstrasser, and O. Pretzl. Leipzig: Dieterich'sche Verlagsbuchhandlung, 1909-1938.
Ochser, Schulim. 'Yemen,' *The Jewish Encyclopedia,* Vol. 12, pp. 592-594.
O'Leary, de Lacy Evans. *A Short History of the Fatimid Khalifate.* London: K. Paul, Trench, Trübner & Co., 1923.
O'Shea, Raymond. *The Sand Kings of Oman.* London: Methuen and Co., 1947.
Oussani, Gabriel. 'Syria,' *The Catholic Encyclopedia,* Vol XIV, pp. 404-406.
Pestalozzi, Carl. *Heinrich Bullinger, Leben und ausgewählte Schriften.* Elberfeld: R. L. Friedrichs, 1858.
Philby, Harry St. J. Bridger. *The Empty Quarter, Being a Description of the Great South Desert of Arabia Known as Rub'al Khali.* New York: Henry Holt, 1933.
Al Qur'ān. Arabic edition. Būlāq, Egypt: Government Press, 1344 A.H. [1925].
Rihani, Ameen. *Arabian Peak and Desert, Travels in Al Yaman.* Boston: Houghton Mifflin Co., 1930.
De Sacy, Silvestre. *Exposé de la Réligion des Druzes.* Paris: L'Imprimerie royale, 1838.
———. *Mémoire sur la dynastie des Assassins, et sur l'étymologie de leur nom.* In Académie des inscriptions et belles-lettres, Paris: 1818.
Sa'd, Ibn. *Kitāb al Tabaqat al Kibīra.* Eugen Mittwoch. Leiden: 1322/1904.
Samné, Georges. *La Syrie.* Paris: Bossard, 1920.
Schacht, Joseph. 'Zakāt,' in *The Encyclopædia of Islam,* Vol. IV, pp. 1202-1205.
Scott, Sidney Herbert. *The Eastern Churches and the Papacy.* London: Sheed and Ward, 1928.
Silver, Abba Hillel. 'Herzl and Jewish Messianism,' as an Appendix to Jeremiah Ben-Jacob, *The Future of Jewish Nationalism.* London: Carmel Publications, 1947.
Sloan, R. C. *Recent Educational Advances in Egypt.* Report prepared for the State Department, Washington, D.C.: April 18, 1946.
Sprenger, A. *Das Leben und die Lehre des Mohammed.* Berlin: 1869. 3 vols.

BIBLIOGRAPHY

Springett, Bernard H. *Secret Sects of Syria and the Lebanon.* London: Allen and Unwin Ltd., 1922.
Stafford, Ronald Sempill. *The Tragedy of the Assyrians.* London: G. Allen and Unwin, 1935.
Stamouli, A. A. 'Maronites,' *The New Schaff-Herzog Encyclopedia,* Vol. VII, pp. 188-190.
Stark, Freya. *The Southern Gates of Arabia, a Journey in the Hadramaut.* Middlesex, England: Harmondsworth, 1936.
Stewart, John. *Nestorian Missionary Enterprise.* Edinburgh: T. and T. Clark, 1928.
Storm, William Harold. *Whither Arabia? A Survey of Missionary Opportunity.* London: World Dominion Press, 1938.
Strothmann, Rudolf. *Das Staatsrecht der Zaiditen* (Studien zur Geschichte und Kultur des islamischen Orients). Strassburg: Karl J. Trübner, 1912.
Ṭabari, Abou-Djafar-Moʻhammed, *Chronique.* Traduite par M. Hermann Zotenberg. Paris: Imprimerie Nationale, 1867-1874. 4 vols.
Tertullian. *To Scapula* in the Ante-Nicene Fathers, Vol. III, pp. 105-108. New York: Charles Scribner's Sons, 1918.
Tritton, Arthur Stanley. *The Rise of the Imams of Sanaa.* London: Oxford University Press, 1925.
Weigall, Arthur E. P. Brome. *A History of Events in Egypt From 1798-1914.* New York: Charles Scribner's Sons, 1915.
Weir, T. H., 'Sadaqa,' in *The Encyclopædia of Islam,* Vol. IV, pp. 33-35.
Wensinck, A. J., and J. H. Kramers. *Handwörterbuch des Islam.* Leiden: E. J. Brill, 1941.
White, Wilbur W. *The Process of Change in the Ottoman Empire.* Chicago: The University of Chicago Press, 1937.
Wigram, William Ainger. *The Assyrians and Their Neighbours.* London: G. Bell and Sons, 1929.
——————. *An Introduction to the History of the Assyrian Church.* London: Society for Promoting Christian Knowledge, 1910.
Wilson, Sir Arnold Talbot. *The Persian Gulf.* Oxford: Clarendon Press, 1928.
Yearly Report of the Ministry of Education of the Republic of Syria, in Arabic, 1946.
Zwemer, Samuel M. *Raymund Lull.* New York and London: Funk and Wagnalls Co., 1902.
——————. *The Law of Apostasy in Islam.* London, Edinburgh, and New York: Marshall Brothers, Ltd., 1924.

PERIODICALS

Al Bilād al Suʻudiyya. Daily Paper. Makka al Mukarrama, 1947, 1948.
The Moslem World. Vols. 1-37. A Christian Quarterly Review of Current Events, Literature, and Thought Among Mohammedans. Editor

BIBLIOGRAPHY

Samuel M. Zwemar. Published by the Hartford Seminary Foundation, name changed to *The Muslim World*. A Quarterly Review of History, Culture, Religions, and the Christian Mission in Islamdom. Editor E. E. Calverley, Vol. 38, 1948.

Adams, C. C. 'Trends of Thought in Egypt.' *The Moslem World*, Vol. 34, p. 271, 1944.

Ingrams, Harold. 'A Journey in the Yemen,' *Royal Central Asian Journal*, Vol. XXXIII, January, 1946.

Liebesney, Herbert L. 'International Relations of Arabia,' *The Middle East Journal*, Vol. I, No. 2, 1947. Published quarterly by The Middle East Institute, Washington, D.C.

ADDITIONAL BOOKS RECOMMENDED FOR STUDY

Besides the books mentioned in the bibliography, the following are recommended for further study:

Pre- Islamic Period

Biruni. *Chronology of Ancient Nations*. Edited and translated into English by M. Sachau. London : 1879.

Cheikho, L. *Le Christianisme en Arabie avant l'Islam*. 2 vols. Beyrouth: 1912-1923.

Margoliouth, D. S. *The Relations Between Arabs and Israelites Prior to the Rise of Islam*. Schweich Lectures, 1921.

Nöldeke, T. *Die ghassanidischen Fürsten*. 1887.

O'Leary, de L. *Arabia Before Muhammad*. New York: E. P. Dutton, 1927.

Perceval, Caussin de. *Essai sur l'histoire des Arabs avant l'Islamisme*. Paris: 1847.

Rothstein, J. *Die Dynastie der Lakhmiden*. Berlin: 1899.

Smith, W. R. *Kinship and Marriage in Early Arabia*. Cambridge: 1885.

Wellhausen, J. *Reste arabischen Heidenthums*. Berlin: 1897.

Early Christianity and Other Religions

Badger, G. P. *The Nestorians and Their Rituals*. London: 1852.

Berthold, W. *Zur Geschichte des Christentums in Mittel-Asian bis zur mongolischen Eroberung*. Tübingen: 1901.

Burkitt, F. L. *Early Eastern Christianity*. London: 1904.

Cheikho, L. *Le Christianisme et la littérature chrétienne en Arabie*: Beyrouth: 1919.

Dhalla, Maneckji N. *Zoroastrian Civilization from the Earliest Time to the Downfall of the Last Zoroastrian Empire 651 A.D*. New York: 1922.

Iselin, E. L. *Der Untergang der christlichen Kirche in Nordafrika*. Basel: 1918.

Kopp, C. *Glaube und Sakramente der koptischen Kirche*. Rome: 1932.

BIBLIOGRAPHY

Labourt, J. *Le Christianisme dans l'empire Perse sous la dynastie Sassanide.* Paris: 1904.
Stahl, Robert. *Les mandéans et les origines chrétiennes.* Paris: 1930.

ISLAM, HISTORY

Blochet, E. *La conquete des Etats Nestorians de l'Asie Centrale par les Schi'ites et les influences Chrétienne et Bouddhique dans le dogma Islamique.* Paris: 1926.
Brockelmann, C. *History of the Islamic Peoples.* New York: 1947.
Gibb, H. A. R. *The Arab Conquest in Central Asia.* London: 1923.
Hitti, P. *History of the Arabs,* London: 1940.
Lane-Poole, S. *The Mohammedan Dynasties.* Westminster: 1894.
Le Strange, G. *Lands of the Eastern Caliphate.* Cambridge: 1905.
———. *Palestine Under the Moslems.* London: 1890.
Mikusch, D. von. *Muhammed, Tragödie des Erfolgs.* Leipzig: 1932.
Weil, G. *Geschichte der Chalifen.* 5 vols. Mannheim: 1846-1862.
Wellhausen, J. *The Arab Kingdom and Its Fall.* Calcutta: 1927.
Wüstenfeld. *Geschichte der Fatimiden-Chalifen.* Göttingen: 1881.
Zaidan, G. *Umayyads and Abbasids.* (English Translation by D. S. Margoliouth, Gibb Memorial series, vol. 4.) Leiden: 1907.

ISLAM, RELIGIOUS ASPECTS

Becker, C. H. *Islamstudien.* 2 vols. Leipzig: 1924-1932.
Bell, R. *The Origin of Islam in Its Christian Environment.* London: 1926.
Bergstrasser, G. *G. Bergstrasser's Grundzüge des islamischen Rechts.* Berlin: 1935.
Blair, J. C. *The Sources of Islam.* Madras: 1925.
Brown, J. P. *The Darvishes.* London: 1927.
Casanova, P. *Muhammed et la fin du monde.* Paris: 1911.
Dermenghem, E. *Vies des Saints Musulmans.* Alger: 194-?
Donaldson, D. M. *The Shi'ite Religion.* London: 1933.
Eklund, R. *Life Between Death and Resurrection According to Islam.* Uppsala: 1941.
Fischel, J. W. *Jews in the Economic and Political Life of Medieval Islam.* 1937.
Fritsch, E. *Islam und Christentum im Mittelalter.* Breslau: 1930.
Geiger, A. *Judaism and Islam.* English translation of *Was hat Muhammed aus dem Judenthume entnommen.* Madras: 1898.
Grunebaum, G. von. *Medieval Islam,* Chicago: 1946.
Lammens, H. *Islam, Beliefs and Institutions.* London: 1929.
Lane, E. W. *Arabian Society in the Middle Ages.* London: 1883.
Leszynsky, R. *Muhammedanische Traditionen über das jüngste Gericht.* Heidelberg: 1909.
Levonian, L. *Studies in the Relationship between Islam and Christianity.* London: George Allen and Unwin Ltd., 1940.
Macdonald, D. B. *Aspects of Islam.* New York: 1911.

BIBLIOGRAPHY

McPherson, J. W. *The Moulids of Egypt.* Cairo: 1941.
Muhammed 'Ali. *Islam, or the Natural Religion of Man.* Qadian, India: 1912.
―――. *The Religion of Islam.* Lahore, India: 1936.
Muhammed Ikbal. *The Reconstruction of Religious Thought in Islam.* London: 1934.
Nicholson, R. A. *A Literary History of the Arabs.* Cambridge: 1930.
―――. *Studies in Islamic Mysticism.* Cambridge: 1921.
Roberts, R. *The Social Laws of the Qur'ān, Considered and Compared with Those of the Hebrew and Other Ancient Codes.* London: 1925.
Servier, A. *Islam and the Psychology of the Musulman,* London: 1924.
Torrey, C. C. *The Jewish Foundation of Islam,* New York: 1933.
Tritton, A. S. *The Caliphs and Their Non-Muslim Subjects.* Oxford: 1930.

ISLAM, MODERN, AND MISSIONS

Arberry, A. J. *Islam Today.* London: 1943.
Brown, L. E. *The Prospects of Islam.* London: 1944.
Cash, W. W. *Christendom and Islam.* New York: 1937.
Constitutions, Electoral Laws, Treaties of States in the Near and Middle East, ed. by Helen Miller Davis, Durham, N.C.: 1947.
Gairdner, W. H. T. *The Reproach of Islam.* London: 1911.
Harris, G. K. *How to Lead Moslems to Christ.* Philadelphia: 1947.
Jones, L. E. *The People of the Mosque.* London: 1932.
―――. *Christianity Explained to Muslims.* Calcutta: 1938.
Kohn, H. *Nationalism and Imperialism in the Hither East.* London: 1932.
―――. *Western Civilization in the Near East.* New York: 1936.
Padwick, C. *Henry Martyn, Confessor of the Faith.* New York: 1923.
―――. *Temple Gairdner of Cairo.* London: 1929.
Presbyterian Church in the U. S. A. Iran Mission, *A Century of Mission Work in Iran.* Beirut: 1936.
Shields, R. F. *Behind the Garden of Allah.* Philadelphia: 1937.
Some Aspects of Religious Liberty of Nationals in the Near East. Edited by Helen Clarkson Davis. New York: Harper Brothers.
Tisdall, W. St. Cl. T. *A Manual of the Leading Muhammedan Objections to Christianity.* London: 1915.
Titus, M. T. *The Young Moslem Looks at Life.* New York: 1937.
Yonan, I. M. *The Beloved Physician of Teheran.* Nashville: 1934.
Watson, C. R. *What Is the Moslem World?* 1937.
Zwemer, S. M. *The Moslem Christ.* London: 1912.
―――. *Studies in Popular Islam.* New York: 1939.

NEAR EAST GEOGRAPHY, TRAVEL, FOLKLORE, BIOGRAPHY

Antonius, G. *The Arab Awakening.* 1939.
'Arif al 'Arif. *Beduin Love, Law and Legend.* Jerusalem: 1934.
Armstrong, H. C. *Grey Wolf.* Editions 1933, 1944.

BIBLIOGRAPHY

Bein, A. *Theodor Herzl*. Philadelphia: 1940.
Bell, G. L. *The Desert and the Sown*. New York: 1907.
Brown, P. M. *Foreigners in Turkey*. Princeton: 1914.
Burckhardt, J. L. *Travels in Syria and the Holy Land*. 1822.
Bury, G. W. *Arabia Infelix, or the Turks in Yemen*. London: 1915.
Cleland, W. *The Population Problem in Egypt*. Lancaster, Pa.: 1936.
Coan, F. G. *Yesterdays in Persia and Kurdistan*. 1939.
Cromer, Earl of. *Modern Egypt*. 2 vols. New York: 1908.
Edib, Halidé. *Memoirs*. New York: 1926.
————. *Turkey Faces West*. New Haven: 1930.
Ekrem, Selma. *Turkey: Old and New*. New York: 1947.
————. *Unveiled*. New York: 1930.
Foster, Henry A. *The Making of Modern Iraq*. Norman, Okla.: 1935.
Glanville, S. R. K. *The Legacy of Egypt*. Oxford: 1942.
Glück, N. *The Other Side of the Jordan*. New Haven: 1940.
Hourani, A. H. *Syria and Lebanon: A Political Essay*. New York: 1946.
Hessein, Taha. *An Egyptian Childhood*. New York: 1946. Cairo: 193-?
Lane, E. W. *An Account of the Manners and Customs of the Modern Egyptians*. Everyman's Library.
Lawrence, T. E. *Revolt in the Desert*. London: 1927.
Lloyd, S. *Twin Rivers*. Oxford University Press, Indian Branch, 1947.
Lowdermilk, W. C. *Palestine, Land of Promise*. 1944.
Luke, H. C. J. *Prophets, Priests, and Patriarchs, Sketches of the Sects of Palestine and Syria*. London: 1927.
Luke, Sir Henry. *The Making of Modern Turkey from Byzantium to Angora*. London: 1936.
Mattern, J. *Les villes mortes de Haute Syrie*. Beyrouth: 1933.
Meulen, D. van der. *Aden to the Hadramaut*. London: 1947.
Miller, W. *The Ottoman Empire and its Successors, 1801-1927*. Cambridge: 1936.
Morier, J. *The Adventures of Hajji Baba of Ispahan*. New York: 1937.
Morris, Jastrow, Jr. *Zionism and the Future of Palestine. The Fallacies and Dangers of Political Zionism*. New York: 1919.
Mosharrafa, M. M. *Cultural Survey of Modern Egypt*. London: 1947.
Nasr-ed-Din. *The Khoja*. Translated by H. D. Barnham. New York: 1924.
Niebuhr, M. *Travels Through Arabia and Other Countries in the East*. Translated by Robert Heron. Edinburgh: 1792.
Philby, J. B. *Arabia of the Wahhabis*. London: 1928.
————. *A Pilgrim in Arabia*. London: 1946.
————. *Sheba's Daughters*. London: 1937.
Rihani, A. *Around the Coasts of Arabia*. Boston and New York: 1930.
Rihbany, A. M. *The Syrian Christ*. Boston: 1916.
Ristelhueber, R. *Les traditions francaises au Liban*. Paris: 1925.
Stark, F. *The Southern Gates of Arabia*. 1936.
Storrs, R. *Lawrence of Arabia*. London: 1940.
Stripling, G. W. F. *The Ottoman Turks and the Arabs*. 1942.

BIBLIOGRAPHY

Sykes, Sir P. *A History of Afghanistan.* New York: 1942.
———. *A History of Persia.* 2 vols. New York: 1922.
Thomas, Bertram. *Arabia Felix, Across the 'Empty Quarter' of Arabia.* New York: 1932.
Tobin, C. M. *Turkey, Key to the East.* 1944.
Ward, B. *Turkey.* 1942.
Wilson, Sir A. *South West Persia.* Oxford: 1941.

INDEX

Aaron, 60
Abadītes, 119
'Abbāsids, 88, 105, 127, 170, 190, 191
'Abdallah, father of Muhammed, 19
'Abd-al-Muttalib, 19
Abraha, 104
Abraham, 28, 60, 124
Abu Bakr, 27, 29, 45–46, 61, 81, 82, 86
Abū Hanīfa, 74
Abu Hurayra, 52
Abu Tālib, 19
Abyssinians, 84, 104, 114
Aden, 113–114, 116
Adventists, 133
Aelius Gallus, 110
Afghanistan, 87, 128, 187, 192, 198
Afiq, 61
Africa, 83, 92, 166, 167
Agha Khān, 145
Ahl al Kitāb (people of the book), 73, 75
Ahmad ibn 'Isa, 115
Ahriman (Angra Mainju), 188
Ahura Mazda, 188, 189
'Ā'isha, 27
Alamut, 145
Alcohol, 78, 79
Alexandretta, 138
Alexandria, 166, 169, 172, 173
Algeria, 96, 119
'Alī, caliph, 40, 119, 126, 143
Allah, 17, 30, 47, 53, 67, 69, 82
Alms (zakāt, sadaqa), 50, 51
Alphabet, 139 ; Latin, 182–183
Americans, 106
Amida, 76
Amīna, mother of Muhammad, 39
Amīr al Mu'minīn, 112
'Ammān, 164
'Amr ibn al 'Ās, 74, 170

Ancient of the Mountain, 145
Antichrist, 61
Antioch, 137, 138, 140
Antonius, 169
Apamea, 140
Apostates, 76, 77
'Aqaba, Gulf of, 102
'Arābi Pasha, 173
Arabia, 16, 81, 90, 97, 102–109, 111, 114, 118, 119, 120, 122, 124, 136
Arabic language, 46, 86, 91, 124, 128, 150, 153, 167, 183, 190, 206
Arab League, 161
Arabs, 20, 28, 31, 39, 53, 73–76, 80, 81, 94, 110, 113, 115–116, 118, 120, 122, 124, 125, 126, 127, 137, 138, 145, 161, 162, 167, 181, 189, 190, 196, 204
  conquests, 82–85, 190
  culture, 87, 88
  race, 86
Arab State, 160–161
Aramæan States, 139
Aramaic, or Syriac, 130, 140, 141
Ardahan and Kars, 97
Arianism, 17, 84, 85
Armenians, 71, 84, 128, 147, 152, 184, 185, 194
  Catholic, 142
  highlands, 193
  massacres, 96, 184
  Orthodox, 142, 148
Aryan, 127, 187, 188
Ash'arī, Al, 67
Asia
  Central, 83, 87, 88, 90, 193, 194, 198, 199
  Minor, 88, 91, 97
Assassins, 145
Assiut, 176

230

INDEX

Assyrians
 ancient, 139
 modern, 96, 125, 128, 129
Athanasius, 169
Austria, 97
Avicenna, See Ibn Sīna
Azerbaijan, 193, 194
Azhar, Al, 167, 171

Baalbek, 137, 140
Bāb-al-Rayyān, 52
Babylon, Babylonians, 121, 124, 125, 127, 139
Badr, battle of, 30–31, 36
Baghdad, 13, 87, 88, 105, 127, 128, 129, 131, 141, 170, 187
Baha'al Dīn, 146
Bahai, 162
Bahrayn, 121–123
Bājūrī, 77
Bakhtiaris, 195
Balfour Declaration, 160, 161
Balkan Wars, 97
Baluchis, 118, 193, 195
Bani Ghassān, 103
Barhebræus, Abdul Faraj, 130
Basel, 93, 159, 160, 175
Basra, 82, 130
Bātinīya, 144
Batum, 97
Baybars, Sultan, 77, 145
Baydāwī, 56–57, 59–61, 76
Beduins, 16, 19, 81, 103, 123, 164, 167, 191
Beirut, 140, 149–151
Benedict of Nursia, 169
Bessarabia, 95, 96
Bible, 44–62, 115, 175, 210, 211–212
 biblical concept, 188
 Society, 185
 tithe, 51
 translation into Arabic, 80, 150
 translation into Iranian, 197
Bibliander, 93
Bid'a hasana, 41

Birs Nimrud, 13
Birūnī, al, 191
Bombay, 189
 Presidency, 112
Bosnia and Herzegovina, 97
Budapest, 92
Buddhism, 80
Bukhārī, al, 60–61
Bulgaria, Bulgar, 95, 97
Bullinger, 93
Byzantine Empire (Eastern Rome), 72, 75, 82, 83, 84, 91, 170

Cairo, 105, 166, 170–172
Calendar, Islāmic, 29, 54
Caliphate, 182
Capitulation Laws, 174
Carlyle, 19
Caucasus, 95, 164, 193
Chalcedon, 147, 148
Chaldæans (Christians), 128–130, 134, 142
China (Cathay), Chinese, 87, 92, 128
Christ, 34, 41, 80, 108, 134, 192, 198, 199, 201–203, 204–214
Christian
 attitude towards women, 32
 belief in return of Jesus, 160
 conception of sin, 70
 influence, 20, 21, 81, 152, 177–178, 192
 Lent, 51
 minorities, 92–96
 missionary, 99, 204–207
 point of view, 65
 religion, 95
Christianity, 15, 53, 71, 80–81, 84, 91, 96, 100, 134, 141, 147, 169, 170, 174, 186, 189, 200, 203, 206, 209
Christians, 39, 73, 74, 76, 78, 80, 83, 85, 86, 88, 94, 147, 157, 162, 201, 208, 209, 210
 accepted Islam, 75, 85

INDEX

Christians
  holy war, 90, 93
  in Arabia, 103–105, 107, 108
  in Egypt, 168–170, 172, 173, 174–176
  in Irān, 194–197
  in 'Iraq, 125, 126, 128–130, 132
  in Lebanon, 142, 143
  in Palestine, 162, 163
  in Syria, 140–143
  in Transjordan, 164
  in Turkey, 96, 182, 183–185
  of John the Baptist, 130
Cinema, influence of, 177–178
Circassians, 164
Clermont, council of, 89
Columbus, 72, 92
Confucianism, 80
Constantinople, 75, 83, 91, 95, 184, 185
Converts, 77, 132
Copts, Coptic Church, 76, 84, 147, 170, 174–176
Cordoba, 87
Crete, 97
Crimea, 95, 97
Cromer, Lord, 174
Crusades, 76, 88–92, 145, 174, 195,
Cyprus, 97

Dahnā', 103
Dajjāl, al, 61
Damascus, 46, 87, 103, 104, 105, 138, 139, 141
Daniel, 188
Dante, 17
Dār al-Islām (House of Islām), 14, 53, 55, 79, 90, 94
Day of Judgment, 23–25, 60–61
Day of Resurrection, 25–27
Desert, influence of, 16, 17
Devil worship, 131
Dhikr, 51, 54
Dhimmī (ahl al dhimma), 74–75, 158
Dhu Nawās, 104
Dyophysites, 148, 149

Divorce, 32
Druzes, 138, 142, 143, 145–146, 162, 163
Dufar, 118
Dyck, Dr. C. V. A. van, 150

Eastern Church, 81, 91
Eastern Rome, See Byzantine Empire
Edessa, 128, 140
Egypt, 74, 81, 82, 97, 110, 116, 139, 154, 161, 166–180
Elagabalus, 140
England, See Great Britain
Erasmus, 97
Esther, 188
Evil spirits, 169
Europe, 83, 87–88, 90, 91–93, 96, 97, 98, 99, 172, 182, 187, 195
Europeans, 92, 113, 114, 122, 172

Fallāhīn, 167
Fard (wājib), 69
Fasting, 51, 52
Fatalism, 49, 67, 189
Fātimids, 105, 144, 145, 170, 171
Fatra, 21
Faysal, King of 'Iraq, 164
Fēz or tarbūsh, 182
Fiqh (science of Islāmic law), 74, 77, 79
Firdausi, 189, 190
Fire worship, 188
Food, unclean, 78
France (French), 83, 89, 96, 97, 137, 138, 153, 172
Free will, 67
French, Bishop Valpy, 120
French influence, 153
Fu'ād, King of Egypt, 174

INDEX

Gabriel, 21, 40, 44, 56, 57, 60,
   as the Holy Spirit, 62
Gabrs (Parsees), 189
Gairdner, W. H. Temple, 176
Genghis Khan, 90, 189
George, Bishop of the Arabs, 130
German Empire, 93
Gerra, 121
Ghafārī dynasty, 120
Ghazālī, al, 191
Gibraltar, 101
Ginza, 130
Gobat, Samuel, 175
God, 16, 53, 69, 70, 80, 98, 107, 201, 202
   his relationship to Jesus, 59, 148
   in Christian thinking, 47–49, 201–202, 213
   in Druze thinking, 145, 146
   in Iranian thinking, 188
   in Ismaʿīlī thinking, 144
   in Jewish thinking, 47
   in Muslim thinking, 47–50, 59, 67, 68
   in Nusayrī thinking, 143
   in Yazīdī thinking, 131
Gospel (Injīl), 73
Great Britain (England), 97, 113, 114, 116, 120, 122, 125, 129, 138, 153, 160, 165, 171, 174, 194, 195
Greece, 84, 86, 95, 96, 125, 141, 182, 184
Greek Catholic or Rūm-Catholic, 142, 148, 164
Greek fire, 83, 101
Greek Orthodox Church (Rūm), 75, 84, 142, 147, 148, 164, 170
   Orthodox Christians, 95

Hadīth (tradition), 22, 27, 38, 51, 60, 61
   around Muhammad, 38, 39
   collections, 42

Hadramaut (Hazarmareth), 110, 113, 114–117
Hāfiz, 191
Hajjāj, Al, 88
Hākim bi amr illah, 145, 170
Halāl, 69
Hama, 137, 139, 149
Hamadan, 129
Harām, 69
Harrison, Dr. P. W., 120, 121
Harūn al Rashīd, 127, 190
Hasa district, 106
Hasan al Banna, 179
Hasan, grandson of the Prophet, 126
Hasan ibn Sabbāh, 145
Hāshim, Hāshimīs, 19, 28
Haurān, 137
Hawārī, 58
Hell, 24, 66, 144
Heraclius, 149
Herzl, Theodor, 159
Hijra, al, 29
Hilāl, Al, 155
Himyār, 104, 110, 112
Hinduism, 80
Hindu Kush, 83, 193
Hira, Kingdom of, 104
Hittites, 139
Hocker, Friedrich Wilhelm, 175
Holy Spirit (*ruh al qudus*), 62
Homs, 137, 149
Hormuz, 121
Hūd, prophet, 115
Hulaga Khan, 128
Hume, 97
Husayn, grandson of the prophet, 111, 126, 192
Husayn of Hijaz, 106, 126

Ibādīs, 119
Iblīs, See Satan
Ibn Batūta, 119
Ibn Hanbal, 74
Ibn Saʿd, 31, 38
Ibn Sīna (Avicenna), 191

INDEX

Ibn Suʻūd (Ibn Saud), 105–107
Ibn Taymiyya, 146
Igmāʻ, 105
Ignatius of Loyola, 93–94
Ikhwān al Muslimīn (Muslim Brotherhood), 179
Imām
  of al Yaman, 110, 111
  of Ismaʻīlīs, 144
  of mosque, 49–50
  of Shīʻa, 143
  imamate, 192
Imām Yahya, 111, 112
Immaculate conception, 55
India (Hind), 87, 92, 100, 102, 110, 116, 117, 128, 145, 187, 189
  East India Company, 122, 197
Indian Ocean, 110, 113, 118
Indians, 113, 114, 122
Ingrams, W. H., 112–113, 116
Iqbāl, Indian thinker, 186
Irān, 82–84, 121, 122, 128, 129, 131, 145, 187–199
Iranians, 83, 86, 120, 122, 125
  language, 187, 188, 190, 196
ʻIrāq, 97, 101, 115, 124–135, 166
ʻIsa, See Jesus
Isaac, 124
Islām, 15, 16, 51, 62, 78, 81, 90–91, 94, 98, 102–105, 111, 141, 145, 167, 171, 181, 182, 183, 187, 189, 200, 201, 209, 214
  on alcohol and foods, 78, 79
  change of aspect, 38
  Christianity, 80–101
  culture, 86–88
  and Druzes, 146
  early spread, 82–85
  empire, 91–92
  fundamentals, 44–54
  Jesus, 55–62
  little horn of Daniel, 18
  mystics, 40
  predestination, 65–68
  Qurʼān, 46
  religious liberty, 71–78
  sin, 68–70

Islām
  sword, 31, 73, 83
  treatment of apostates, 76–78
  women, 31, 32, 33
Ismāʻīl (Ishmael), 50, 124
Ismāʻīl, Khedive of Egypt, 172, 173
Ismaʻīlīs, 142, 144–145, 170
Israel, 124, 139
Istanbul, 184
Italy, 91, 97

Jabal Akhdar, 103, 118
Jabal Druze, 137, 145
Jabal Sinjār, 130, 131
Jacobites, 75, 84, 128, 130, 147
Jaʻfar al Sadīq, 144
Jalāl al Dīn al Rūmī, 191
Janissaries, 94
Java, 116
Jazīra district, 129, 137
Jerusalem, 11–13, 53, 76, 82, 93, 127, 162, 163
  kingdom of, 90, 161
Jesuits, 94, 130, 149
Jesus (ʻIsa), 21, 84, 148, 192, 212
  in Druze thinking, 146
  in Muslim thinking, 55–62
Jews, 73, 75, 78, 103, 113, 124, 129, 157, 158
  influence, 21
  messianism, 159
  in Egypt, 169, 172
  in ʻIrāq, 126, 127–128
  in Madīna, 29, 51, 52
  in Palestine, 158–162
  in Syria, 142
  in al Yaman, 110–111
Jidda, 106
Jihād (Holy War), 105
Jinn, 41
John of Damascus, 17
Joseph, 60
Justinian II, 140, 149

Kaʻba, 53, 126
Kaʼb ibn al Ashraf, 34

INDEX

Kairowān, 83
Kamāl Ata Turk, 181–183, 196
Karbalā, 104, 126
Kasb or *iktisāb*, 67
Keith-Falconer, 114
Khadīja, 12, 19–21
Khālid, 88
Khawārij, 119
Khayzurān, 127
Khorasan, 125, 195
Khyber Pass, 82
Kismet (Fate), 17
Kitāb, al Jilwah, 131
Kitchener, Lord, 174
Koelle, Dr., 185
Kūfa, 46, 104
Kurds, 125–127, 129, 145, 194
Kutchuk Kainardji, Treaty of, 95
Kuwayt, 106, 123

Lactantius, 71
Lādhaqiyya, al-(latakiya), 143, 144
Land-tax (*kharaj*), 74
Latin Church, 81
Latins, 142, 148, 164
League of Nations, 125
Lebanon, 96, 97, 136–156, 162, 163, 172
  centre of Catholic work, 149
Literary awakening, 154–155, 172
Literature work, 150, 175, 176
Locke, 97
Lull, Raymond, 91
Lurs, 195
Luther, 18, 68, 76, 77, 84, 93

Macdonald, D.V., 203
Madīna, 29, 30, 33, 36, 46, 51, 52, 61, 76, 81, 104
  forbidden to non-Muslims, 104
Madkhal, al, 77
Mahdi, 61

Makallā, 114, 115
Makka (Mecca), 17, 19, 20, 23, 29, 49, 52–53, 81, 104, 106, 107, 126
  forbidden to non-Muslims, 104
  newspaper, 106–107
  people of, 25, 27–29
Makrūh, 69
Mālik, law school of, 74
Malik Ta'ūs, 131
Mamlūk Sultans (Beys), 76, 171
Ma'mūn, al, 88, 127
Mandæans (Subbis), 126, 130–131
Mandates, 97, 137, 138
Mansūr, al, 88
Marco Polo, 92
Mark, St., 169
Maronite College, 149
Maronites, 96, 142, 148, 149
Martyn, Henry, 197
Marwa, al, 53
Marwān II, 119
Maryam (Mary, mother of Jesus), 55–57
Maryland, 168
Matrah, 118
Maulid al nabbī, 40, 41
Medes, 127
Medical Mission, 107, 114, 122, 123, 151, 163, 164, 176, 197–198, 202–204
Medicine
  under Muslims, 87
  under Nestorians, 128
Mediterranean, 83, 97, 98, 136–138
Melanchthon, 18
Melitene, 75
Meshed, 198
Mesopotamia, 81, 82, 84, 101, 104
Messiah, See Jesus
Meulen, D. van der, 116
Middle Ages, 72, 75, 78, 98
Millet-system, 183
Minæan kingdom, 128–129
Miracles
  attributed to Muhammad, 38–39
  Qur'ān greatest, 39

235

INDEX

Mission work
  Adventist, 133
  American Presbyterian Board, 151, 175, 197
  Arabian Mission, 107, 121, 122, 123, 133
  Basel Mission, 197
  Bibliander, 93
  British Syrian Mission, 151
  Church Missionary Society, 163, 164, 175, 176, 185, 198
  Danish Church Missionary, 114, 116, 151
  Egypt General Mission, 176
  Ignatius of Loyola, 93-94
  in Aden, 114
  in Egypt, 174-176, 178-179
  in Hadramaut, 116, 117
  in Irān, 192, 196-199
  in 'Irāq, 132
  in Lebanon, 149-151
  in 'Omān, 120, 121
  in Palestine, 162-163
  in Persian Gulf States, 123
  in Turkey, 184-185
  in al Yaman, 112
  modern, 99, 100, 152-153, 202-204
  Moravian Brethren, 175
  Nestorians, 86, 128
  Raymond Lull, 91
  Roman Catholic Missions, 114, 134, 164, 197
    Capuchins, 114, 149
    Carmelites, 134, 149
    Franciscans, 174
    Jesuits, 134, 149
    Lazarites, 150, 197
    Sisters of the Good Shepherd, 114
    Sisters of the Holy Family, 150
    Sisters of St. Vincent de Paul, 150
  Scotland South Arabian Mission, 114
  Syrian Orphanage, 163
  United Missions of Mesopotamia, 134

Mitannis, 139
Mithra, 188, 189
Monasticism, 169
Mongols, 86, 128, 145, 189
Monophysites, 84, 130, 148, 149, 170
Monothelites, 149
Moses, 60
Mosque (*Masjid*)
  Gaylāni, 127
  of Qūm, 196
  influence, 85-86
  schools, Kuttāb, 85, 153
  for women, 120
Mosul, 129, 130, 131, 133
Mount Hirā, 20
Mu'āwiya, 88
Mubāh (jā'iz), 69
Mughīra, al, 39
Muhammad, 16, 17, 28, 44, 50, 51, 52, 58, 61, 65, 66, 73, 80-82, 84, 205, 210, 212
  antichrist, 18
  birthday, 41
  Christians and Jews, 20, 21
  critics of, 17-19
  development of, 33-34
  early life, 19
  in eyes of followers, 37-42
  in Medīna, 29, 30, 33, 34
  in Makka, 27-29
  literacy of, 20
  mediator, 40, 42
  message, 23-28
  miracles, 38, 39
  night journey, 22, 60
  on state of dead, 26, 27
  pre-existence, 39, 40
  revelations, 20-23
  traditions about, 37-38
  women, 31-33
Muhammad 'Abd al Wahhāb, 105
Muhammad al Abdarī ibn Hajj, 77
Muhammad 'Alī Pasha, 171, 172
Muharram processions, 192, 196
Mujtahid, 195
Muqtataf, Al, 155

INDEX

Muslim (commentator), 61
Muslims, 28, 37, 41, 44–45, 52, 67–68, 74, 83, 85, 87, 88, 97, 100, 101, 104, 116, 128, 132, 138, 151, 153, 158, 162, 163, 170, 174–175, 177, 178, 182, 197, 198, 201, 204, 207–209, 210–212
  against missions, 179
Musqat (muscat), 118–121
Mustafa Kamāl, See Kamāl Ata Turk
Mutawalī, 142, 143, 155
Muthanna, 88

Naaman, 139
Najaf, 126
Najrān, 104, 107
Najrāniyya, 104
Nationalism, 152, 161, 179, 181, 182, 185
Near East Christian Council, 151
Nebuchadnezzar, 124–125
Nehavend, battle of, 82, 190
Nestorians, 20, 27, 84, 86, 128–130, 142, 147, 194
Newton, 97
Nile Mission Press, 176
Nisibin, 128, 129
Nizam of Hyderabad, 116
North Africa, 81, 82, 83, 91
Nubians, 84
Nufūd, 103
Nusayrīs ('Alāwīs), 142–144

Oil Companies, 106, 122
'Omān, 103, 110, 118–121
Omar Khayyām, 191
Origen, 169
Original sin, 55

Pachomius, 169
Paighambar akhira zamān, 192
Pakistan, 195

Palestine, 81, 82, 90, 97, 111, 128, 137–138, 157–163
Paradise, 24, 41, 52, 59, 63, 66–67, 144
Parsees, 113, 189
Parthians, 125
Patriarch of Babylon, 129
Paul, Apostle, 48, 103, 201, 202, 211, 213
Pearl diving, 122
Persia, Persians. See Irān, Iranians
Persian Gulf, 102, 106, 110, 118, 121–123, 193, 195
Peter, the Apostle, 212
Peter the Great, 94
Petrie, Dr. and Mrs., 112, 113
Pfander, G., 185
Philip the Arabian, 140
Philistines, 158
Phœnicians, 139
Pilgrimage (*al ḥajj*), 52, 53, 126
Pinsker, Leo, 159
Pirate Coast (Trucial Coast), 122
Poll tax (*jizya*), 74
Polygamy, 31–33, 182
Pompey, 140
Popes, 129
  Clement III, 89
  Gregory VII, 89
  Gregory, XIII, 149
  Urban II, 89, 90
Portuguese, 120, 121, 122, 130
Prayer, 49, 50, 182
Predestination, 65–68
Prophecy, 212
Prophet, idea of, 37
Protestantism, 93, 97, 99, 142, 147, 155, 164, 177
  in Egypt, 175–176
  in Irān, 197
  in Lebanon, 151
  in Palestine, 163
  in Turkey, 184
Psalms (*zabbūr*), 73

Qadasiyya, battle of, 82

INDEX

Qāḍī, 171
Qalat (near Shinraz), 198
Qat, 109
Qatar, 122
Qatn, al, 115
Qias, 105
Qibla (direction of prayer), 53
Qūm, 196
Qur'ān (Koran), 18–22, 37–38, 44, 50, 65, 66, 76, 80, 85, 105, 119, 144, 150, 190, 210, 212, 213
  abrogated verses, 47
  commentaries, 45
  Holy Spirit in, 62
  Jesus in, 55–62
  recension of, 44–46
  translation of, 35, 93
Quraysh, 19

Rahmān, al, 56, 57
Ramadān, 51, 52, 54
Rationalism, 71
Red Sea, 102, 106, 113
Religion, 68, 72
Religious Liberty, 71, 75, 76, 78, 131–132, 164, 165
Renaissance, 97
Reuchlin, 97
Rhazes, or Razi, 87, 191
Riād, 106
Richard, the Dominican, 18
Riza Shah Pahlevi, 193, 195, 196
Roman Catholic Church, 78, 89, 93, 147, 148–150, 174, 176
Roman Empire, 72, 83, 103, 110, 140, 189
Romans, 115, 125, 140, 189
Rub'al Khālī, 103, 113, 118
Rumania, 95, 97
Russia, 92, 94, 95, 96, 97, 129, 194, 195, 198
  Tsars of, 164

Sa'adi, 191
Sabæans, 110
Sabians, 73
Safā, al, 53
Sajjūn, 115
Saladin (Salah al Dīn), 76, 195
Salāt, 49
Salt, al, 164
Samaritans, 162
Samarkand, 87
San'a', 104, 112, 113
Sargon, Assyrian King, 110, 121
Sassanids, 82, 125, 190
Satan (Iblīs), 55, 63, 78, 130, 131,
  his fall according to Qur'ān, 62, 63
Savonarola, 18
Sayyids, 112, 115, 116
Schneller, L., 163
Schools
  al Azhar, 171
  Catholic, 149–150
  Christian, 133, 203, 204
  C.M.S., 162, 164
  Fu'ād University, 172, 173
  Girls School, first, 150
  higher learning, 87
  in Egypt, 172–173, 175
  in Irān, 196–198
  in 'Irāq, 132, 133
  in Syria and Lebanon, 149–151, 153–154
  in Turkey, 184
  Mission, 114, 153
  of Nestorians, 128
  Qur'ān, 85
  Robert College, 185
  St. Joseph University, 149
  Syrian Orphanage, 163
  Syrian Protestant College, American University, 150–151, 184, 185
Secularism, 78
Seleucids, 121, 139, 140
Seljūk period, 194
Serbia, Serbs, 95, 96
Shabak, 120
Shāfi'ī, al, law school of, 74
Shahāda, 47

INDEX

Shah Namah, 189, 190
Sharī'a (Muslim canon law), 77, 195
Sharīfs of Makka, 164
Shaykh 'Ādī, 131
Shakh Hamīd of Qaṭar, 107
Shaykh of Lahaj, 113
Shaykh 'Othmān, 112
Sheba, queen of, 110
Shī'a, 40, 42, 111, 122, 143, 191, 192, 195, 198
Shibām, 115
Shihr, 115
Shī'ī, 39, 126–127, 142–144, 162, 170, 171, 192
Shirāz, 197, 198
Shirk, 69
Shoas, 114
Sicily, 83, 88
Sidra Rabba, 130
Sidra tree, 22
Silver, Dr. Abba Hillel, 161
Sin, 68–70
Sind, 82, 83
Singapore, 115
Smith, Eli, 150
Solomon, 110
Somalis, 113
Spain, 15, 81, 86, 87, 88, 91
Spice Islands, 110
Spirituality
 in Christianity, 47, 48
 in Islām, 47, 48
Storm, Dr., 107, 118, 121
Suez Canal, 99, 113, 172
Sūfī, Sūfism, 40, 41, 48, 191
Sulaymān, the Magnificent, 94
Sulaymania, 127
Sumatra, 116
Sumerian (s), 121, 124
Sunna, 38, 143, 192
Sunnīs, 42, 83, 105, 112, 119, 123, 126–127, 142, 143, 162, 171, 192
Sūra
 general, 44, 53–54
 of Madīna period, 45
 of Makkan period, 28, 45

Sūra
 question about first, 22
 quoted, 21, 22, 24–26, 30, 31, 34, 47, 48, 51, 56–60, 63, 65, 66, 67, 69, 73, 76, 77, 78
Swahilis, 114
Syria, Syrians, 81, 82, 84, 88, 90, 97, 104, 129, 136–156, 162
Syriac (language), 128, 141, 149
Syrian Catholic Christians, 142, 148
Syrian expedition, 82
Syrian Orthodox Christians, 142, 148
Syrians abroad, 154–155

Tabriz, 194, 197
Tā'if, 28
Talmud, Babylonian, 130
Tama, Bishop of, 174
Tamerlane, 129, 189
Tārim, 115, 116
Tāriq, 83, 101
Tartars, 82, 92, 94, 189
Teheran, 193, 198
Tertullian, 71
Thornton, D. M., 176
Thousand and One Nights, The, 115, 190, 191
Tibet, 87
Timothy I, patriarch, 86–87
Tolerance, 73, 75, 76, 120, 177, 196
Torah, 73
Tours and Poitiers, 83
Tradition, see Hadīth
Transjordan, 97, 104, 138, 163–165
Transmigration (re-incarnation), 144, 146
Transoxania, 83
Trinity, 59, 69, 210
Tripolitania, 97
Tunis, 97, 144
Turan, 183, 187,
Turcomans (Turkmenes), Turkmenistan, 125, 183, 195

INDEX

Turkey, 97, 111, 125, 127, 129, 138, 152, 164, 171, 174, 181-186, 192, 198
Turks, 18, 71, 88, 90, 94, 96, 97, 111, 125, 189, 194
   Osmanli Turks, Ottomans, 91-93, 95, 147, 148, 172
   Ottoman Empire, 94, 95, 137-138
   language, 183, 194

'Ubayd Allah ibn Muhammad al Mahdī, 144
Ukraine, 95
'Umar ibn al Kattāb, 27, 74, 81, 82, 88, 104
Umayyads, 88, 105, 119, 131, 141, 190
Uniate Eastern Churches, 129-130, 148, 174
Urmia, Lake, 194
U.S.A. (American), 111, 150, 153, 155, 190
'Utayba, tribe, 122
'Uthmān (caliph), 46, 119

Van Ess, Dr., 133
Vasco da Gama, 92
Vedas, 187
Veil, 32-33, 182, 195
Verdi, 172
Vienna, 93

Wafd Party, 179
Wahhābīs, 78, 105-106
Wāli, 169

Weizmann, Chaim, 160
Wolff, Joseph, 112
Women
   first girls' school, 150
   mosques for, 120
   position of, 31-33, 169, 182, 195-196
   schools, 173
World War I, 111, 125, 129, 135, 137, 160, 163, 164, 174, 181, 194, 198
World War II, 100, 163, 179, 186, 193, 194

Yafā'īs, 115
Yaman, al, (Yemen), (Arabia Felix), 102, 103, 104, 109-113
Yarmuk, battle of, 82
Yathrib, 20, 29, 30
Yazīdīs (Yezidis), 126, 131, 132, 142
Y.M.C.A., 163, 176, 177
Y.M.M.A., 177

Zacharias, 55
Zahrān, 106
Zamzam, 126
Zanzibar, 120
Zarathustra (Zoroaster), 189, 196, 199
Zoroastrians, 73, 74
Zayd ibn 'Alī, 111
Zayd ibn Thābit, 45-46
Zayd, Muhammad's adopted slave, 34
Zaydites, 111-112, 113
Zinzendorf, von, Count, 175
Zionism, 128, 157-160, 162
Zubayda, 127
Zwemer, Dr. S. M., 112, 120, 121

For Product Safety Concerns and Information please contact our EU
representative GPSR@taylorandfrancis.com
Taylor & Francis Verlag GmbH, Kaufingerstraße 24, 80331 München, Germany

www.ingramcontent.com/pod-product-compliance
Lightning Source LLC
Chambersburg PA
CBHW070602300426
44113CB00010B/1364